Wrigley Regulars

D1260357

WRIGLEY REGULARS

Finding Community
in the Bleachers

Holly Swyers

UNIVERSITY OF ILLINOIS PRESS
Urbana, Chicago, and Springfield

Library of Congress Cataloging-in-Publication Data
Swyers, Holly.
Wrigley regulars : finding community in the bleachers /
by Holly Swyers.
p. cm.
Includes bibliographical references and index.
ISBN 978-0-252-03550-0 (cloth : alk. paper) —
ISBN 978-0-252-07740-1 (pbk. : alk. paper)
1. Wrigley Field (Chicago, Ill.) 2. Chicago Cubs (Baseball team)
3. Stadiums—Social aspects—Illinois—Chicago. 4. Communities.
5. Community life. I. Title.
GV416.I32S89   2010
796.357068773'11—dc22   2009044158

Contents

Acknowledgments

A book like this is built with the help of an entire community. At various points in the past several years, many regulars have given their time and energy to this project, and even if they do not appear by name in the pages of this book, they are here, cheering, laughing, crying, sharing. This list is in no way comprehensive, but it reflects regulars who went out of their way to help me, who let me interview them, who read draft chapters and cheered me on when I struggled. They include:

Centerfield: Marv, Judy, Colleen, Bill, Bea, Jeff, Sue, Cyndi, Connie, Linda, Streamwood Linda, Fred, Sal, Howard, Norb, Richie, Fireman Tom, Tom, Tammy, Kathy, Jan, Bobby

Leftfield: Ron, Karen, Mary Ellen, Robyn, Jonathon, Ellen, Tim, Jim, Fred, Donna, Gary, Keith, Anthony, Stephanie, Ken, Jack, Joe

Rightfield: Al, Jeff, Howard, Phil, Linda, John, Billy, Mary Ellen, Cheryl, David, Mike, George, Uncle Mel

Everyfield: Mary, Jimmy, crowd control and concession workers at Wrigley

I want to give special mention to Connie from Centerfield, who passed away in January 2010. She will be missed.

Additional credit is due to Hayley Wolfcale, Ben Zarit, and Emilie Vrbancic, who gave a lot of time to checking readability and proofing later drafts. My thanks also go to the anonymous reviewers who went through two completely different drafts of this book and made it progressively better, and to Dave Zirin, who gave me a new title for the manuscript. I also owe a debt of gratitude to the editors and production and marketing staff at the University of Illinois Press, who worked patiently with me and did a great job getting this text from manuscript to finished book form.

Pregame

When I tell people I am doing a study of community in the Wrigley Field bleachers, I get knowing smiles. Usually, someone will remark, "Uh huh, 'research,'" complete with finger quotes around the word research. Occasionally, I'll hear indignant mumbling about research dollars and crazy professors wasting time and money. Most people, though, will lean back and say, "Okay, explain *that* one to me."

This skepticism has valid reasons. The lure of the corner of Clark and Addison, where Wrigley Field is located, is pretty clear in popular imagination in Chicago. There is the image of sunshine, tanned young bodies, cold beer—an eternal party state reminiscent of frat house keggers. It hasn't always been this way, but it has been for enough of the last twenty years to cement the reputation of Wrigley Field and the neighborhood around it. Wrigleyville is perceived as a place to go to have fun, an entertainment district for the post-college, pre-marriage, predominantly white, professional class demographic. The word to describe it would be something along the lines of carnivalesque rather than community.

There is a much lauded residential neighborhood around the ballpark, distinct from the bar and restaurant scene, although its relationship to the Cubs is fraught. The ways in which this part of the neighborhood is a community are most evident when residents are struggling *against* their famous baseball shrine, fighting for fewer night games, stricter parking rules, and more policing of unruly and drunken fans. Otherwise, the most striking element of the residential Wrigleyville area is obvious and accelerating gentrification, one of many frequently cited bugaboos of urban community.

Some of my interlocutors assume, with some correctness, that I am talking about die-hard *fans*. Cubs fans are notorious for their devotion to their "lovable losers," and whether that devotion is seen as quasi-religious or sadly delusional depends more on the observer than any other factor. Many of these fans treat Wrigley Field as a site of pilgrimage, which brings them into occasional conflict with both the party set and the residents. At the end of the day, though, the die-hard fan does not require a community to validate his or her love of the Cubs. Nor does loving the Cubs automatically create a sense of community in the way that most Americans seem to mean it, imbued with nostalgia for kinder, gentler days from the misty past. Socially speaking, loving a sports team at best lends a lubricant to introductions and business luncheons, providing a topic of conversation that is relatively "safe" for comparative strangers.

Nonetheless, loving the Cubs *can* become the baseline for community, and that is exactly what we see among the bleacher regulars. These die-hard fans claim their piece of bleacher bench two hours before every home game, ready with heckles and cheers even during batting practice. They count one another among their closest friends and will say to anyone who asks, "We are a community." This is the community I have studied.

By this point, the question could be fairly asked, "What the heck is a 'community' anyway?" An argument could be made that it does not really matter what academics think community is; a person who experiences a community knows s/he is in one. Likewise, a case can be made that too much scholarly ink has been spilled over the question of community already. Countless movements on all sides of the political spectrum have mobilized around one definition of community or another, and almost invariably, community is treated as a cause, a site of potential or actual loss that must be shored up or empowered. This is as true of the American "family values" movement as it is of various anti-gentrification campaigns in major cities. "Community" has become a buzzword, as laden as "freedom" or "patriotism" and as relatively empty of content.

And yet, I propose to write about community.

Why bother?

The first answer is derived from the morass described above in politics. Contemporary world politics holds on to two strong, interrelated myths. The first is that industrialization and globalization are the enemies of community, and the fast-paced world of the twenty-first century has destroyed our abilities to connect with one another. The second is that any indigenous or disadvantaged group has the "power of community" over the forces that would exploit them. The problem with letting politics dictate how Americans think about community is that it encourages people to substitute an abstract concept for their actual experience. In much the same way that education has become a political football, panic over the state of community has replaced common sense. In the case of education, surveyed Americans have given "the nation's public schools" consistently low grades, while the same Americans gave their own local schools high marks (Berliner and Biddle 1995: 112).[1]

With rare exception, my conversations with people about community have followed this same pattern. Most Americans I have talked to have agreed that we have lost our sense of community, and that this is the cause of many social ills. At the same time, they will boast of the exceptionalism they enjoy; most can point with confidence to their own communities, citing themselves as lucky.

While the results of several hundred conversations over the course of a dozen years may not hold the esteem in the United States that is accorded to hard statistical data, it is a mistake to disregard the information gleaned from these conversations. This brings me to the second reason for troubling myself with writing about community: respect for ethnographic methods.

Ethnography has long been the method of anthropologists for learning about cultures. In recent years, other disciplines have recognized some of the value of ethnography, although most have modified it to their own needs. The primary change has been in terms of the length of ethnographic study, a move that I feel directly contradicts the spirit of an ethnographic enterprise. But this begs the question, what is ethnography?

A short definition would steal the title of Clifford Geertz's essay on the topic and say ethnography is "thick description" (1973). It relies on "the kind of material produced by long-term, mainly (though not exclusively) qualitative, highly participative and almost obsessively fine-comb field study in confined contexts" (23). To my mind, ethnography is a necessary companion piece to the sweeping generalizations made possible by statistical study. Most Americans have had the experience of taking a survey or answering multiple-choice questions and realizing that they are choosing the option *closest* to what they think or believe rather than an exact match to their opinions. Similarly, most people have had the experience of agreeing with someone else's conclusions for completely different reasons than the other person has presented. Surveys and polls have limited scope for shades of gray, but that is part of their value. They can give us an idea of general trends, with the necessary caveat that the questions being asked originate from the survey designers.

Ethnography, in contrast, starts from extreme specificity. Ideally, an ethnographer assumes nothing, noting everything s/he sees, hears, smells, tastes, and touches and describing each with care. Nothing should be taken for granted. As Ruth Benedict explained, when things are taken for granted, the observer "does not explore the range of trivial habits in daily living and all those accepted verdicts on homely matters, which, thrown large on the national screen, have more to do with that nation's future than treaties signed by diplomats" (1969 [1946]: 11–12). These trivial habits in daily living are the bread and butter of ethnographers, who both describe them and ask people about them.

So we return to Wrigley Field and the question of the community I claim to be studying there. I have already discounted the park itself, the neighborhood, and the die-hard fans, not because they are not capable of supporting or even behaving as communities, but each entity in itself is not necessarily a community. I make this contention because after several years of research, I have reached the conclusion that the term "community" needs to be understood in terms of habits and actions rather than in terms of names and places. Communities, like any other collective of individuals, are dynamic institutions, although they may go to great lengths to appear constant and relatively unchanging. Such is the case of the bleacher regulars, a group that I first met in 1997.

I started going to Wrigley Field in the summer of 1995. I was a recent convert to the Cubs, discovering them when I returned to baseball after the 1994–95 strike. The Cubs had always been my grandmother's team, but my father was a Dodger fan, and I was raised with Los Angeles broadcaster Vin Scully on the radio. Adolescent rebellion took me away from baseball, but when I finished college and settled in Chicago, I found myself nostalgically tuning in to the available games. Before I knew what had happened, I had fallen in love with the Cubs.

A year later, in 1996, I had moved to New York, but I took my love of the Cubs with me. I went to Shea Stadium whenever the Cubs played the Mets, completely decked out in my Cubs gear and cheering loudly against the home team. That was how Linda found me.

I was standing in the field boxes of Shea, a triumphant sign hoisted in my hands: "CUBS WIN!" Unhappy Mets fans streamed past me, but I also was meeting Cubs fans, exchanging high fives and happy acknowledgments as they filed by. Among those fans was Linda. She stopped by my seat, and we chatted Cubs, recapping the game highlights. We talked about Chicago and how much we missed it. In the course of that conversation, we discovered that we both planned to be at the next day's game and made tentative plans to meet when we got to the ballpark.

The next day, I was settling into the same seat I'd occupied the day before when Linda appeared. She sat down next to me, and we talked more baseball. When someone appeared to claim the seat Linda occupied, we shifted to find two vacant seats together in the same area. At the end of the game, we exchanged phone numbers and planned to see each other for the next series.

By the end of the 1996 season, I knew I could count on going to Cubs games with Linda—or rather, meeting Linda at Cubs games. We made a point of arriving early for batting practice and staying until the final out, talking about anything and everything during the course of the game. It was during these conversations that I learned about the bleacher regulars.

Linda, as it turned out, was (and still is) a bleacher regular. She had stories and more stories about the group of friends she had in the bleachers of Wrigley, and at the end of the 1996, she brought me a copy of *Bleacher Banter*, the newsletter of the regulars. I eagerly subscribed, enjoying the opinionated baseball savvy of the regular writers. I tended to skip the large "News and Notes" sections focused on gossip involving the regulars themselves. That, however, would quickly change.

The story of how I found my way into the bleachers will be recounted later in this book, but for now it is enough to know that I got there. On Opening Day 1997, I met the centerfield regulars, and over the course of the next few years, I came to know many more members of the bleacher regulars.

The bleacher regulars profess the belief that they *are* a community. I have taken this as a given. My questions focus on the how and why of this community. How do people come to feel they are a part of the community? What do they do to cement their relationships within the community? How do they establish who is in or out of the community? Why is the community important to them? In short, rather than starting from a definition of community and seeking to find an exemplar, I am starting from a self-described community and trying to unpack the intuitive knowledge that it is a community.

The role of ethnography in this project should be clear enough. It is only through fine-grain observation and long-term involvement in day-to-day life that my questions can be answered. What I would like to achieve is a book that allows people to examine their own relationships to community. One argument I make is that human beings find ways to connect no matter what the situation, but community now may look very different than it did twenty years ago or will look twenty years hence. What remains constant are types of interaction and the subjective sense of belonging. An attempt to bring back a particular type of neighborhood-based community may well be doomed. An effort to find where and how community is manifesting in the present moment and to nurture its better qualities strikes me as a wiser course.

Ultimately, though, I leave the decisions of how to use the information in this book to its readers. Having presented my rationale for writing this book in the first place, it behooves me to address the question of my methodology—and my research ethics—more specifically. My objective over the next nine chapters will *not* be to reveal what should be done, but rather to present a study of what *is*. To understand how I've gone about constructing this study, it is important to first understand the relationship between my project and the people who are its object.

As I have implied above, I did not join the bleacher regulars with any intention of writing about the experience. Initially, the ballpark was a site of desperate defiance. I moved back to Chicago in 1997 to attend graduate school, and my time at Wrigley Field proclaimed me as something more than a person who read social theory and anthropology all the time.

Over the course of years, however, my involvement in the bleacher regular community became a major source of questions for existing social theory about community. I found myself checking theories against the real world. Did they capture what I knew was out there? Could they describe it accurately? What would the regulars say if they had a chance to debate with this theorist? I broached the idea of studying the regulars in 1999 in centerfield. At the time, the thought was to write a paper or two, using the bleachers to concretely demonstrate some theoretical points I wanted to make about the nature of community. The centerfield regulars both teased and supported me. Every time the topic of my research came up, Marv from Centerfield would say, "She came out here to dig up old fossils, and she found us."[2] Sue from Centerfield, another regular, compared my efforts to those of primatologists Jane Goodall and Dian Fossey. "We're like the gorillas in the mist," she remarked, often sparking nature-channel style voice over narrations of my activities.

It was near the end of this first season of research that I realized I had become a regular. This pronouncement might give some readers understandable pause. If I am a bleacher regular, how can I approach the community with objectivity? Being a regular has certainly influenced how I approach my research; among other things, I wish to maintain my own position in the community. I also have very different relationships with different members of the community, and this colors my perception of events. I submit, first and foremost, that this is something that is true of any research involving human beings. We all have personality types we deal with better than others, and even the most objective research protocol will be influenced by such preferences. I would also argue that a native has an enhanced awareness of the ethical relationship between a researcher and his/her informants. In research as much as in medicine, the principle "First, do no harm" should apply, and it is harder to lose sight of potential harm when the researcher is a part of the research.

This was all on my mind when I decided to write this monograph. I circulated a book proposal, and many regulars responded enthusiastically. I expanded my research activities to include leftfield and rightfield. I also began collecting formal interviews to supplement my earlier research work. I explain this history to give context for my actual note taking and other research work.

Throughout my note gathering and writing, I have been careful to allow regulars to request that certain things not be included or to supply pseudonyms to protect their identities. Because I am writing from inside this community, I have had more or less unfettered access to some dirty laundry, and I have agreed to be as circumspect as possible in handling such material, carefully separating relevant from prurient.

What have I decided is relevant? That will of course become evident in the succeeding chapters, but my general rule of thumb questions are, Does this example demonstrate a characteristic of a community? Will another example serve as well? Are details necessary to make the point? The conversations among bleacher regulars frequently touch on close personal matters like marital problems, substance abuse, and medical conditions. In these cases, it is enough to know such conversations are had. Where I have felt it necessary to discuss a particular example, I have been as circumspect as the involved parties have requested.

In addition to these kinds of personal matters, there have been some developments in recent years that have affected the community as a whole. These include increasing ticket prices and decreasing ticket availability, the gentrification of the Wrigleyville neighborhood, questions about the structural integrity of Wrigley Field, and the sale of the Cubs franchise to the Ricketts family. I have not engaged in an analysis of these trends beyond the ways in which they figure into regulars' conceptions of the community. There have been some conspiracy theories floated about the various pressures the community has been experiencing, and their inclusion here without more thorough research could be read as libelous. I anticipate future researchers will be more able to present a nuanced explanation of the push and pull of various economic forces that are at play in Wrigley Field, and I will leave such analysis to them.

The various ethical decisions I have made about this research give some sense of the scope of this project. I have been a voracious note taker, although the nature of my notes has varied over the years. In my initial two years in the bleachers, my notes consisted of journal entries made after games, newspaper clippings, letters, copies of the *Bleacher Banter*, and scorecards. The scorecards are the most important of this collection in the long run, since scorecards became the center of my note taking for the duration of my research.

My methodology has included participant observation, archiving, formal and informal interviews, and literature review. Participant observation has partly meant sitting in the bleachers writing down literally everything that was going on around me, and for that purpose, the scorecard has been an admirable tool. I have some scorecards that are several pages, although in recent years I have gotten more adept at jotting notes that work mnemonically, allowing me to unpack entire conversations into my computer after each game ends. Because keeping a scorecard is such a classic baseball activity, it has been possible to take notes while remaining involved in the game and in the banter that accompanies it. On occasion, my scorecards have been snatched away by others to be read mid-game, or perused by people covering the game for me when I made a rare in-game trip to the concession stand or the bathroom.

I returned one day during the 2004 season to find Jeff from Centerfield squinting at my handwriting. "What does this say?" he asked.

"Take the field: *Jump*," I read off to him, identifying the Van Halen song that played over the PA when the Cubs ran onto the field at the start of the game.

"But they always take the field to 'Jump,'" he pointed out.

"They haven't always," I reminded him.

"I *know* that," he replied, "but they have this year." He shook his head at me. The detail is small, but it matters. The Cubs started playing "Jump" when they took the field at the start of the 2004 season. They had played it before, of course, but it had special significance for some regulars. On another day, "Jump" was playing, the Cubs were running out, and Mary Ellen from Left-field, standing at the rail behind me, said, "It makes me nervous that they keep doing all this 1984 stuff." In 1984, the Cubs had come within two games of going to the World Series, collapsing in the playoffs, and regulars still say the name "Steve Garvey" as if it were a curse.

The significance of a date, a song, and a ballplayer: these things are part of the day-to-day knowledge that make the regulars a community. Notes of thousands of such tiny details form the backbone of this study.

There has been more to my research than note taking, however. I have collected an archive of newspaper and magazine articles in addition to my notes. I've also amassed a collection of baseballs, ticket stubs, party flyers, ballpark giveaways ranging from hats to toy trains to porcelain figurines, a sample size bottle of Canadian whiskey, a foam finger from Banco Popular, a voodoo doll, and more plastic souvenir cups than anyone could conceivably need. Many of the items have stories of their own; the whiskey, for example, dates to the closing of a bar that had once been part of a circuit of bars frequented by some regulars. Souvenirs are part and parcel of the culture of the regulars, concrete evidence of their commitment to baseball, to the Cubs, and to one another.

Interviewing is an obvious and important method in documenting any community. Much of my interviewing has been informal, spur of the moment questions prompted by the events going on around me. In the last four years, I have done more formal interviewing, particularly in rightfield and leftfield, where I have spent far less time. In the course of these interviews, I have had people map their seating history in the bleachers as well as tell their stories, and the maps have become an important part of my notes.

Finally, I have spent a fair amount of time reviewing the literature available on baseball, community, and American culture and history. This has been, unsurprisingly, a rather large undertaking, and I cannot claim to have comprehensively covered every possible item I could have read. However, I have faithfully followed leads that I felt could shed light on how best to analyze the way bleacher regulars interact and how that interaction can be understood as community building and sustaining activity.

Ultimately, like any writer, I would like this book to be read by many people. Its themes and subject matter strike me as of wide interest. At the same time, however, I have had to make a choice in my writing regarding my audience. This decision has had more to do with the structuring of the book than with any decision about content or style.

I have written this book to be easily taught to undergraduates. This means the heaviest theoretical themes and literature review portions of the book are concentrated in the first chapter. Each successive chapter is designed to expand upon and exemplify different points discussed in the first chapter. For teachers, this allows for picking and choosing of assigned readings. The later chapters are rich in ethnographic detail, and any of them could be taught in combination with the first chapter to create a compact unit around a given theme.

For readers who are coming to this book outside the context of a class, the later chapters will certainly be more fun to read. For some people, it may be worth reading the book backwards, coming back to the more theoretical discussion after experiencing the examples in the later chapters. Such a strategy will actually give readers more of the feel that I have had in researching the book. My conclusions came only after I had spent years in the Wrigley Field sun, and it is my hope that I can give others a vicarious sense of what that has been like.

There is one final comment to be made in this preface, and it relates to the working title of this book. During the long phase of development, this book was known to all the regulars by the title "And Keep Your Scorecard Dry." Reviewers of the draft pointed out that while the title might be meaningful to insiders, it was not a great choice for describing what this book is about. The current title of this book emerged from a conversation with sportswriter Dave Zirin, for which I remain grateful, but I also think it is worth explaining where the original title came from.

Among regulars, keeping a scorecard is a relatively common activity. Some regulars have decades of scorecards saved, and most know how to keep score even if they opt not to. The more compulsive scorekeepers will keep score under any conditions and check their scorecards against the box scores in the next day's paper. To not keep score at a game one has attended is regarded by these regulars as a personal shortcoming. A scorecard-keeping regular will keep score no matter what—even if it's raining.

Rain obviously creates problems for note taking of any kind. Even a couple of drops of water will cause paper to disintegrate under the pressure of a pen or pencil. In the bleachers, however, there is very little shelter when the rain comes. What shelter there is is tightly crowded, and few regulars will leave their carefully staked-out seats just because of a little (or a lot of) rain. Instead, they open umbrellas, climb into rain suits, or pull on ponchos and hunker down to wait out any downpour. For a regular who keeps a scorecard, it is virtually guaranteed that said scorecard will be in the driest spot under the rain gear. I have lost count of the number of times I have heard a regular say, "Whatever happens, you've got to keep your scorecard dry."

I will have more to say about scorecards later in this book, but lest this seem extreme, understand that regulars know that any game can end up becoming special. In my own collection, I have a scorecard with water-crinkled edges. It is from May 6, 1998, a Wednesday afternoon game between the Cubs and the Houston Astros that I cut class to attend. Baseball aficionados might recognize the date or the matchup: it was the game in which the rookie Kerry Wood tied a major league record by striking out twenty batters. I could have stopped keeping score when it started to rain in the sixth. The persistent drizzle was difficult to deal with, and it was a cold rain.

But it was a magical game. The umpires must have realized it, because they kept the game going despite the rain. If they had doubts, Judy from Centerfield was explaining the situation at the top of her lungs. "REAL MEN PLAY IN THE RAIN!" she yelled. None of the regulars was actually mentioning the mounting strikeout total; no one wanted to jinx it. But we gave each other knowing glances as we clutched our scorecards to our chests under our ponchos between outs. And like everyone else in the ballpark, we groaned when the second out in the ninth was a ground out and we realized Kerry could only tie the record and not break it. The rain had stopped by then, but we had kept our scorecards dry, and we were able to record the twentieth strikeout in real time, as it happened, because *we were there*. As I will show, the being there is important in more ways than one.

In addition to its significance among the regulars, "And Keep Your Scorecard Dry" evoked *And Keep Your Powder Dry*, the title of a book written in the 1940s by anthropologist Margaret Mead (2000 [1942]). Mead's "ethnography of America" was written during World War II as part of an effort to help Americans recognize their own culture and the qualities that would help them win the war. While my book has less of a triumphalist bent, I share Mead's mission to give Americans the tools to recognize their own culture. Not every American will identify with the nominally sports-centered community of the bleacher regulars, but most will recognize the day-to-day behaviors that make the regulars a community.

As Charles Darwin pointed out in 1871 (1981), humans are social animals by nature, and they will find ways to connect with one another in almost any situation. The conditions of the twenty-first-century United States may well promote lifestyles and values that undermine the rootedness of hearth and home. Families may well be dysfunctional, and bonds of blood kinship may feel far thinner than water. The world is changing, and people are both participating in changing it and adjusting to the unforeseen consequences of the changes they have instigated. They still need one another, however, and they find one another. The bleacher regulars offer one example of how this process happens, how a seed of shared experience can be nurtured into ties that bind people as thoroughly as any neighborhood association. The important message of this book is this: what makes a community is the belief and commitment of the people who are participating in it. Any time we insist community must look a certain way, we will miss hundreds and thousands of communities that do not fit our mold. It is my hope that this book will help us avoid that mistake.

1

Community as Experience and Practices

My interest in community is long standing. I was a navy brat in my childhood, and as a consequence, I learned young that every new home included a new code of rules to crack. Like most children raised in mobile families, I had mixed success with the various communities I passed through. Two things were very clear to me: every place we ended up had some sense of community, and the nature and permeability of each community varied dramatically. I encountered small towns that offered open-armed welcome and others that closed ranks. I found the same extremes in urban centers. I discovered a variety of oxymoronic interaction styles, ranging from an icy kind of "niceness" to a brusque type of acceptance.

The knowledge of so many types of community proved invaluable in my early career when I worked in community organizing. It also gave me an ability to quickly gauge the different kinds of communities that were lumped together into school districts when I was doing my dissertation research. During that research, it became clear to me that one of the problems facing schools was deciding which of the plethora of communities claiming ownership of a school should determine the direction of the school. In essence, years of life and work approaching communities from the outside made me aware that communities were flourishing even though there was a great deal of hand-wringing going on about the demise of community.

During these same years, I was finding my own adult communities. I was gradually settling into a career path and the people within it who would become my professional community. I began training in aikido, a martial art, and found myself in a tight-knit group. First, though, I was in the bleachers with the regulars.

Examining communities from the inside challenges a lot of received notions about what a community is. British anthropologist Raymond Williams pointed out in 1983 that the key characteristic of the word community is that "it seems never to be used unfavourably, and never to be given any positive opposing or distinguishing term" (76). The reason so many people talk warmly about community is that it has been constructed in U.S. culture in utopic terms. For Americans, the word conjures up images of natural affinities and easy conversations, close emotional ties that are effortlessly maintained between people who almost always get along. While experience teaches us that this idyllic vision is off the mark, the idealized vision of community continues to have rhetorical sway. It also creates unrealistic expectations of what a community is, a point worth noting when we consider the aforementioned hand wringing about community demise.

One quality of community, though, that seems to be consistent, is the feeling that seems to accompany membership in a community. Anthropologist Anthony P. Cohen, in his 1985 book *The Symbolic Construction of Community*, described this as a community's consciousness of itself, an awareness among individuals that they were in a group that could be thought of as a unit. This kind of group self-consciousness is understandably difficult to measure or produce at will, resulting in a relative paucity of theorizing about community as lived. There have been countless studies of particular communities and perhaps more studies about how to mobilize communities. There have also been descriptions of traits that seem to be consistent across communities, although possessing any of these traits does not guarantee that a group is a community. What is needed is an exploration of how group self-consciousness arises and is maintained. People certainly know when they are in a community, but if the reason they know is "just a feeling," how can we study it?

Cohen's text is helpful, and I will refer to it again, but its focus on the symbolic dimensions of community amount to asking, "How does this community represent itself to itself?" This is an important question, especially given the problem of discovering a community's self-consciousness, but it leaves aside this point: what is it that people do together that prompts them to see themselves as an identifiably unified group in the first place? This is a large part of my project here: I seek to understand how people create and maintain the experience of community.

This book goes step by step through the different activities of the bleacher regulars in order to demonstrate that community needs to be conceptualized in terms of practices, that is, behaviors that become part of everyday life. These practices range from the simple act of gathering in the same location to elaborate rules of ticket distribution and seating arrangement. They include symbolic behaviors, like the easy embrace of superstition and magical thinking and the habit of referring to regulars as "family." Many of the practices of the regulars encode a moral stance toward the universe at large, often as ticklish and contradictory as any moral stance can be. In brief, I claim that community is best defined as a set of practices through which participants arrive at self-consciousness of themselves as a group with a particular relationship to the larger world.

This claim does two important things. First, it moves away from the idea that only specific practices or traits can legitimate a group as a community. This gives my definition flexibility to handle the changing social realities that cause community to look very different across generations. Second, it offers an analytic lens beyond the "warm fuzzy" idea of community. This is an important quality given the late-twentieth- and early-twenty-first-century interest in grassroots campaigns and community initiative. With so much hope invested in community, it behooves us to have a means of recognizing what brings a community together—and what keeps it together.

Bowling Alone—A Measure and its Limits

I have already said that I take for granted that the bleacher regulars are a community. I have experienced a sense of belonging in the group, and I am working backwards to understand its wellspring. In this work, the regulars have been active participants, discussing, arguing, bringing me news clippings, and passing along book reviews and things they heard on the radio. It was Fred from Centerfield, with whom I share my season ticket, who first mentioned *Bowling Alone* to me.

In 2000 Robert D. Putnam published *Bowling Alone* as a follow-up to his 1995 article of the same name. The book gathered a wide array of statistical evidence to demonstrate that American civic engagement has undergone a steady decline since the 1950s. For the regulars, Putnam's thesis, widely picked up by the American mass media, validated the claim that what was happening in the bleachers was rare and special, so it is not surprising that it was a hot topic of conversation. The regulars were not alone in discussing Putnam's findings: by 2002, the phrase "bowling alone" had become a familiar metaphor for "not participating in the social life of a community" (Word Spy 2003).

Putnam has been the inheritor of a long-standing scholarly focus on community dysfunction, most famously advanced in the United States by the Chicago School of Sociology in the Progressive Era. This tradition is unsurprising; between the warm-fuzziness of community as a catchall word and the hopes popularly invested in community, we would expect to see community fall under close scrutiny. And so it has, and the resulting reports reflect concerns about communities failing to act in their own interests, or, perhaps more alarmingly, communities failing to exist at all. The latter position has bemoaned the destruction of social connections in the ill-defined "modern" era. As people become more individualistic, or as the world industrializes, or as capitalism spreads, or as moral education falters (the bugaboos are numerous and frequently polemical), then, the arguments run, people become lonelier. Interconnectedness is no longer understood, and society suffers as a result.

Putnam deserves great credit for the assemblage of data he presents in his 2000 book. He seeks out statistically measurable aspects of American social life and demonstrates persuasively that on many counts, Americans are less socially engaged than they were in the 1950s. He then claims that this downward trend is neither irreversible nor perpetual. Rather, he argues that "American history carefully examined is a story of ups and downs in civic engagement, *not just downs*" (2000: 25).

In Putnam's work, civic engagement is the defining quality of community and a lynchpin of successful democracy. He writes, by his own account, in an effort to shore up failing American institutions, to reverse the downward spiral his statistics reveal. Unfortunately, Putnam's model of what constitutes community is time bounded; the link he posits between civic engagement and community is specific to the immediate post–World War II era of American history. Much of what he seeks to restore appears to hinge on the existence of stay-at-home housewives (2000: 194–203), white racial hegemony (17–18), and strict demands for conformity (257–65). His most recent research, using the same measures, has led Putnam to claim that ethnic diversity has been a big contributor to the erosion of American social cohesiveness (2007: 138).

Putnam's analysis shows that the United States has been suffering a "collapse of community" when considered according to civic engagement of a *particular, measurable type*. That type of engagement was one that emerged in the United States during the early cold war, and Putnam's reliance on it as a baseline represents a key fallacy of his thesis. During this era, "American" was being aggressively defined in a way that is very different from what we see in the late twentieth century. The post–Civil Rights era, post–cold war world of the twenty-first century has presented the United States and its citizens with a wholly different set of issues and concerns. Putnam himself argues that there are signs in his data of a resurgence of community mindedness in the 1990s. What such data suggest to me is that American culture supports an array of models of social connectivity that operate in different combinations to meet the demands of different eras. This is a good argument for finding a definition of community that is less pegged to the community indicators of a particular era.

To his credit, Putnam recognizes that he is dealing with social change. He acknowledges that the bleak picture he paints conflates social connection with civic engagement, and states, "The average American in recent decades has been far from isolated civically or socially, but we seem more engaged with one another as friends (or *schmoozers*) than as citizens (or *machers*)" (2000: 97).[1] In other words, for Putnam, some kinds of community behaviors are better than others, and the good ones are the 1950s type behaviors that are fading in relevance.

I detail this problem to highlight the need for a model of community that is not so reliant on measures that may lose relevance over time. Putnam's statistics reveal a variety of countertrends to his claim of community decline. For example, sports spectatorship has been "rising rapidly" (2000: 113). For every drop in club meeting attendance, there has been a concurrent increase in concert attendance (114). He even notes that his central metaphor of "bowling alone" is misleading: he tells us "between 1980 and 1993 the total number of bowlers in America increased by 10 percent" (1995: 70), and those bowlers *weren't* bowling alone, they just weren't bowling *in leagues* (2000: 113). However, because the activities that are on the rise are less formally organized, Putnam dismisses them as relatively "asocial" and "passive."

My critiques of Putnam are far from unique. Nor do they decisively discredit Putnam's claims so much as offer an example of how a dispute over definitions can alter how we interpret statistics, and how the popular gloss of a scholarly argument can miss its nuances. Beyond the debate about method and definition, however, I find myself in deep disagreement with Putnam's preferred theoretical frame for understanding community. That framework— the idea of social capital—has become the most recognized mode for analyzing community at the start of the twenty-first century.

Social capital, like most models for discussing community, has serious limitations. As defined by Putnam, social capital "refers to features of social organization such as networks, norms, and social trust that facilitate coordination and cooperation for mutual benefit" (1995: 67). In other words, the problem of community for Putnam is that Americans have suffered a decrease in their social capital over the past fifty years. Thus, they are less able to coordinate and cooperate for mutual benefit than they have been in the past. A more cynical read would suggest Americans are less able to grease the wheels and manipulate "the system" in their own self-interests than in times past. Such a reading does not appear to be Putnam's intent, but it highlights the problem of trying to think of community by means of the metaphor of capital.

If the purpose of being in a community is the ability to get what one wants more easily, community becomes something instrumental. The framing assumption about human interaction in this case takes us back to Adam Smith's famous formulation of human motivation in terms of "what's in it for me?" (see 1976: 18). While a person could argue that companionship and human connection are ultimately only indulged out of material self-interest, such Machiavellian approaches to friendships and family relationships are popularly decried. Instead, we talk in more emotional terms of sympathy and love that lead us to see ourselves reflected in others and often to behave altruistically toward one another.

The social capital model has the advantage of appearing rational—hence its appeal. A claim that low voter turnout in the United States can be traced back to a cost-benefit analysis regarding community offers the soothing illusion that people are behaving in a systematic and predictable fashion. The story is made all the more compelling when accompanied by statistical data, since the ready comparability of numbers appeals to U.S. audiences. The problem is that community is a profoundly emotional and often irrational experience. Putnam's dismissal of informal "schmoozing" makes sense in this context; it is difficult to correlate hours at the movies with friends with tangible benefits like career advancement or better schools.

These difficulties and limits are what prompt me to use qualitative rather than quantitative measures. Unlike a statistical measure, which requires that a set of behaviors be identified to be measured before any survey can be done, a qualitative approach can be more flexible. Instead of reading community with the model of a balance sheet, I seek to identify the conditions of possibility for community and the practices required to make the possibility of community into a reality. How, in short, can emotional connection and group self-consciousness arise?

Communities and Their Conditions of Possibility

Theorists writing about the industrial age of the nineteenth and twentieth century tend to agree on one point: rapid change is a defining trait of an industrial (or postindustrial) nation. Each person is born into a world in which certain conditions are true: people make their livings in factory jobs, or Victorian architecture is all the rage, or it is possible to travel across oceans in a matter of hours. In the last few hundred years, the rapid pace of technological and economic change has practically guaranteed that the world that a person was born into would be startlingly different by the time s/he had children of his or her own. Children coming of age in the early years of the twenty-first century are inheritors of the digital revolution of the late 1990s, and with a facility startling to their elders, are adept at navigating the world of information via the Internet. The tools laboriously developed and learned by people only fifteen to twenty years their senior are taken for granted by these youngsters, and their way of life is necessarily affected.

It takes little enough imagination for us to see the generation gaps we encounter on a daily basis, whether those gaps are between us and our elders or our juniors. Certain changes in how we run our affairs become *conditions of possibility* (see Marx 1978 [1846]; Weber 1949) for new ideas and new ways of handling our lives. The widespread use of cell phones was a condition of possibility for a culture that expects to be able to reach anyone, anywhere, at any time. Then, as Jean-Jacques Rousseau so clearly recognized 250 years ago, yesterday's convenience has become today's necessity (1997: 165). As people become accustomed to instant connectivity, they become less patient with people who are not immediately available, and the cell phone simultaneously becomes an increasingly necessary part of life and an instrument that changes standards of sociability.

The idea of conditions of possibility gives us a means for developing a way of seeing community that is sensitive to different eras. If we work from the fundamental assumption that humans are inherently social (an idea presented in empirical terms by Charles Darwin in 1871 and generally supported by subsequent research), the question we are asking is what forms their social interactions tend to take under any given set of conditions. The condition of possibility for human survival in any time or place is the simple act of finding food to eat and shelter from the elements. In the twentieth- and twenty-first-century United States, the ability to find food and shelter has increasingly depended on the ability to find—or more usually earn—the money to pay for it. Because this effort to find or earn money is so crucial to our existences in the United States, our social lives are going to be shaped to a certain degree by how we have to adapt them to our jobs. In the 1950s, a way to create community feeling that worked with the basic desire to put food on the table was to have bowling leagues and belong to the PTA. In the twenty-first century United States, those community-forming mechanisms work less well, so new patterns are emerging.

I have sought in the following chapters to isolate conditions of possibility for community that transcend the specifics of any given era. What I have determined is on some level fairly self-evident. People need the space (whether physical or virtual) to come together (chapter 2) and the time to establish and deepen relationships (chapter 3). Less obviously, a group must have some sort of effervescent potential (chapter 4), some idea or thing about which all members feel passionately. The most important part of this passion is that people are confident that everyone in the group *shares* the same passion. This as much as anything serves as a social glue, and it explains to some extent why the bleachers are a good site to find community. As social psychologist Daniel Wann has demonstrated convincingly, a high identification with a sports team produces a high level of social well-being (Wann et al. 2001; Wann and Grieve 2008), in large part because sports fans know their fellow fans share their passion.

Once we have addressed the conditions of possibility for forming community, we must also consider the active role community members must take in producing and maintaining community. I have been characterizing community throughout this introduction as an "experience" derived from "practices," and that is not accidental. We frequently discuss communities as if they are simply repositories of individuals who can be labeled with the same term. In studying the bleacher regulars, it becomes immediately apparent that whatever else characterizes community membership, passivity is not among the traits.

The Practices of Community Formation and Maintenance

I have a standard line to explain the bleacher regulars to people who ask me what exactly it is I research at Wrigley Field. It begins like this: "I know this isn't what you think of when you think of the bleachers at Wrigley, but there's this group of regulars out there who regard themselves as one of the last true communities in the United States. And it's not like they're just saying that; the group dates back to World War II, and they get together for weddings and funerals and birthdays and look after each other's kids . . ."

I was launching into this spiel one muggy day in June when I looked to Marv from Centerfield for confirmation.

Marv gave me a look that might have been a comment on my naiveté or idiocy or both. "World War II?"

"Well, not the *same* regulars, but, you know, regulars. Other people were sitting out here back . . ."

"*I* wasn't even sitting out here back in World War II. The bleachers didn't *exist* in World War II."

The bleachers were actually built in 1937, and I knew Marv had been to games before the bleachers were built, but this was a difference of book history and lived history, and one of semantics. I was embarrassed, but I tried to save face with a challenge. "Look, when did you start coming out here?"

"I didn't start coming out here regular until '46, '47."

"Well, since the *end* of World War II, then," I decided a bit grumpily and ungraciously, turning my attention away from Marv and burying myself in my scorecard.

There is, of course, no real way to say when the community of bleacher regulars actually started. I have collected stories from many regulars, formally and informally, and the narratives without fail have one of two structures. In version one, the regular in question (like Marv) had been sitting in the bleachers by him or herself or with a couple of friends for some number of months or years. Eventually, this individual or small group would merge with another, larger group that was *always already* there. The second version of assimilation is also my own—I met a regular in a context other than the bleachers, and she introduced me to the regulars as a group. Over time, I and others sharing this narrative came to be a part of the regulars. Describing the group as dating back to World War II was a bit of license I had taken to explain the bleacher regulars to people *outside* the group. It was not, strictly speaking, a lie. But the truth—that for the regulars, there had *always* been regulars—would not stand up to a factual test. After all, how could there always have been regulars when there hadn't always been a ballpark or a team or even a city of Chicago?

I raise this point because it helps explain why we talk about community differently than we experience it. When we reflect on community for an outsider, we tend to use language derived from our feelings. There are undoubtedly thousands of groups like the regulars in the United States. They are informal groups, relatively undocumented outside their own membership, who likely think of their activities as "just what we do." There are not really founding members or codified rules of belonging. There is just a perception of something "real" and "organic" that simply exists.

This sentiment of organic-ness, of a community as something that develops of its own accord, has been the dividing line set between society and community all the way back to 1887. That was when German sociologist Ferdinand Tonnies (1957) started trying to distinguish between the kinds of groups that are created as social institutions, like schools and armies, and the other kinds of groups people seem to form without deliberate organization. Some theorists, like Miranda Joseph (2002), have argued that the organic community is a romantic ideal that masks practices of capitalist consumption and production. She joins other postcolonial and feminist theorists in critiquing the warm-fuzziness of community, noting the appropriation of the term in Nazi Germany and the attendant violence of forced belonging (xxix). In a similar vein, critical theorists have argued that the presumed organic quality of community works to stifle dissent by making a failure of "like-mindedness" a cause of schism.

These critiques of community are useful cautions. To the extent that community membership becomes a demographic category for marketers or becomes a holy grail for people who feel outside community, it has the potential to do harm. As previously noted, if the problems of the current age are dumped at the feet of community, the term is left empty, and by playing to people's fears and hopes of community, politicians and leaders of industry can leverage quite a bit of power. All of this is important, but as a framework for understanding community, it misses the mark in the opposite direction of Putnam's quantifiable social capital. Where social capital theorists fetishize a particular type of data, the critical theorists of community tend to neglect empirical data. Regardless of the potential mystifying effects of community, regardless of how the concept might be used to manipulate or control populations, the fact remains that people not only claim to experience it, but experience it in positive terms. They do so in a way that is not easily dismissed as "false consciousness," a distraction from the real problems in their lives. In fact, communities often organize precisely around such real problems. What community members fail to do is express the amount of work they do to make community happen.

This work is the subject of the middle chapters of this book. I consider the practices of boundary maintenance and gatekeeping in chapter 5, showing how principles of inclusion and exclusion develop and change in practice. Even while such boundaries are established and a system is developed for maintaining them, a community focuses attention inward to organize itself. These internal tasks of organization are explored in chapter 6.

In addition to the structural work of community, the regulars engage in behaviors that on the surface serve no practical purpose. These are rituals and superstitions, habits of day-to-day life that are quirky and entertaining to witness. Chapters 7 and 8 examine these practices, showing how the everyday becomes the stuff of community, and how the extraordinary becomes evidence of the community's orientation toward the larger world. Taken together, rituals and superstition serve to produce the group self-consciousness that is central to community. While members of a community tend to use the language of what they *are,* the existence of their community hinges crucially on what they *do.*

In chapter 9, I offer a snapshot of what life looks like among the regulars and how the family metaphor has taken root among them for describing their community. These are the practices I mention in my usual descriptions— weddings, funerals, birthdays, childcare, vacations. They are the practices most American readers will recognize as common to their own communities, and I maintain that the practices outlined in the earlier chapters—in form if not content—are preconditions for what we witness in chapter 9.

I reiterate this point in the conclusion, but it bears repetition: what is community? Community is a word that describes a set of long-term social relations that are self-consciously and regularly maintained by all participants in the relationship. Those relations are predicated on a (frequently inchoate) sense of something shared. Members of a community act within a prescribed (usually implicit) set of practices and discourses that index their membership. Community acts to establish a person in a comprehensible social role through which s/he can choose to interact with a larger, more diverse social milieu. That social role includes a set of moral presuppositions about the way people should operate within the world. It involves trust in the face of situations that entail risk, and a basis for self-understanding. The degree to which such community is felt to be "real" or "true" by its participants is contingent upon an affective sense of connection between a person's "real self" and others.

In short, community is the means by which we navigate the larger complexities of our late capitalist culture. While we use the word *community* as a noun, our experience of it is of a verb, of a doing more than of a being. The more we are able to understand this as the underpinning of the term, the more we will be able to find (or build!) community if we desire it, and the more we will be able to recognize ways of getting communities to work together. By looking at what the bleacher regulars do, we can learn a broader lesson about how community works.

2

Social Space

It almost goes without saying that a community requires space. After all, how could a community exist at all without some place to bring people together? However, simply having a space where people can gather does not guarantee community. To complicate things further, there seems to be little consistency with regard to what kinds of spaces will stir community sentiment. A street corner can serve (Whyte 1993), and in recent years, a compelling case has been made for cyberspace as the starting point for communities (Rude 1996; Holmes 1997; Stoecker 2002). The questions to be answered, though, include "What qualities of space make it viable for a community? Are some spaces more apt than others to enable relationships and connections among individuals?"

I contend that part of the bedrock of any community is a sense of shared ownership of some space. I do not mean by this that people own their community in a private property sense, but rather that the space has taken on a specific social significance that allows it to both represent and mediate links between people. I have written elsewhere about the theoretical dimensions of understanding Wrigley Field as a social space (Swyers 2005), and here I recap some of those arguments. I also want to ground the idea of Wrigley as a social anchor in the world of the bleacher regulars in concrete examples from the ballpark and its environs.

The relationship between bleacher regulars and Wrigley Field is an objective human relationship, which is to say that Wrigley has a life in the imaginations of the regulars (and, indeed, in the imaginations of many other people as well) that goes beyond the simple physicality of its existence. The ballpark embodies and is implicit in generations of interactions between regulars. The regulars *know* the bleachers of Wrigley Field from long-time familiarity, and that knowledge has produced a kind of ownership of the place. Its history is deeply intertwined with their history, and events in the ballpark get woven into the life stories of regulars. Memories are shared and fixed upon the geography of the ballpark in ways that make them collective property of a special sort.

The balance of this chapter focuses on the specificities of Wrigley Field, both as generally constructed for public consumption and as particularly understood by the regulars. I open with a discussion of the marketing of Wrigley itself, a complicated and sometimes contradictory affair that makes Wrigley widely adoptable as a symbol for different kinds of communities. I follow with examples of lived experience of the regulars and the ways in which select aspects of the Wrigley legend have been incorporated into the community. I conclude with the regulars' handling of significant changes to their space: the 2006 renovation of the bleachers. Throughout, I will highlight how the social quality of Wrigley Field affects the possibilities of community.

Wrigley Field:
Baseball Cathedral or Playground for [Unprintables]?

To understand the regulars, a person must first understand Wrigley Field and its bleachers. There is no doubt that the park enjoys mystique in baseball circles, often described as a "cathedral." It is the second oldest ballpark where Major League Baseball is played.[1] It was the last major league park to get lights.[2] For the regulars, Wrigley is a crucial element of the community. As Bill from Centerfield explained, "People bond quickly because they are avid Cubs fans. This is a place where you can let your hair down. It doesn't really matter what field of work you are in or what nationality, religion you are. We don't talk business a lot; we don't talk politics a lot. It's a Cub thing. It's a baseball thing. It's a Wrigley Field thing. It was not the Cubs who drew me out here originally, it was Wrigley Field."

Note that despite Bill's assertion that the quality that makes people bond at Wrigley is their shared devotion to the Cubs, it was not the Cubs that drew him out initially. It was Wrigley Field. So why the field and not the baseball?

Part of the answer can be gleaned from a quick history of Wrigley Field. Wrigley Field with its grandstand was originally built in 1914 as Weeghman Field for the Chicago Whales, a team in the Federal League. When the Federal League folded in 1915, the owner of the Whales, Charles Weeghman, blended his team with the National League's Cubs, who began to play at Weeghman Field in 1916. Four years later, William Wrigley bought the team and the ballpark, renaming it Wrigley Field in 1926. Six years later, William Wrigley died after extracting a promise from his son, P. K. Wrigley, that he would never sell the Cubs. Peter Golenbock's excellent history of the Cubs, *Wrigleyville* (1996), covers much of this story in great detail, and we pick up from him some important information about the Cubs' new owner. P. K Wrigley, who apparently had no passion for baseball:

> [He] made it clear that his first priority in running the Cubs was to make his father's ballpark a monument, and he set about refurbishing it and making it the most beautiful ballpark in America.
>
> The reason he did this, he told Bill Veeck [Jr.], the son of the Cubs' late general manager, was that "a team that isn't winning a pennant has to sell something in addition to its won-and-lost record to fill in those low points on the attendance chart" (268).

Wrigley is also quoted as saying, "The fun, the game, the sunshine, the relaxation. Our idea is to get the public to see a ball game, win or lose" (268).

Wrigley Field, then, had the benefit of the marketing geniuses of Bill Veeck Jr. and P. K. Wrigley. Bill Veeck Jr. is perhaps most widely known for his publicity stunts; he was the man responsible for sending three-foot-seven-inch Eddie Gaedel to the plate as a pinch hitter in a 1951 game between the St. Louis Browns and the Detroit Tigers (Veeck and Linn 2001: 11–22). P. K. Wrigley is the man who convinced the U.S. government that chewing gum was an essential wartime industry during World War II (Golenbock 1996: 267).[3] Together, the two men managed to make Wrigley Field a green island in the middle of the city. Veeck planted the ivy that still climbs the outfield walls of the park. Wrigley mandated that radio announcers refer to the "friendly confines of beautiful Wrigley Field" (Golenbock 1996: 268), a tagline that continues to the present. For decades, the virtues of the ballpark were extolled above the (frequently poor) quality of the team.

In 1977, P. K. Wrigley died, but his ballpark vision by that point was well cemented in Chicago. When the Tribune Company bought the Cubs from the Wrigley estate for $20.5 million in 1981, they promised winning baseball, but they did not propose to alter Wrigley Field. Even as new revenue streams were developed from other stadiums (cf. Schaaf 2003), the Tribune proceeded cautiously. They maintained the hand-operated scoreboard installed by Veeck in 1937. To this day, advertising inside the ballpark walls remains relatively scarce. The games are still accompanied by organ music despite the existence of a sound system that could—and sometimes does—pipe in prerecorded music. These decisions have helped ensure that Wrigley Field retains the power of nostalgia, and more than one first-time visitor has remarked to me how much they can imagine it being "just like this fifty years ago."

Nostalgia, though, is not the only marketing factor at play with regard to Wrigley Field. While the Tribune Company savvily recognized it could sell "old tyme" baseball to fans, thus continuing the tradition of luring spectators to the park for the park itself, there were too many competing options for Chicagoans' entertainment dollars. In the 1970s, according to the regulars, there were days when the bleacher crowd numbered in the hundreds and a person could "count the house." The upper deck of the grandstand was closed off most of each season. While the Tribune Company might have hoped to remedy the empty-seat problem with winning baseball, they also had the sense to recognize they might not have a winning team overnight. Thus, one of the first moves the Tribune Company made was hiring Harry Caray to do the broadcasts of Cub games in 1981.

Caray had previously been a broadcaster for both the Cardinals and the White Sox, which initially upset many fans since the Cards and Sox are regarded by Cubs fans as rivals, if not actual enemies. Nevertheless, Caray brought a fun-loving, hard-drinking sensibility to the booth that quickly won people over. He also imported the tradition of leading the singing of "Take Me Out to the Ballgame" in the seventh-inning stretch. The cameras of WGN television, one of the first superstations, played to his appreciation of beautiful women and his unique brand of joie-de-vivre, showing off the "fun" to be had at Wrigley. Harry himself was promoted as "Cubs fan, Bud man," and his iconic connection to Wrigley led many to emulate his style of baseball appreciation.

What we see emerging here is a double marketing of Wrigley Field (for more on this, see Swyers 2007). On the one hand, there is the idea of a baseball cathedral, where the game is still played in a setting a person's grandparents could recognize and enjoy. The sanitizing quality of American nostalgia implies family-friendliness and traditions of deep respect. On the other hand, there is a party zone, a place that combines beer, sports, and scantily clad women.[4] American ideas of "hard play" away from the influences of family promote rowdiness, violence, and public drunkenness. A strongly mixed message was being sent about what constituted the Wrigley experience.

Into this mix exploded something that could not be anticipated: the now infamous "Lee Elia rant" in 1983. The 1983 Cubs had lost fourteen of their first nineteen games, and the players were receiving a particularly harsh razzing from the fans in the Wrigley Field bleachers. I have heard from regulars there that day that there might also have been an issue of beer being dumped on an outfielder, but I have been unable to confirm that from published reports. Lee Elia, the manager at the time, had had enough. At his postgame press conference, he lashed out:

> Fuck those fuckin' fans who come out here and say they're Cub fans that are supposed to be behind you, rippin' every fuckin' thing you do. . . . They're really, really behind you around here . . . my fuckin' ass. What the fuck am I supposed to do, go out there and let my fuckin' players get destroyed every day and be quiet about it? For the fuckin' nickel-dime people who turn up? The motherfuckers don't even work. That's why they're out at the fuckin' game. They oughta go out and get a fuckin' job and find out what it's like to go out and earn a fuckin' living. Eighty-five percent of the fuckin' world is working. The other fifteen percent come out here. A fuckin' playground for the cocksuckers.[5]

Ironically, Elia may have done the Tribune Company an enormous favor. Although his words were widely printed and replayed, rather than alienating fans, they galvanized bleacher fans into a more united body and gave them a recognizable identity. Regulars to this day refer back to Elia's rant, and buttons circulated in the bleachers in the mid-1980s read "working Cubs fan." The strong identification of the bleacher fans with Elia's rant had a twofold effect: first, it gave visibility and credibility to the idea of a party zone in Wrigley; and second, it implied a division between the "respectable" grandstand and the hard-partying bleachers. While this later idea has never been given official voice, it is striking that when incidents of fan misbehavior at Wrigley are widely publicized, the response has tended to be a limitation of beer sales in the bleachers, regardless of where the problem occurred.[6]

When the Cubs finally did begin winning in 1984, "the Cubs [drew] more fans than any year in their history . . . [and] the Cubs were the top-rated show every day of the season from mid-June on—regardless of the time of day they played" (Golenbock 1996: 472). At this point in Cubs history, WGN was carrying almost every single Cubs game and broadcasting it nationwide through early cable networks. A backdrop to every game was the bleachers, awash in sunshine and replete with happy fans, raising their beers and screaming their love of their team.

Here it is worth noting how the bleachers were *backdrop.* This matters because the multistage construction of Wrigley Field made the bleachers and the grandstand entirely separate structures. Through 2005, in the left- and rightfield corners, the bleachers met the grandstand in narrow seating sections only four rows deep that older regulars referred to as "the catwalks." The resulting bottlenecks made it unsafe to move masses of people through the space. This meant that bleacher fans could not enter the ballpark through any of the grandstand gates, and vice versa.

The end result of the mixed marketing and the distinct worlds of the bleachers and the grandstand is the creation of multiple Wrigley Fields in people's imaginations. The marketed "Wrigley experience" figures into the conceptions people have of the ballpark, so when people visit the ballpark, they are bringing together the physical space, their impression of the marketed Wrigley experience, and their own emotional reactions and interactions in the stands. The preconceived notions of what Wrigley *should* be like help people interpret their individual experiences, and this in turn gives them a vocabulary for talking about that experience with others who share a similar template.

The possible shared understandings of Wrigley Field are always tempered by lived experience. For people like the regulars who are at Wrigley far more often than the typical fan, the lived experience of the ballpark creates a very specific idea of what the park represents, and that is often deliberately placed at odds with the available marketed versions.

Wrigley as Lived by the Regulars

Because of the structural qualities of the bleachers and the grandstand, bleacher fans have to enter through a specific gate: Gate N. Gate N is at the corner of Waveland and Sheffield Avenues, and it has the feel of a back entrance. Aside from Murphy's Bleachers directly across Sheffield Avenue and a small parking lot kitty-corner from the gate, the streets leading to the corner are residential. Less than half a block down Waveland and clearly visible from the gate are the trestles of the El train with a couple of port-a-potties tucked underneath. The back of the centerfield scoreboard looms above, the words "Chicago Cubs" picked out in neon, but the intended audience is the riders on the El, not the people on the street.

For many years, bleacher tickets were only available as day-of-game sales.

There are boarded up sales windows by Gate N, remnants of those days. People would arrive before dawn to line up for tickets, settling along the red brick exterior of the outfield walls. Advanced tickets were made available in the mid-1980s in response to neighborhood concerns about people camping against the ballpark walls. However, because the bleachers are general admission, people still arrive well before the gate opens, lining up for the best chance to claim their favorite seats before anyone else can.

It is clear, then, that bleacher fans are set apart from other Wrigley spectators even before they enter the ballpark. This sense of being set apart and subject to different rules helps to create a certain esprit de corps among bleacher fans, and that spirit is pronounced among the regulars. The shared experience of waiting at the bleacher gate, a behavior dictated by the spatial qualities of Wrigley Field, has become part of what it means to be a regular.

Because of the long history of the park, other spatial features have figured into Wrigley Field's image and have been subject to interpretation by the regulars. There have been significant structural changes, including the additions of lights, luxury skyboxes, electronic scoreboards (small, but nonetheless present), and rows behind home plate. In the winter of 2005–6, the bleachers were almost entirely demolished and rebuilt. Each of these changes has served to punctuate time and orient the regulars, demonstrating the ways in which spatial change features in communal memory. The ability to use this history also distinguishes the regulars because they are self-consciously able to see through marketing histories that promote the unchanging quality of the ballpark.

These practices demonstrate the importance of space for community maintenance and ordering. For example, when regulars are telling stories, often they incorporate information about how the bleacher space was different during the era from which the story originates. This cements how long different regulars have been part of the community and positions regulars in an informal hierarchy. As an example, a regular might start a story by saying, "This was a while ago now, back when the men's room was right where that concession stand is now . . ." Other regulars will interject: "Oh, yeah, I remember that," or "I've heard it used to be that way." The first response establishes a regular of relatively equal authority to the storyteller, while the second reaction marks a newer regular who has been around long enough to know the history but not to have lived it. A third response—an incredulous "The bathrooms used to be up here?!"—would signal a much newer regular or a fan from outside the community.

This way of using history is available to any social space where people have long-term attachments. In this way, a space effectively becomes a mediator of the relationships among individuals. For the regulars, the geography of the bleachers not only mediates their relationships, but it provides a map of how the community understands itself.

The bleachers of Wrigley Field cover a boomerang-shaped space that is raked toward the playing field. Long benches follow the arc of the outfield wall with occasional aisles allowing access. This seating pattern is interrupted in two directions. In centerfield, a wide aisle with a concession area splits the bleachers into an upper and lower level. Also in centerfield, an entire section of seats has been replaced by a "batter's eye"[7] that has been variously draped with Astroturf, filled with shrubbery, and, most recently, become the site of a luxury box.

What we see in the bleachers, then, is a seating area for approximately four thousand informally mapped into four quadrants by the regulars. The quadrants are leftfield, centerfield (or right-centerfield, depending on who you ask),[8] rightfield, and upper centerfield. Each quadrant has its own regulars, although in recent years, upper center seems to have faded as a presence in the bleacher regular cosmos. Regulars identify themselves by their seating area, and this identification produces a social map of the regular community.

How does this work? Let me take my own case as an example. I sit in right-centerfield, and I call myself a centerfield regular. When I meet a regular I do not know, I will introduce myself thusly: "I'm Holly from Centerfield." This will generally produce one of two reactions. The first is an "Oh! Okay," since regulars frequently talk about each other, and a person might be known by name rather than by face. The second alternative is an "Oh, so do you sit by X?" The other regular will then name one or more people from centerfield in order to place my social connections. Almost every regular knows at least one person in each of the other fields, and this getting-to-know-you ritual can begin to sound like the "six degrees of separation" game.[9]

To unpack this a little further, "centerfield" serves in place of my surname in bleacher regular relationships. It identifies not just where I tend to sit, but also allies me with a certain social network. While I have friendships with regulars in left- and rightfields, it is understood that my primary loyalties and connections are with the other centerfield regulars. I am expected to be relatively up on centerfield gossip, to have a rough idea of what sorts of things are going on in the lives of centerfield regulars, to know the likes and dislikes and internal connections and animosities that define life in centerfield. By a certain way of reckoning things, if the bleacher regulars are my kin group, then centerfield is my immediate family.

That said, my membership in the bleacher regular community is not a product of relationships I formed outside of the context of Wrigley Field. Instead, the relationships I have with regulars outside the ballpark are all based on the relationships formed during ballgames. Those relationships grew out of *proximity* as much as anything else; my social connection to the rest of the centerfield regulars grew out of a spatial seating arrangement.

This is where the general admission character of the bleachers becomes significant. The piece of bench I end up sitting on each game is determined by one of two things: how quickly I can get into the park, and/or whether or not someone has saved a seat for me. If I can arrive at Wrigley Field when the gates open, two hours before game time, I more or less have my choice of seats. Otherwise, I am at the mercy of the seating patterns of the people who have arrived before me.

The same is true of every bleacher regular. A small percentage of regulars are able to arrive for gate on a consistent basis,[10] but most are juggling other responsibilities and can only arrive early occasionally. Almost every bleacher relationship involves, at some level, the desire to secure a seat with pleasant company. This motivation drives both regulars who cannot arrive for gate and those who regularly appear when the gates open, and it makes seat-saving arrangements mutually agreeable. It also marks a certain impatience among the regulars for aspects of the "party-zone" appeal of the bleachers. Regulars are pointedly baseball fans, and surrounding themselves with other people who are likely to be watching the game more than the party scene is a way of exerting control over their environment.

What this highlights is one of the more unusual characteristics of the regulars; most regulars have spent some portion of their baseball lives going to games solo. Eventually, each found the regulars in closest proximity to his or her seat of choice, usually because s/he has realized that the same group of fans is in the same seats at every game. Because the bleachers offer freedom of movement, the soon-to-be regular can sit next to the regulars and begin to integrate into the group. Through the regulars in whatever field the person starts in, s/he will be made aware of other groups of regulars and may decide to sit in a different field.

This last step in the process is part of what creates the sense of different fields having different characters, adding a depth of meaning to the social map of the bleachers. Leftfield, for instance, has a reputation for being tremendously more organized than either center- or rightfields. Centerfield is stubborn and can be curmudgeonly, while rightfield seems to attract a more independently minded, live-and-let-live-type of regular. When I identify myself as a centerfield regular to another regular, I not only reveal my social network, I also make a statement about qualities of my personality.

Space as Anchoring and Mediating

From the above discussion, we begin to get a sense of how the space of the bleachers gets folded into social relationships. Because the ties between space and people are part of a geography of relationships and seating patterns have become meaningful on an interpersonal level, we can say the regulars have appropriated Wrigley Field (or at least the bleachers). The ballpark has become a part of each regular's identity, and this in turn gives regulars a sense of ownership. It is a *part* of each regular, and as such, it forms an anchor point for the community.

Bleacher regular relationships are complex, often involving close personal involvement with one another's lives. This seems a startling claim when we have already seen the apparent contingency of these relationships. With very few exceptions, bleacher friendships *began* at Wrigley Field. As a result, Wrigley Field is not only a part of each regular, it is a crucial element in the relationships *between* regulars.

A classic example of this is the friendship between centerfield regulars, Judy and Colleen. Judy and Colleen met in 1975 in rightfield. Together with a few other young women around the same age, they attended hundreds of games, making a point of sitting together. They used to play Uno on the bench between them while they watched the game and kept score. "I don't know how we did it," Colleen confessed. "If we tried it now we'd miss plays." Over the years, they got to know one another well, confiding in each other during slow games and rain delays. They traveled across the country to watch the Cubs play, every trip adding to the store of stories demonstrating the strength of their friendship. As they grew older and got married and had kids, their friendship deepened, and today they still are best friends.

Throughout this friendship, the ballpark has figured prominently. It is not unusual to have them break out ballpark chants from an earlier era during a game, laughing as they share inside jokes. They compare levels of loyalty, Judy talking about bringing her infant daughter to a game, Colleen outdoing her by stopping by the ballpark on the way home from giving birth to one of her sons one Opening Day. While they are in daily contact throughout the year, it is clear that the continual returns to Wrigley evoke decades of memories and serve to renew the bond they share.

This idea resonates with a similar story told to me by another set of longtime ballpark friends, Sue and Cyndi. We were standing in the bleacher line on Opening Day 1999, when a pull-down door in the wall behind us was lifted a couple of feet by someone on the inside. We jumped, startled, but the door opened no further. After a moment it slammed shut. Then Sue looked at Cyndi. "You remember that time . . . ?" she began.

Cyndi began to laugh, and I looked mystified, cuing a classic bleacher story.

"We were younger and thinner then," Sue began, Cyndi still laughing beside her. "It was right about dusk, and we were walking by and we saw the door"—she held her hands out about two feet apart—"it was open only about this far. So Cyndi says we should go in."

Cyndi picked up the story. "Sue didn't want to do it. She was afraid we'd get arrested or something, and I replied, 'This is a public park and the door was open.' Sue just gave me this look and said, 'You've been watching too much *L.A. Law.*'"

"So we looked around," Sue continued, "and we looked at each other and we got down and squeezed right under and into the park."

I was incredulous. "What did you do?" I asked.

"We sat in the bleachers, reminiscing and admiring the field from that vantage point," Cyndi recalled. "Then we decided to go into the regular stands."

"We ran all over the park. Cyndi, you remember you had on that skirt—"

Sue was laughing as hard as Cyndi at this point. "Yes!" Cyndi agreed. "It was this little short skirt and we're running all over. We swung around the leftfield foul to get to the grandstand, and I'm hanging there, my butt in the air—"

"I know someone got a thrill out of that," Sue interjected.

"Oh yeah, we know people were watching us in there. They could tell we weren't going to do anything, though. So we got in the grandstand and sat there a while."

"And then we went out onto the field." Sue's tone began to get more serious and dreamy.

"I put my face in the grass," Cyndi said in the same tone. "It was so soft . . ." Then she paused and added in a more joking voice, "Sue was running around like a ballplayer catching the winning out in a crucial ballgame." Her eyes got a conspiratorial glint. "We even went into the dugout."

"Remember how you used the toilet?" Sue prompted.

"You didn't!" I exclaimed. "In the dugout?"

"We went into the dugout and it was right there," Sue began.

"We got down there because we just wanted to check out the dugout, and I saw that toilet and I said to Sue, 'I really need to go.'"

"And I'm going, 'Oh my god, are you going to use it?'"

"And I'm like, 'why not?' So I used the toilet in the Cubs dugout."

We all laughed for a bit, and then Sue said, "So anyway, we kept running around the park for like twenty minutes before we got out the same way we got in. And as soon as we were out—"

"This is the freaky part," Cyndi put in.

"As soon as we were out from under the door," Sue continued with a sense of drama.

"The door came slamming down!" Cyndi revealed.

"And I mean as soon as we were clear."

"So we know someone was watching us the whole time."

"Man, security must have gotten such a thrill watching the two of you run around," I teased, and we continued in that vein for a bit. Then Cyndi and Sue began to speculate that maybe the Cubs don't really mind if people get in there as long as they are not destructive.

This of course elicits the question of how security (or anyone) would know a pair of young girls running around the ballpark would not be destructive. Maybe those years ago, when Cyndi and Sue had their opportunity to lie out in grass of Wrigley Field in the gathering dusk, people were more trusting, or security was confident they could catch them if they did anything awful. I think it is something more basic than that. Sue and Cyndi speculated that they were allowed to play because someone believed they wouldn't be destructive. More accurately, both Sue and Cyndi knew *themselves* that they could never be destructive to Wrigley Field. They projected their self-knowledge onto security, and maybe whoever was operating the cameras and check stations that day did recognize a pair of regulars when s/he saw them. The point is a regular would never harm the ballpark or anything attached to it. In fact, a regular would be more likely to *repair or improve* the ballpark than do anything to harm it.[11] After all, for the bleacher regular, Wrigley Field is a second home.

Wrigley Field is in this sense a participant in the lives of regulars, and that participation is significant. The bleachers color every relationship in particular ways and become part of the identities of regulars. The space is the context that makes many of the relationships possible in the first instance, and it is almost always a third party in the relationship between any two regulars. It is also a third party in the community more generally, something that becomes clearer by considering the example of "the death seat" in centerfield.

Space and Changing Social Orders: The Death Seat

Over the course of the past few years, knowledge of the death seat has slipped beyond the circle of bleacher regulars. Part of this is my fault; I have used it as an example in interviews and in published work, so its existence is becoming public record. Its legend has taken on a life of its own, evident in a YouTube video that appeared in 2007.

The YouTube version of the death seat legend is particularly entertaining, as the video's creator states, "They told 'em over in leftfield that forty people died in this seat." Norb from Centerfield sets the record straight, but the initial exaggeration is an example of playfulness by people in the know at the expense of credulous newcomers. The regulars own the death seat as a social artifact inasmuch as they structure social relations around it, using it to mark the connections they share with one another.

So what is the death seat? It is eighteen inches of bench at the end of the top row of what is now section 311. Over the course of the last several decades, this piece of bench has been inhabited by the oldest of the centerfield regulars. As each of these older regulars has passed on, abandoning the ballpark due to failing health or death, the next oldest regular has claimed the seat; at least, that was the case through 2006. The seat has intense and ambivalent meanings for centerfield regulars. It is simultaneously a seat of honor and a reminder of one's mortality—hence the "death seat." The seat has carried that designation for decades, and it has become storied as if it had powers of its own.

Through 2005, the death seat was oddly configured by bleacher standards. It was at the end of a row, and the rail that backed the bench ended in the middle of the seat and pitched forward a little. There was also a step down in the foot space, so when a person sat in the seat, his or her feet were at different levels. To a person unaccustomed to sitting there, it was an uncomfortable seat. It was impossible to lean back comfortably, and the uneven footing put the fan at risk anytime s/he jumped up to cheer something.

When I first began sitting in the bleachers in 1997, only one person ever sat in the death seat: Marv. Marv turned eighty during the 2004 season, and at the time, he was among the most well known of the regulars. He is not a tall man, thick in the torso with a bit of a beer gut. He still has a full head of snow-white hair, though, and he always sported a half-smoked (but unlit) cigar at games. These features and his seat near the concession stand made him highly visible, and his acerbic wit made him easy to remember. When I met him, he was the resident elder in centerfield, although he would correct me here to point out we sit in *right*-centerfield. *Center*field has been blocked off for decades to make a batter's eye, but years ago, Marv used to sit there with the gamblers. Those gamblers bet on every pitch, Marv has told us more than once, and they are among the characters featured in the play *Bleacher Bums*, conceived by Joe Mantegna and written and performed by the Organic Theater Company.

Marv's health began to fail in 2002, and as a consequence, he began to miss games. This was jarring to centerfield regulars. Positioning someone at the end of the row was important to maintaining both the established boundaries of the regulars' section and to signaling and maintaining the social organization of the section. But who was the appropriate inheritor of the death seat? For years, Tom from Centerfield (a.k.a. Marv Junior) had been the heir designate, but he had left Chicago. Judy was the next logical candidate for the seat by virtue of game attendance and seasons in centerfield, but she steadfastly refused to sit there.

To complicate matters, volunteers who sat in the death seat tended to trip or stumble, falling from the seat into the aisle in dramatic fashion, adding to the mythology of the seat. It appeared not only to be reserved for the eldest member by convention, it increasingly seemed to reject anyone who had not "earned" the right to sit there. For a time, the seat was left vacant during games, protected by a warning to anyone who sat there: "The last four people who sat there died." The warning and the inherent discomfort of the seat usually worked to keep the seat empty during Marv's absences.

Since the bleachers were reconfigured in 2006, though, the death seat has become a more viable seat. In addition, Marv has attended fewer and fewer games, and what has emerged is the daily problem of managing the death seat. Centerfield regulars, led by Judy as the acknowledged elder, developed a roster of death seat volunteers from its existing membership. As we can see, dealing with the death seat among the regulars involves knowledge of its relationship to the regulars and the regulars' relationships to it. Regulars from other sections respect the death seat, and when Marv is not at a game, they will ask, "Who's sitting in the death seat?" The seat helps to order relationships, and it allows for a way of talking about situations when the section feels out of order. Its past becomes a part of the present, dictating what can and cannot be done and who can and cannot sit there.

As 2007 began, new dimensions emerged in the death seat drama. Marv had not been at any games early in the year, and Judy had had a brainstorm. To avoid conflicts over the death seat, she decided to seat Howard, one of the blind regulars who sit in centerfield, in the death seat. This seemed an excellent solution, as it moved Howard up a row from his previous seat, which had always had a lot of traffic. Howard was happier because he was jostled less by fans climbing past him on beer and bathroom runs, Judy was happier because she was freed from daily death seat arrangements, and the section was happy to be settled into a new routine.

Then Howard developed health problems. When word got around, Judy began hearing from other sections about her decision to put Howard in the death seat. Worry grew as Howard missed weeks of games, but happily, he recovered fully and returned to the bleachers. During his absence, however, a new set of issues developed.

One of the consequences of the 2006 bleacher renovation was a dramatic change to leftfield. Previously only four to six rows deep in the corner where the leftfield regulars sat, the section had become fourteen rows deep. The section was accessed from the top, which meant to sit in the regulars' old seats required walking down several steps. For a couple of leftfield regulars, the stairs were an impossible hurdle. However, sitting at the top of the section meant sitting too far away from the other regulars to benefit from their company.

These sorts of seating issues appear periodically among the regulars. The need for a backrest during games, for instance, drove many regulars to the back rows of sections from backless benches closer to the field. One regular's migration, though, might not be enough to persuade others to leave their long-time seats, and groups have splintered and reformed around such seating concerns, sometimes amicably and sometimes not.

In this case, the leftfield regulars who were unable to join the group next to the field decided to shift to centerfield where the death seat was known to be open. Suddenly, the death seat's social meaning had changed. Where for centerfield, the seat represented an absent elder and a shift in leadership from Marv to Judy, to the newcomers from leftfield, it represented integration into a group after feeling orphaned from their previous section. While the leftfield regulars respected Judy's authority to make the final call, they also put her in the middle of choosing the death seat's occupant and of negotiating between people to ensure harmony within the section. In key ways, the death seat has become an early test of Judy's leadership, mediating a changing of the social order in centerfield as surely as any individual has.

While these recent developments may produce an image of squabbling children more than of an established community, it does serve to illustrate my point: the death seat itself has a very real life in the imagination of regulars. While none of them *own* it, each has a stake in the social message connected to *occupying* it. That social message only matters in the context of the community. There are plenty of aisle seats in the bleachers. The seat itself is nothing special. Most fans, if not for recent media attention, would not know anything called "the death seat" exists.

The feeling of ownership that emerges from daily experience and practice is crucial to any community—and to the creation of social space. To take a simpler example, it is unlikely that any of the legal owners of Wrigley Field knew that among the things they destroyed when they renovated the bleachers was a nametag affixed to the wood under the fiberglass of row 6 in section 144. I know about the nametag, announcing the seat in question as Jeff's, covered in commentary from fans sitting in row 6 in the late 1980s on days when Jeff was not there, because Jeff from Rightfield told me about it. Jeff no longer sits in row 6, or even in rightfield (the renovation moved him to left), but the nametag remains in his memory as part of the landscape of the bleachers. He *owns* the memory and is able to share it with people who appreciate its significance and will incorporate the memory into their own mental maps of the bleachers. The concrete feeling of *being there,* of claiming a moment of time in a place, is a central element of this kind of ownership.

This ultimately leads us to material that I will cover in chapters 3 through 5, the issues of time, of shared emotion, and of boundary creation and maintenance. Here, though, is a good place for recap. We have seen throughout this chapter how the bleacher regulars have a particular sort of ownership relationship to Wrigley Field, and that relationship helps them construct a feeling of community. What is crucial to understand here is that this *feeling* is both real and anchored to a particular version of Wrigley Field. It is precisely this *feeling,* this *consciousness* of community, that makes the regulars describe their community as "true" and "real."

How does the social space of Wrigley Field help constitute this feeling? In the first instance, it is available to be constructed as social space by features of its geography and history. Because the bleacher regulars are set apart from the rest of the fans, and because they are allowed to sit where they choose within the bleachers, they are able to engage in practices that help construct community. These practices, which we shall see played out throughout the rest of this book, are the habits of social mapping. The relative permanence of Wrigley Field has made it a stable point of reference, a place to return to in order to mark the changing of the seasons and the years and to renew social ties. Its rhythms and cycles make it a predictable force, a knowable entity in the lives of regulars, and regulars use their shared knowledge to affirm their sense of community with one another.

The bleacher regulars *own* Wrigley Field, not in a legal sense, but in the sense of being intimately connected to it. They have appropriated it and made its space their own. It is a crucial component of their community, bringing them together and marking their commonality. In these ways, the creation and maintenance of social space is intimately connected to establishing "real" communities. The ties that hold groups together need an environment within which they can form, and it behooves us to discover the sorts of spaces that allow for human appropriation. Among our questions in studying community should be, "What is this community's Wrigley Field? What space do they own?" For the purposes of this book, this is the opening that also allows us to ask precisely what it is that regulars do in their space that makes them a community. First and foremost, though, it opens the question of how they come to give enough time at Wrigley to create a community, the subject of my next chapter.

3

Baseball Time

"It's like we were saying," Judy from Centerfield began, "no matter how long you've been out here, there's something you've never seen before."

On this occasion it was raining. A lot. An unpredicted, thoroughly drenching downpour had begun with one out in the bottom of the ninth inning, right after the Cardinals' shortstop had performed a circus catch in short leftfield, complete with a near collision that was avoided when the leftfielder leapfrogged over him. We scrambled into ponchos and put up umbrellas, and the game continued. The Cubs' Jeromy Burnitz singled, Ben Grieve struck out, and the rain kept falling. I had turned to Judy and said, "It would be the height of absurdity for them to call a rain delay in the bottom of the ninth with two out."

Two batters later, the Cubs had the bases loaded, largely because the field was playing like a slip-and-slide, and the Cardinals fielders were having a hard time keeping their feet. The umpires convened in the middle of the field, and at 9:54 pm, with the Cubs losing 6–1 and two out in the bottom of the ninth, a rain delay began.

Those of us remaining in centerfield began laughing. The height of absurdity had been reached. We were sitting in the pouring rain, waiting for the last play of a game we were almost certain to lose. It was raining hard enough that no one was sure when the game was likely to start again. We had already been at the ballpark for almost five hours when the rain started. Many of us had also been at the ballpark for six hours the night before, for five and a half hours the night before that, and for four and a half hours the night before that. In the space of eighty hours (from 5:05 pm Monday to 9:54 pm on Thursday), regulars who had attended all four games had potentially spent as many as twenty-one hours inside Wrigley Field.

For those of us sitting in centerfield, it was a moment of decision: stay or go? Connie from Centerfield, facing a bike ride home, opted to go before it got any wetter, as did many other regulars. In fact, most of the 37,000 plus fans who had been at the game had long since gone home. A crowd control member began loudly counting the individuals still visible in the bleachers and came up with a number in the low twenties.

Judy and I decided to stay, which is when she made her comment about something never seen before. We concluded that if the game resumed and we weren't still in our seats, we would betray our die-hard reputations.

The rain delay lasted fifty-eight minutes. During that time, we stayed in our seats and entertained regulars from left- and rightfields as they stopped by to laugh. Anyone who opted to stay was of the same mind: we all wanted to see what was going to happen. In years to come, people might not remember the specific game, but they would remember that there was a time that some regulars stayed in the rain to see a single out. It would be a badge of honor,[1] the kind of thing that could become part of bleacher lore.

This rain delay is worth noting for three reasons. The first and second are implied in Judy's observation that every year we see something new. Judy's remark contrasts with a far more common statement in the bleachers: "We've seen this movie before." The bleachers are a place where time moves in decided cycles within cycles, and events recur with a fair bit of regularity. However, even as the years roll into one another with a steady repetition of events, every year there is something entirely novel, entirely unanticipated, some anomalous event that becomes a marker in time. The rain delay we were sitting through when Judy made her comment also became an occasion to remember Mother's Day 2003. That day the Cubs were playing an afternoon game against the Cardinals in horizontal rain (blowing at forty miles per hour), conditions that defied any explanation for why the game was being played at all. After four innings, the game was called, at least in part because of a devastating injury to the Cardinals' Eli Marrero, who broke his ankle slipping on the outfield grass. Such events give a sense of history, albeit history tinged with a bit of mythology, as we shall see.

In addition to these two qualities of time suggested by Judy's comment—its cyclical nature and its ability to be marked—there is simply the matter of time itself. That Thursday night, we sat in the rain for what would appear to be an entirely unproductive hour. Tack on commute times to the already observed twenty-one hours in the stands, and it is clear that being a regular is no small time commitment.

The first question people ask when they begin to understand how much time is involved in being a regular is: "Who are these people who can afford to go to so many ballgames?" The question is one of both time and money. Some of the underlying incredulity of the question reflects a disconnect between how an outsider views baseball time and how a regular sees it. Otherwise, the question is entirely fair.

Who are the regulars? In the United States, we tend to answer this question in terms of what people do for a living. On that basis, a surprising diversity reveals itself. The list of regulars' occupations includes retail worker, nurse, retiree, lawyer, bartender, teacher, postal worker, CEO, artist, flight attendant, secretary, mom, television producer, marketer, and student. This is not an exhaustive list, yet to compile it, I had to work carefully around a bleacher taboo. I had to ask people about their careers.

I had understood the taboo before I heard it articulated. In essence, it is an unspoken ban on talking about work. I heard it best explained by Norb from Centerfield on a bus trip to Milwaukee in 1999. As Norb and I discussed what it was that made the regulars a community, Norb pointed out, "You can be sitting next to the biggest bum in the world for years and find out later they're a CEO of a company or a great artist or something. But we never talk about that stuff, so you'd never know what they do. We only talk about the important things."

Norb's observation was repeated six years later when I interviewed Ron from Leftfield. We were discussing the same point—what makes the regulars a community—and Ron said, "One thing that's noteworthy that Karen [Ron's wife] points out year after year is that it takes a long time before we know what people do outside the ballpark. Sometimes we even get elected officials out there but nobody cares what anyone does. Even so, we're there for reasons that go beyond the ballpark."

The "important things" and the "reasons that go beyond the ballpark" are events and people that will weave through this book. What is of interest here, though, is what is being left out of regulars' accounts of themselves and one another. In the context of contemporary American society, "What do you do?" is among the first getting-to-know-you questions a person is likely to ask. Different values are attached to different occupations, and a subtext of the "What do you do?" question is, "How do you contribute to the economy?" and "Are you as important as I am?"

This question as a means of identifying and classifying a person is one that only makes sense in a society characterized by specialization and an advanced division of labor. In short, it is an identifier that belongs to the logic of capitalism and/or bureaucracy. As life in the United States necessarily engages people in both capitalism and bureaucracy, this raises three questions: what are the regulars eschewing in avoiding discussions of occupation and social status outside the community? and why do the regulars mark the distinction between their bleacher experience and their work-a-day lives? and how are they making the distinction in practice?

While these questions may seem esoteric, they get at the heart of how the regulars "are able" to go to so many games. For the regulars, baseball time is often dearly purchased. Regulars have quit jobs and broken off relationships that interfered with baseball. Many have deliberately structured their careers to maximize their opportunities to go to Cubs games. This is no easy feat, since the Cubs play the majority of their games during the day. As ticket prices increased,[2] I know of at least one regular who gave up phone service in order to afford tickets.

This information only heightens the "why?" and the answer is found in the issue of "the important things" mentioned by Norb. A key point about time in the bleachers is that it is *passed,* not *spent.*

Time Passed—Not Spent

During the already mentioned bus trip to Milwaukee in 1999, Norb and I talked almost the entire way to Milwaukee County Stadium. It was a long trip, featuring traffic jams and a failing optimism about the possibility of tailgating before the game began.[3] I do not have a record of the entire conversation, but at some point, our discussion turned to the question of community. Norb was among the most adamant of the regulars in pointing out the virtues of the bleacher community. "It used to be," Norb began as Milwaukee County Stadium finally became visible through the bus windows, "it used to be that people would look out for each other, everyone in a neighborhood would know and care about each other. Now you can only find it in the bleachers."

We kicked around this idea for a while, and while I do not necessarily hold to the idea that community exists exclusively in the bleachers, Norb had picked up on a strongly felt sentiment. There is an idea current in the United States that there was a simpler time in our history characterized by something called community, and we tend to look for it in "traditional" societies. Later in this book, I will actually use examples developed in the study of small-scale societies to help understand some of the ways that the regulars interact and create community. However, in contrast to the small-scale societies usually studied by anthropologists, the regulars do *not* include their daily sustenance among their activities as a community. While the world of the bleachers can and does bleed into their lives outside of the bleachers, for the regulars, the bleachers exist as a separate kind of time.

A useful way of understanding the distinction regulars draw comes from sociologist Emile Durkheim. As he argues, most people divide their lives into "sacred" and "profane" aspects, with work-life most often designated as "profane" (1995: 33–39, 118–26, 216–25, 310–13). If we accept for the moment that the bleachers represent a kind of "sacred" space, a discussion of a person's career would "pollute" bleacher time and be inappropriate. By this logic, there is also a risk involved in bleacher time spilling into profane time, and inasmuch as regulars contort their lives to include bleacher time, this risk is real. While most regulars are upfront about their bleacher loyalties and the centrality of baseball in their lives, outsiders often don't understand until an otherwise responsible regular skips work for a game against the Cardinals or misses a wedding because the Cubs were home. This makes baseball time all the more striking: what is so valuable about this time within the community that it should be both protected from life outside the community and occasionally come at the cost of ties and responsibilities outside the community?

I argue that the regulars value many of the same things outside the regular community as they do within the community: loyalty, commitment, attention to detail, respect, passion, and love. However, in the world outside the bleacher community, the regulars are less able to demand those virtues of the people around them. The wider world is more subject to the pressure of "industrial time" (see Tamara Hareven 1982, E. P. Thompson 1993), the historical reality of living in an industrial society.

The consequence of participating in industrial time is that the logics of efficiency and productivity necessarily affect all decisions. Because a job in this kind of society is, for most people, a prerequisite for staying alive, every person sells control of his or her time to an employer. Thus, in the contemporary

United States, as historian E. P. Thompson explains, we see a world in which "all time must be consumed, marketed, put to *use*" (1993: 395). This contributes to our tendency to discuss time with the common idioms of "spending" and "wasting" time.

In direct contrast to the time of the world outside the ballpark, the regulars treat baseball time not in terms of how it is *spent*, but in terms of how it is *passed*. It is as if the community offers a distilled essence of everyday life, returning a perception of control of their time and resources to the regulars. This kind of personal control of time requires a careful fiction that workaday life cannot disrupt baseball time, which helps to make sense of the taboo on career discussions. It has also contributed to a dual notion of time itself among the regulars.

To borrow again from E. P. Thompson, in bleacher time, the world of the regulars is *task* oriented rather than time conscious. In essence, task-orientation ignores time. A task, like an inning, takes as long as it takes. In part because the clock is not part of the equation, there is less need to separate work and social time. Obviously, the regulars *do* separate work and bleacher time, but within bleacher time itself, "work" and "life" easily commingle. Finally, Thompson points out that to a time-conscious society, task-orientation looks like a frightful waste of time. A quick review of bleacher activities reveals that task orientation is the presumptive relationship to time.

Time in the bleachers is often expressed in terms of the length of time it takes to complete a task, like the time it takes to record an out on one's scorecard or the time it takes to get into and use the bathroom. The start of the game itself is the only clock-oriented time marker; beyond first pitch, regulars make plans to meet in the "pregame" or in the "late innings," amorphous stretches of time that are more recognizable for the energy of the ballpark than by the sweep of a minute hand. Upon entering the ballpark, most regulars surrender to this time. Families are prevailed upon to watch the game if they need to know when to expect a regular home. Dinner plans come with a caveat that they are always tentative if the Cubs are home. Occasionally, a regular will watch the clock, confessing that s/he must leave at a specified time for some obligation, but this is the exception rather than the rule.

Baseball time, though, is far from empty and unmarked. Once the gates open each game, the regulars make their way to their seats and engage in a variety of socially necessary tasks. The more urgent tasks (e.g., getting to the seats and spreading towels across them) are determined to be urgent by the competition for seats in the bleachers. The less urgent "tasks" (e.g., showing pictures, visiting other fields) happen at the leisure of the regulars. The obligations of the ballpark have their own force in regulars' lives, and they must be fitted into baseball time. However, within the context of baseball time, the various tasks performed at the ballpark are just "what we do," regardless of how ritualized or obligatory. Life and "work," however loosely defined such work may seem, become relatively seamless.

Certainly, it is true that the regulars are in baseball time for hours together without doing anything our postindustrial society would deem productive. Rather, they are productively building and maintaining friendships and community, activities that *are*, in the contemporary United States, seen as "wasting time." They are also diverting a significant number of resources in order to "waste" this time. However, it would be difficult if not impossible to find a regular who would agree that his or her bleacher hours should be understood as time wasted.

To sum up, the avoidance of work-talk in the bleachers is a way for the regulars to distance themselves from the world that values them for what they can do to make a living. In so doing, the regulars enable themselves to assert that they are not *controlled* by the constraints of time that the capitalist system demands. Rather than allowing their leisure time to be controlled by the clock that governs many of their work lives, the regulars retreat into baseball time.

Baseball time is not "quality time" in the way that term was constructed in the United States in the 1980s. The idea is not to cram social activities into a set period in a regular's schedule. It is instead as large a quantity of time as can be begged or borrowed, shared with people who have similarly begged and borrowed hours that they owe to no one but themselves and the community.

In addition, once entered, baseball time exerts a palpable force. It is not just time set aside, it is time reckoned differently. I have felt the pull of it on the rare occasions when I have had to leave the ballpark at a specific time, and I have watched the same emotions play on the faces of other regulars in the same situation. The logic of baseball time fights the logic of clock time, making it difficult to leave in the middle of an inning, for instance, no matter how important it is to leave on time. I have had occasion to curse decisions I made in baseball time as I snapped back into clock time and found myself running late or buying a game ticket for a day when I should have remembered I could not attend easily. At the same time, I could still feel the comprehensibility of my baseball time logic. I contend that this is because baseball time is cyclical time.

Cyclical Time

Various calendars from various cultures feature a notion of time that is running a cycle, numbering years not in an ongoing, infinite series, but rather establishing elaborate cycles within cycles. In many of these systems, it is ultimately factually possible to live the same year over again, albeit at such great intervals that said year is unlikely to recur within a single person's lifetime.[4] Some cultures show no evidence of numbering years at all, making the issue of sequential time irrelevant.

In a society such as exists in the United States, the idea of cyclical time is confusing. We are accustomed to hours and minutes and fixing dates in time. However, cyclical time is still evident in annual religious festivals and events. The standard English formulation, "Christmas is a magical time," highlights this phenomenon. A listener knows that the speaker is not referring to a *specific* Christmas; rather, there is a time of each year that is designated "Christmas." In a similar fashion, the regulars experience cyclical time at the ballpark.

Baseball is very much tied to its long season. The regular season is 162 games, starting in late March or early April and ending in late September or early October. The season splits loosely into early, mid, and late, each attended by various predictable events like the All Star Game and trading deadlines. The daily grind of the season eliminates some (although not all) of the "big game" energy that is more familiar to American football, and between the relative parity of teams and the fact that baseball games tend to be played in series of threes,[5] losing teams can say with some accuracy, "We'll get 'em tomorrow."

All of these qualities of the sport, when combined with its relatively long history in the United States,[6] contribute to a sense of repetition and regularity. Spring comes every year, and with it comes spring training, and then Opening Day. For the regulars, Opening Day is a "high holy day of obligation," a ritual feast of renewal. Everyone pours into Wrigleyville in the morning, making a traditional round of visits to bars and diners and morning barbecues. Parents and grandparents know to have recent photos of their children and grandchildren on hand. Regulars at every stop ask who else has been seen where and are informed of who has been looking for them. Glasses are raised to regulars who have died; news is passed about anyone who is missing for any reason. Forced changes to the routine are remarked, and plans are made for the day, the week, and the season. As noted in later chapters, the predictability of the experiences is a comfortable indicator of a healthy community as far as the regulars are concerned. Their way of life as embodied in Opening Day ceremonies is intact, and life goes on as it always has.

We have already seen how baseball time is valued, and for the regulars, the baseball season is part of a larger cycle of life. It contrasts the off-season, when social engagements with other regulars as a group require advance planning and must be more fully organized and arranged and thus occur with less frequency. The off-season is also a time of bitter cold and long hours of darkness in northern cities like Chicago, and the idea of the baseball season as a harbinger of warm and happy summer months is one that is more generally felt by the population at large. In fact, the traditional greeting of regulars on Opening Day is "Happy New Year!"

Not only the season, but also the games proceed in cycles. Lineups bat around, and a starting rotation of pitchers determines who will pitch on any given day. By midseason, regulars appear with the words, "Well, here we are again." The rhythm of the game quickly asserts itself, and not only the years but the games begin to blur together. The resulting steady and repeating cycle is part of what produces the amorphousness of time noted earlier. The effect is one of timelessness.

In anthropological studies, this timelessness is roughly comparable to the idea of being a "people without history." Although it could be argued that of course the regulars have history, to construct a historical timeline of the community would be an exercise in conflicting and contradictory accounts.[7] Important events are tied less to the calendar than to their defining features, and regulars can recount games in startling detail while completely misremembering the years in which they happened. The point is less *when* something happened than that it happened at all, and the shared memory of key events is less about the objective history of the regulars than it is about the experience that holds them together. In this sense, the regulars are what anthropologist Claude Lévi-Strauss called a "cold society" (1966: 233): they are a group of people who are determined that no matter what happens, the society will continue unchanged.

Even events that empirically do produce change are narrated in a way that allows the people in the community to maintain the idea that the change is just a new manifestation of something old and known. Over the past twenty years, the bleachers have seen the advent of advance ticket sales, the imposition of night baseball, a season-ending players' strike, a rapid increase in ticket prices, a startling increase in ticket demand, and a consequent renovation and expansion of the bleacher seating area. Each of these things has had a profound effect on life in the bleachers, and yet in a certain way, none of them has mattered.

In 2005, for example, the end of the season approached with a wrecking ball waiting to tear down the old bleachers. The regulars, armed with blueprints of the new seating area, knew their social map was about to be irrevocably changed. The community response is detailed in a later chapter, but for now, it is enough to know that people were worried about what would happen when the old seats were gone. It was a constant topic of anxious conversation after the All Star break, especially in leftfield. One September afternoon, I stood with Mary Ellen from Leftfield against the chain-link fence that ran along the back of the bleachers until 2006. We knew the new bleacher configuration would eliminate this gathering place, but Mary Ellen was philosophical. "We'll still be here," she pointed out. "We outlasted the Wrigleys, and we'll outlast the Tribune." Regardless of the changes, within the park or outside its confines, the implied argument was that there would still be baseball, the team would still be the Cubs, and the regulars would still gather in the bleachers.

In a society that values progress, this attitude is often described as "traditional" or even primitive. The idea, though, is a valuable one for considering the nature of community. This kind of time privileges *continuity* over change. While some faces may have changed, and some patterns may have been adjusted, within their own way of thinking, the regulars are always as they have always been.

The regulars work this magic by focusing on the steady rhythm of the baseball season and the strict structure of the game. Any season is a progression of wins and losses, and each win or loss is anchored within a realm of plausible scenarios. Within the context of these wins and losses, regulars' lives unfold against a steady backdrop of baseball that is regarded as unchangeable in certain fundamental ways.

A couple of examples will demonstrate how that steady backdrop is constructed. Take, for instance, a game in which the Cubs were down by fifteen runs in the seventh. When they started to come back, scoring five runs, centerfield regulars were far from optimistic. Marv called out, "Save 'em for Friday, you don't need 'em today." Marv's comment successfully weighed the potential for loss against the desire to win another day, when the slate would be clean. While it was not inconceivable that the Cubs could win, it was far more likely that they would lose—and they did.

Beside Marv, Connie slumped in dejection as the Cubs made their final out of the inning, still down by ten runs. "It's like watching *Lucy*," she remarked, referencing the television show *I Love Lucy*, perpetually in reruns on syndicated television. The idea of knowing exactly what was coming next fit the scenario of the impending loss and reinforced the sense of the game moving according to an established rhythm.

"Yeah," Judy agreed, "except *Lucy* is funny."

That got a laugh and murmured agreement, all tinged with an undercurrent of long-suffering. The shared sense of déjà vu, articulated as such, relegated the game to a familiar script. It was not the kind of loss that could change anything, no matter how much it might hurt.

As it happens, the more painful losses (or thrilling victories) serve to temper one another and produce a sensation of a season proceeding at even keel. One August game in 2004, the opposing team had batted around and was still hammering away at Cubs pitching.[8] One of the centerfield regulars, his or her name unrecorded in my scorecard, said, "They batted around so much the pinch runner is up,[9] that's a new low."

Another voice chimed in, "This is bad, but that 11–8 Cardinal game was worse."

The "11–8 Cardinal game" was one the Cubs had been leading 7–1 at the end of the second inning. It was the kind of game where someone would ask Marv, "Is this lead blowable?" and get his usual answer, "Yes." On this occasion, Marv would have been right. In the sixth, the score was 8–6, with the Cubs still holding the lead. The Cardinals scored again in the seventh, making it 8–7. Then they tied the game in the eighth. In the ninth, they scored three runs. We had gone from elation to anxiety to despair in four innings. The drubbing we were getting a month later was nothing in comparison. By the same token, the worse loss served to put the game in perspective, reminding us all that there are more games, and losses are just a part of the cycle of the baseball season.

Once the comparison started, however, it was hard to stop. Suddenly, Colleen shouted out, "7 to tie, 8 to win, we ain't dead yet!"

As I burst out laughing, Judy turned to glare at Colleen. "You're lucky no one's got a gun," she remarked, and Colleen just grinned back at her. The shout was a modified version of words made famous among regulars during a particularly humiliating 1984 playoff loss to the San Diego Padres.[10] Several regulars had traveled to San Diego expecting to watch the Cubs win a trip to the World Series. As it became clear that the Cubs would not win a single game of the three they played there, one regular spent the late innings of the last game running up and down the aisles trying to start the "*x* to tie, *y* to win" chant.

In terms of perspective, Colleen had trumped everyone. She had invoked a benchmark event against which the present could be measured. The regulars had witnessed countless losses since 1984, and it built character. This had happened before, and as before, it would pass.

Benchmark Events

A benchmark event, as seen above, is an occurrence unusual enough to stand out amid the hundreds and sometimes thousands of games regulars attend. While occasionally such benchmarks become historic, recognizable to outsiders as part of the narrative of the Cubs, they function differently within baseball time. By dint of steady repetition, a regular might remember what happened on June 23, 1984. However, it is far more likely to get his or her instant comprehension by referring to "the Sandberg game."[11] And while the regular might well use that opportunity to launch into a discussion of the 1984 team, it is more likely that the ensuing conversation will be free-ranging across decades of games without regard for any apparent temporal order.

Benchmark events serve to classify time, to mark moments as exemplars of the extremes that can be and have been experienced in the bleachers. The *when* is less important than the *what happened,* and the lesson is fairly consistent. On the one hand, the benchmark event serves as a measuring instrument for the present moment in baseball time. Is this the coldest I've been at the ballpark? The worst loss I've seen? The best win I've experienced? On the other hand, the benchmark is a reminder that baseball time continues, that this moment may be worth savoring, but the regular rhythm of the game and the season will reassert itself.

Some benchmark events are relatively local or confined to smaller groups of regulars. Some are held in esteem because they show how the regulars continue to behave like regulars regardless of the circumstances (the rain delay that opened this chapter is a case in point). Most benchmark events, though, are either shared memories, or they become the stories retold so often that they become required telling under the right circumstances. As an example, when a pitcher loses his no-hit bid by giving up a hit, the conversation automatically turns to no-hitters the regulars in attendance have witnessed.[12] Milt Pappas's near perfect game in 1972 will be mentioned, always including a harsh word for home plate umpire Bruce Froemming.[13] Marv from Centerfield invariably invokes Sam "Toothpick" Jones's no-hitter in 1955. "He walked the bases loaded in the ninth and then struck out the next three," Marv tells everyone, his tone managing to convey both the anxiety and the triumph of the moment even fifty years later.

One of the striking features of most benchmark events is the deep *sympatico* that tends to emerge between the regulars and the team on those occasions. In 1998, for example, Bill from Centerfield was assigned a seat in leftfield for the one-game playoff between the Cubs and the Giants. The Cubs had backed into the playoffs,[14] and the general sentiment was that the potential wildcard win was a gift from Harry Caray and Jack Brickhouse, Cubs broadcasters who had died that year. The team was playing far above its potential, and the standard explanation was that Jack and Harry were asking God for a favor up in heaven.

Because the playoffs were entirely unexpected, and because the season had ended in a tie, forcing this single-game contest between the Cubs and the Giants, the electricity in Wrigleyville was palpable. During the game, someone floated a giant balloon printed with a likeness of Harry Caray behind the bleachers,[15] and many photos from the night feature the eerie floating head looking down on the field. The general excitement increased to a fever pitch as the Cubs took the lead, and when they won, the crowd exploded. The Cubs ran around the field, spraying the fans with champagne and joining in the general reluctance to go home.

During this celebration, Bill was cheering with everyone when Cubs pitcher Terry Mulholland appeared on the field below and tossed up a bottle of champagne. Bill recalled, "Everyone in the stands around me wanted some of the champagne, but no one had any cups and I wasn't going to let go of that bottle for anything. So I opened the bottle and everyone came up to me like birds with their mouths open. I poured champagne into their mouths until the bottle was empty." The Cubs victory and the shared emotion afterward served to tighten the sense of Bill's—and everyone else's—connection with the team. In the same way that the team itself is ultimately whoever is wearing the uniform, the binding of the fans to the team contributes to the "eternal" sense of the regulars.

By using ballgames to create a sense of time (or more properly, timelessness), the regulars serve to cast their experience into something more akin to mythological history than objective history. I mean this not as a slight, but as a way of making bleacher history comprehensible. As Bronislaw Malinowski points out: "myth is not a dead product of past ages. . . . It is a living force, constantly producing new phenomena. . . . As there is a body of legends already fixed, standardized, and constituting the folklore of the tribe, so there is always a stream of narratives in kind to those of mythological time" (1954: 83). The "body of legends" of the regulars are the benchmark events, retold in terms that grow increasingly standardized with each retelling. Each story, each bit of folklore, connects by implication to a time immemorial, time characterized by curses and larger than life figures, as we will see in chapter 8. The events and activities that bleacher regulars experience are perceived and narrated as continuations of the way things have always been. The outward form of these events might be modified to deal with changing circumstances, but they still retain enough of their essence to be demonstrably the same as the days when Babe Ruth didn't call his shot,[16] and the regulars of that era, before the bleachers, razzed the players with the same efficiency as the regulars of today.

Passing Time and Community

While the above deals with how the regulars use baseball time to protect the continuity of the community and suggests why regulars strive to keep baseball time in their lives, it does little to explain how time is actually passed in the bleachers. Obviously, there are the games, but there are hours of pre-game time, between-inning breaks, and rain delays. This time is filled with conversation, much of it not related to baseball, all of it contributing to the building of community.

First, despite the taboo against it, it is not strictly accurate to say the regulars avoid discussing work at all. Many regulars blow off steam within their sections, venting about office politics, particularly if they've arrived directly from work. Such discussions about work, though, tend to focus entirely on the relationships within the work place, rarely touching on what the person actually does for a living. This pattern reflects a relatively conscious effort to minimize the influence of social standing outside the ballpark. When what someone does for a living does appear in conversation, the contexts tend to be specific conversations that touch upon their expertise or activities that require explanation.

A case in point is Jeff from Rightfield, revealed to be a flight attendant when the Cubs raised the price of scorecards to two dollars. The situation unfolded like this: the price increase on scorecards reflected a 100 percent price hike from the previous season. Unsurprisingly, this was greeted with shock and resentment among regulars who keep score. In what appears to have been an effort to mollify the customers who complained, a "free" pencil was offered with every scorecard. The catch was that a person had to ask for the pencil; it was not automatically handed over.[17]

Many regular scorekeepers asked for the pencil out of principle. Most, however, bring their own pencil or pen and score with it with superstitious diligence, and relatively early in the year, several regulars decided their rapidly increasing pencil collections were more of a nuisance than a value. By midseason, very few regulars were still requesting a pencil. I was discussing this with the rightfield regulars one day, and Jeff revealed he always took the pencil. Why? "I take them to Peru," he replied.

Not surprisingly, this statement required elaboration. This is when I learned that Jeff, whom I had already known for over a year, was a flight attendant. On international flights to Lima, he and other airline employees had discovered children waiting at the airports to beg for school supplies. "Pencils, pens, whatever can write," he explained. "We collect them and every time someone flies down to Peru, they take a whole batch of pencils and pens down."

"Do you want my pencils?" I asked.

The answer was yes, and I began to ask for my pencil every game. When other regulars heard the story, they, too, began saving their pencils, and at regular intervals, handfuls of pencils are delivered to Jeff, prompting observations that eventually the entire population of Lima's schools are going to be Cubs fans. What is worth noting here is that Jeff's career revelation was made to explain a behavior that otherwise seemed aberrant. It also created a situation that allowed regulars to recast their actions. Claiming a pencil had begun as an action of pique for many regulars, motivated by a desire to minimize the profit the Tribune Corporation made by "gouging" the regulars. Sustaining such pique, however, was difficult for the regulars. It warred with their self-perception as good people, and sat uneasily with the idea of loyalty in face of all adversity. The unofficial pencil drive offered the benefit of a shared activity that was driven by something other than anger.

Fireman Tom's[18] job was revealed in a similar fashion, albeit much earlier in his bleacher life. In the late 1990s, long before it was acceptable among the regulars to admit ownership of a cell phone (see chapter 5), let alone have it at the ballpark, Tom appeared with his phone attached to his belt. Accusations that he might be a yuppie were quickly averted by the explanation that he was an emergency worker. Fireman Tom has been the exception that proves the rule, a regular who is encouraged to share work stories. Often his anecdotes are cautionary tales, tied into news events and the history of the city and touching regulars lives directly. He will weigh in on discussions of safety and health with well-respected authority. When Illinois began issuing tickets to motorists who failed to wear seatbelts, for instance, Fireman Tom carried the point in the debate with a firm gaze and the words, "In twenty years, I've never unstrapped a dead body."

As implied by Fireman Tom's intervention, debates about current events are also part of the bleacher repertoire. "Did you see that story in the *Sun-Times* today?" someone will ask, detailing the events. Stories culled from radio, television, and the daily papers are thrown into the mix, opinions offered and alternate versions rehashed. Big events figure into the taunts thrown onto the field, as when a bullpen pitcher gave up multiple runs and someone yelled, "Send him to Abu Ghraib!"[19] Tragedies are often chewed over for possible preventative measures, and debates over correct action often grow quite heated. Such debates are among the forces that occasionally lead people to change sections, but as often as not, several different sides of an issue will be aired without any general agreement being reached.

One area where the regulars do tend to find agreement is when news breaks of someone "snapping" and causing bodily harm to others. While the perpetrator of violence might be reviled or be the source of sympathy, eventually some regular will say, "This probably wouldn't have happened if the person had something like this." The "something like this" includes a gesture encompassing the bleachers, encompassing the regulars and their community. Assenting nods will meet that pronouncement, even if disagreement on other points continues. The regulars, then, are far from insular or divorced from the external world. Rather, they see that world as colored by their bleacher experience and their confidence in the human capacity for community—if it is given the opportunity to flourish.

So how do these notions of time figure into the idea of community? How is maintaining baseball time a key to a flourishing community, and how can baseball time be transferred to other communities?

The key to baseball time, as I see it, is that it is maintained separately from capitalist, monetary time. This is largely an illusory act, since even attending a ballgame means participating in a capitalist economy. Being a regular means being able to buy tickets to games that have increased in price up to 300 percent in twelve years. Baseball time must be purchased, which has its own impact on how regulars budget and plan the rest of their lives. This cost is often discussed at games, but it is rarely if ever linked to the time passed at games. The clear time distinction is fairly rigidly maintained.

The artificial separation, the deliberate energy given to letting the time unfold as it will, apart from other considerations, marks a conscious effort to control one's own time. The fact that that time then gets folded into the time of other regulars in a series of obligations and responsibilities is one of its virtues rather than its flaws. The spirit of reciprocity and generosity that characterizes most bleacher interactions is seen as a counterpoint to corporate interests that disregard people in favor of profits—and in a sense, the cost of tickets offers a tidy foil for such comparisons. Profit-mongering is not uniformly condemned; it is, rather, acknowledged as the nature of the beast. In baseball time, however, regulars can let their concerns about money and profit and debt take second place to concerns about friends and community, and that is what makes baseball time valuable.

It strikes me that most communities must have some mechanism for signaling time that is about relationships rather than things. Capitalism and industry and globalization run by their own logics of profit and loss, and there is little space in such logics for fellow feeling. It may require some capital investment to claim time back from industrial clock-time, but finding time that does not *need* to be sold for survival and prioritizing human interaction—not for what it can do to advance a person's interests but for its own sake—seems to be a crucial component of community feeling.

4

Effervescence

Two thousand one could have been the Cubs' year. They spent a seventy-six-day stretch in sole possession of first place in the National League Central Division—all of June and July and part of August. They had overcome a devastating injury to third baseman Bill Mueller in May (an injury that had sent them on an agonizing eight-game losing streak), and the resilience they had shown had been enough to make people believe. Even the regulars had manic gleams in their eyes as the conversations in the bleachers turned to playoff tickets and October baseball.

Hope built so high takes time to dissipate. The Cubs spent the stretch of August 13 to 18 struggling to stay ahead of Houston, and on the 18th, Houston took firm control of first place. Ten days later, on August 28, Houston still had a three game lead, but the Cubs faithful knew that just a few wins could make all the difference. With only four and a half weeks left in the season, every game counted. Over the weekend, the Cubs had won two of three games over their archrivals, the St. Louis Cardinals, and the sub-.500 Florida Marlins were coming into town.[1] It seemed a certain recipe for a much-needed winning streak, and 38,744 fans packed into Wrigley Field for the 7:05 game.

Baseball purists will argue that the best games are 1–0, fast-paced, well pitched, filled with sparkling defensive plays. Honest purists will acknowledge those games are less fun when their teams are losing. At a game like the one on August 28, 2001, the fifth through eighth innings were nerve-wracking. The Cubs had managed to fall behind 3–2 in a game they could not, in the imagination of the fans, afford to lose. Every batter for the other side was a threat; getting even one run was proving difficult for the Cubs, and if the Marlins were to score more? That would not do at all. The tension ratcheted up in the seventh, when Florida's Alex Gonzalez hit a screaming line drive toward third base for the Marlins. But Bill Mueller was there, catching the ball on the fly, and a tight, punctuated "OH!" escaped the crowd, starting on a note of panic and ending on one of relief. The emotion in the air was one of a dodged bullet, tinged with a quiet despair that the next time the Cubs would not be so lucky. Even though the Cubs were only losing by one run, the regulars, like other Cubs fans, could feel what had been a glorious season slipping away.

But the game was far from over. Very very far from over, as it turned out.

In the bottom of the eighth, Fred McGriff doubled[2] off the Marlins' new pitcher, Armando Almanza. Augie Ojeda,[3] more fleet of foot, was sent in to pinch run.[4] Michael Tucker sacrificed Augie to third, and Marlins manager Tony Perez pulled Almanza from the game,[5] replacing him with Braden Looper. Looper promptly gave up a single to Ricky Gutierrez,[6] driving Ojeda in. The score was tied, 4–4.

The ballpark erupted. Most of the 38,000 had stayed, despite the fact that the seventh-inning stretch had already been sung and beer sales had been cut off for the night.[7] Tie game! If the Cubs could score another run or two and then hold the Marlins, our faith would be rewarded. Fans stood, hands clasped, imploring another run.

It was not to be. The eighth inning ended tied, as did the ninth, the tenth, the eleventh . . . This was baseball at its highest drama. For away teams in a tie game, the bottom of the ninth and every subsequent inning is sudden death. If the home team scores, that's it. Game over.[8]

In narrating this game, it is hard not to get caught up again in the emotions that rolled through the ballpark that night in August. Every inning was a roller coaster, each top half filled with desperate anxiety that the Marlins might score, each bottom half thrilled with the prospects of a Cubs win. By the twelfth, however, the mood had become more grim. The Marlins kept threatening, and after the Cubs' Michael Tucker was run down between third and home in the tenth,[9] the Cubs bats seemed to die. The crowd doggedly hung on as the game entered its fifth hour, already aware that Houston had won earlier in the evening. It had become a do-or-die game, the season in microcosm.

When Ricky Gutierrez struck out to end the twelfth for the Cubs, the ballpark was deathly silent. City ordinances prevent the playing of music at Wrigley after 10 pm, and 10 pm was long past. Every remaining fan, still a substantial crowd, was literally sitting forward in his or her seat, leaning in toward the field. There were no lines at the concession stands, no wandering fans. There was only an intense focus on the field, so palpable that we were using hushed voices in centerfield.

In the top of the thirteenth, the whistling started. The first whistle seemed to come from somewhere over in the rightfield area of the grandstand, a single short note, not sustained for longer than a second. From some other corner of the ballpark, another fan echoed the sound. Soon there were whistles coming from all corners, exact echoes of the first sound, each independently offered into the eerie silence of several thousand focused fans and somehow intensifying that silence. Florida got two hits in that odd whistling silence, and with two outs and a runner on second, Charles Johnson hit a ball to leftfield. Mike Lowell headed toward the plate to the sound of a collective gasp, and the remaining crowd held its breath as the Cubs leftfielder threw home, the baseball racing him to the waiting catcher. The baseball won; Mike Lowell was out at the plate. A weak cheer came from the crowd as people collapsed back into their seats.

There was more. It ultimately took fourteen innings for Florida to win this game. I could write at length about the Jon Lieber at bat that had the crowd chanting in an outpouring of affection, or the pin-drop intensity of the moment when the Marlins loaded the bases in the fourteenth. I could explain the raw, hollow feeling that accompanied the final out, recorded at 11:58. I dashed an email off in a fury that night when I got home, describing to a friend how angry I was that after all that, the Cubs couldn't at least have had the decency to get their last out on the dot of midnight.

So why have I spent so much time detailing a game that ended so miserably? What was striking about the night of August 28, 2001, was not so much that it was an extra-inning game, or that it happened at a time when the Cubs were in a pennant race, or that almost every player on both teams was used in some capacity or another, including the starting pitchers who were supposed to have the night off. What makes this 2001 game stand out in memory is the energy of the crowd, both good and bad. To be at Wrigley Field that night was to have every emotion heightened, to feel the influence of the crowd on every gesture. The experience is similar to what Emile Durkheim described in *The Elementary Forms of Religious Life*:

> The very act of congregating is an exceptionally powerful stimulant. Once the individuals are gathered together, a sort of electricity is generated from their closeness and quickly launches them to an extraordinary height of exaltation. Every emotion expressed resonates without interference in consciousnesses that are wide open to external impressions, each one echoing the others. The initial impulse is thereby amplified each time it is echoed, like an avalanche that grows as it goes along (1995: 217–18).

Of course, we don't need Durkheim to tell us that crowds can have an incredible energy, an *effervescence,* to use his word. Most of us have had the experience of being caught up in something that feels larger than ourselves. Wrigley Field often possesses what Cubs broadcasters call *electricity* for big games. On more than one occasion, I have seen centerfield regulars Judy and Colleen turn to one another and exclaim "Goose bumps!" holding out their arms to show they really do have goose bumps in reaction to something going on at the ballpark.

When the crowd began whistling in the middle of the night on August 28, something "supernatural," for lack of a better word, was happening. I could look around me and see a reflection of my emotions on the faces of everyone seated around me. I saw people with pursed lips continue the whistle, their expressions otherwise fixed in the same intense stare. The crowd, myself included, felt possessed by something larger than any of us, a state Durkheim describes with great accuracy: "it is as if [we were] in reality transported into a special world entirely different from the one in which [we] ordinarily live[d], a special world inhabited by special forces that invade[d] and transform[ed us]" (1995: 220).

Simply being a part of the crowd that night compelled sudden roars of reaction, tense silences, the random whistling. In the thirteenth inning, the entire crowd, unprompted by anything outside its own membership and the circumstances on the field, began to spontaneously chant, "Let's go, Lieber!" The chant was infectious and somehow *mandatory* once begun. Everyone I could see was participating, and the unison was perfect enough that the words were easily distinguishable despite being yelled by several thousand people. In some sense, everyone present was transported to a special world, where everything hinged on the next pitch, and ordinary life was forgotten.

This kind of effervescence serves to form some sort of bond between the people who feel it. "For this reason all parties—be they political, economic, or denominational—see to it that periodic conventions are held, at which their followers can renew their common faith by making public demonstration of it together" (Durkheim 1995: 211–12). While it may seem extreme to claim that a Cubs game is a demonstration of faith, the ability to affirm one's connection to a larger body of Cubs fans is certainly part of the appeal of attending a game at the ballpark rather than watching it on television or listening to it on the radio. However isolated a fan might feel, s/he will always retain the memory that in a particular moment in a particular game, s/he was perfectly *sympatico* with however many thousand held their breath for a play at the plate.

This brings us around finally to the real purpose of exploring this phenomenon; we have already seen that one quality of community is that it includes a sense of belonging or connection. Although there are numerous ways to develop that sense of belonging, few rival the immediacy of collective effervescence. Indeed, Durkheim goes so far as to suggest such effervescence is essential to creating any sense of social cohesion (1995: 421). The bleacher regulars are in a position to regularly experience this kind of collective effervescence, collective *energy*, although not every game produces such energy in the same way or of the same intensity. This raises two related questions: how important is collective effervescence to creating a sense of community? and what are the conditions of possibility for collective effervescence?

To begin this exploration of effervescence, it is important to understand that it is far from a wholly positive force. Durkheim's pleasant phrase aside, the actions of a crowd are as likely to be decried as products of *mob mentality*, an uncontrollable madness. Journalist Bill Buford's book, *Among the Thugs* (1993), excellently demonstrates a bonding effervescence among European soccer fans built around violence. Indeed, most scholarly explorations of the mob or the crowd have focused on how being in a crowd leads otherwise law-abiding, rational human beings to acts of destruction and extreme violence. This kind of mob behavior is all too familiar in Chicago, not just in the examples of race riots or the 1968 Democratic National Convention, but in relation to sports. The elation of the crowd after the 1992 Bulls championship win led to a night of crazed looting and property destruction at an estimated cost of $14.1 million (AABar 1992), and the Chicago Police Department reported that their "entire communications board lit up within 60 seconds" (quoted in AABar 1992). The suggestible crowd of that June 14–15 was immortalized in television coverage of a mass of celebrants turning a car end-over-end down a pedestrian clogged street.

Intriguingly, Sigmund Freud compared the suggestibility of the crowd to the sensation of being in love (1959: 58–61). This idea gives us a useful extension of Durkheim's implication that the frenzy of the crowd may well be attached to the feeling of being in a community. The gist of Freud's argument is that a group subject to a crowd mentality, the unified mind identified by Le Bon (2001), represents people who have all taken the same love-object. In place of the jealousy we might normally expect in such a situation, the crowd members have formed *identifications* with one another, and each member recognizes him/herself in the others. In short, the collective effervescence of the crowd serves notice that whatever else is true of the participants, they share some values, are in some way the same (see McPhail 1991: 211–13).

But are those values enough to form a community? By themselves, certainly not. However, the ability to *experience* effervescence is not necessarily a foregone conclusion whenever a crowd gathers. Thus, I will return to my first question regarding the importance of collective energy to community by way of my second question: what are the conditions of possibility for such effervescence?

"No Wave at Wrigley"

Those are the words printed on the back of a matchbook from Jimmy and Tai's Wrigleyville Tap, the former central meeting place of the bleacher regulars outside the ballpark (see chapter 7). The sentiment fits well with the hard-nosed purism of the regulars and many of Wrigley Field faithful. The wave referred to is a crowd phenomenon familiar to most American sports spectators. It begins with a section of fans rising to their feet and throwing their hands in the air with a shout, then sitting again. In a successful wave, their action is picked up by the next section of fans no more than a second later, and then the next section a beat after that, until the behavior goes all the way around the stadium. The effect is an undulation that moves around the ballpark, both visibly and audibly. It has nothing whatsoever to do with the action on the field, although it is most likely to occur during a "boring" game.

Why shouldn't the crowd enjoy the wave at Wrigley? There have been attempts to start waves; in the bleachers, regulars routinely shout these attempts down with, "Sit down and watch the game," or, "If you want a wave, go to the lake!" On the radio, WGN announcers Pat Hughes and Ron Santo occasionally comment with disdain when the wave begins at other ballparks, noting that the crowd is not into the game. Similarly, when crowd noise swells inexplicably in the background of a Cubs away broadcast, Hughes will observe that an electronic scoreboard is urging the noise. Almost invariably, this observation is followed by a prideful rumination on how Cubs fans don't *need* to be told when to stand up and cheer. Cubs fans, by implication a superior breed of fan, understand the rhythms of the game and react appropriately to the on-field action.

The stimulus of the wave or the provocation of the scoreboard certainly produces a type of energy, although one might argue that fans inspired to participate in such activities are too self-consciously "having fun" to truly lose themselves in the moment. While this may be true of some participants, I think it is more likely that collective effervescence is neither homogenous nor inspired by the same factors in the same crowd. For a regular, the mere hint of the wave is a source of deep aggravation. It challenges their identification with Wrigley Field as a "real" ballpark, where fans gather to watch their team play baseball and appreciate the stakes of every game. On the flip side, the hostility of the regulars (and other longtime Wrigley denizens) to the wave can make other fans perceive them as killjoys.

Despite my bias in favor of the regulars (I confess to shouting down wave starters), neither side is entirely in the right. Even the regulars would be forced to admit that their perception of what Wrigley Field stands for has been strongly challenged by an increasing "party crowd" that has deemed the ballpark a hot social scene. The White Sox fan's caricature of a Cubs fan as a cell phone–toting, Mai Tai–drinking fashion plate, at the ballpark to be seen, has its origin in reality. I have been in bleacher crowds at Wrigley that are best described by the oft-quoted line, "I was at a beer garden, and a ball game broke out." It is clear enough that many people in this kind of crowd are experiencing collective euphoria, that they are bonding, caught up in an effervescent state.

This carnivalesque atmosphere, however, is only coincidentally at Wrigley Field.[10] The ballpark, snuggled down into a city neighborhood, is one more entertainment option on a stretch of Clark Street that includes concert venues, live theaters, upscale bars, neighborhood taverns and local dives, restaurants for any taste and budget, and easy access to public transportation. It offers an open-air environment, energized crowds, and a taste of nostalgia. For the current crop of young professionals in Chicago, these qualities make Wrigley a good summer hangout. If there is winning baseball, so much the better, but at the end of the day, it is the social scene that matters to the majority of this crowd.

This does not mean that baseball does not have the power to affect the party crowd. At any given game at Wrigley, the majority of fans will be there for the baseball. The Cubs have a substantial fan base, made more sprawling by the ubiquitousness of WGN in the early days of cable and the lack of teams in the Mountain Time Zone before Major League Baseball's 1993 expansion. In addition, Wrigley's increasing status as a purist's park and a baseball cathedral brings in lots of visiting teams' fans. The broadcasters' assessment of Wrigley fans is largely accurate; there are enough knowledgeable fans at any game to ensure the crowd reacts appropriately to the action on the field. The social crowd, ready to have a good time, is also ready to give itself over to the cheering and booing of the more baseball-focused fans.

This distinction between the social and baseball-savvy crowds is an over-generalized description of the people who usually fill Wrigley Field, but the categories fit well enough to demonstrate the different types of effervescent experiences that might be going on at a given time. The people in the stands who are focused on the game, distributed throughout the ballpark, are watching for key game situations. While the social crowd around them flirts and drinks, the baseball focused fans will mind the batting order and the pitch counts, shouting encouragement, advice, or criticism toward the field. When the game reaches a critical moment, the baseball devotees will rise to their feet, clapping and yelling. Enough standing, cheering fans will draw the attention of the social crowd, a certain percentage of which will turn to the field. If the reason for the excitement is obvious enough, the cheering will increase as socializers join in. If the moment is one of anticipation (the at bat of a Cubs slugger with runners on base), everyone watching will explode into more frantic cheering if the desired outcome is realized (the slugger hits a home run). The excitement of the roaring crowd will spread to the less attentive spectators, fueling a more general effervescence that appears uniform on the surface. In truth, in this grossly simplified model, there are three different experiences of effervescence. There are the fans of the game, swept away by an anticipated success that has implications for the chance of victory. There are the newly attentive social fans, who are caught up in a part of the game they find exciting. Then there are the less attentive spectators, excited less by what has happened on the field than by the pleasure of the crowd around them.

This may seem to contradict the ideas of other theorists regarding the group mind of the effervescent crowd. I submit that it does not. Once caught up in the frenzy, the crowd has the suggestible qualities Le Bon (2001) and others identify. This explains the ease with which chants and clapping rhythms are disseminated through large stadium crowds, frequently started by very few fans. The importance of these different ways of getting swept into the energy of the crowd becomes apparent if we return once more to

Durkheim: "When [the crowd] is dissolved and we are again on our own, we fall back to our ordinary level and can then take the full measure of how far above ourselves we were" (1995: 212). The exact moment of effervescent experience may wrap an entire crowd in the same group mind, but their memories and interpretations of the significance of the experience will be colored by their understanding of how they got swept up. The recounting of the electricity of the moment may allow them to feel closer to anyone who shared the moment, but it will have a greater bonding effect for people who share the same interpretation of what happened to carry them away.

So what does carry them away, to speak in generalizable terms? I contend that there are three crucial elements to prompting a crowd of people to abandon themselves to a group consciousness: anticipation, knowledge, and triggering actions.

Of these three factors, anticipation strikes me as the most clearly important. Such anticipation, generally speaking, can be hopeful or fearful. It is easy to imagine being caught in a crush of human beings and worrying that in such a crowd, "something" might happen. The atmosphere of an un-unified crowd will carry the tinge of the expectations of the individuals participating. For instance, the cross-town rivalry between the Cubs and White Sox has a hostile undertone, exacerbated by stereotypes about the North- and Southsides of Chicago and by politics of race and class.[11] Because the games the two teams play against each other are constructed as major, can't-miss events, with bragging rights to the city at stake, the attending crowds are large and aggressive. The games are well policed, but fights still happen, and the crowd energy easily prompts cruel taunts and provocative behavior. Regulars regard White Sox fans with disdain, and answer most taunts from White Sox fans at Wrigley with, "When was the last time you supported your team at *your* ballpark?" The low attendance at U.S. Cellular Field (formerly Comiskey Park) is notorious, and I am as guilty as any regular of suspecting that several of the supposed White Sox fans attending cross-town games at Wrigley are less fans than people spoiling for trouble.

In contrast, the visit by the Red Sox to Wrigley Field in 2005 was a lovefest. Considered *the* event of the season, the three June games were symbolically significant. The Red Sox, recently freed from the Curse of the Bambino with their 2004 World Series victory,[12] brought Boston fans to Chicago in droves to share hope with the still curse-laden Cubs fans. While Boston came to town annually to play the White Sox, the games against the Cubs were different. It was the first meeting between the Cubs and Red Sox since the 1918 World Series—the last World Series the Red Sox had won prior to 2004. Of course, both teams came to win, and both teams' fans wanted victories, but the anticipatory atmosphere going into the series was more of hosts preparing to receive honored guests. Regulars approved of the baseball knowledge of the visiting fans, and when the Cubs steamrolled over the Sox in the first game, Red Sox fans gained respect by dissecting the flaws of their own team. Wrigley Field indulged Red Sox traditions, and between the fifth and sixth innings of the Sunday game, the PA system began playing Neil Diamond's 1964 hit, "Sweet Caroline."[13] The crowd of 39,138 picked up the song instantly, singing along and managing to delay the start of the sixth inning in order to belt out the second chorus. The ready adoption of the Red Sox home tradition, despite the fact that at the time the Cubs were losing 2–0, spoke to the crowd's anticipation of friendly bonding with the opposing team's fans.[14]

This highlights how anticipation might predict the nature of a crowd's effervescence, but it does less to demonstrate how anticipation might be crucial to the experience of effervescence in the first place. For this, I return my account of the 2001 game at the start of this chapter. Within the account, there are many effervescent moments, ranging from squealing joy to intense silence. Note, however, how I set up the account. The game was at a time when the Cubs season was perceived to be at stake. The Cubs had lost their hold on first place, but they could regain it. The opposing team had been performing poorly before playing the Cubs. While certainly some fans were attending the game socially, a large percentage of the attendees were anticipating an *important* game. Important games, whether good or bad (and this one turned out to be bad), are ones that will play the emotions of the crowd ... provided the crowd is knowledgeable.

This brings me to the second condition for effervescence, and that is knowledge. I do not claim that every member of a crowd has to know what is going on, or even that a majority has to be aware of the situation that is mobilizing them. However, the anticipation attached to that night game in August of 2001 was predicated in part on fan knowledge that it was a game that might matter. Some percentage of the capacity crowd that appeared that night anticipated not just the typical potential for excitement that graces any sporting event, but they were ready to feel more. Many likely purchased their tickets when the Cubs were still in first place, and they wanted to be given cause to feel they would be in first place again.

Short of a quick lead by either team, the game would have been tense regardless. However, the tie game loomed large for the cognoscenti. As noted, the game became a metonym for the season. Dozens of effervescent moments captivated the crowd for four innings *in which no team scored.* The thirteenth inning, with the whistling, with the play at the plate, with the roaring approval of Cubs pitcher Jon Lieber being put into the game as a pinch hitter—all of the energy that the crowd produced for these moments depended on some portion of the crowd cuing the rest of the watching fans that *this moment matters*.

And this in turn brings us to the idea of a triggering action. I refrained from discussing the Lieber at bat earlier, but it is worth going through now. In baseball, while some pitchers can hit fairly well, pitching is a specialist position. A good pitcher is not expected to hit well, and in the American League, the notorious problem of weak-hitting pitchers is eliminated by the designated hitter rule.[15] In the National League, pitchers do take their place in the batting order, and Jon Lieber in 2001 was a decent enough hitter. Nonetheless, putting a pitcher in as a pinch hitter is very rare. Even a good-hitting pitcher is unlikely to have as good an at bat as a regular player off the bench.

In the twelfth inning of the game against Florida, it became clear that the pitcher's spot in the order was coming up in the thirteenth. In centerfield, we began going through the Cubs roster; my scorecard shows the remnants of the conversation: lines through the numbers of players already used, the letters "DL" by those on the disabled list, "C"s next to coaches' names. The picture became clear; there was no one left on the bench. There were only pitchers, and we had already used most of the relievers. We knew David Weathers should not hit for himself; he'd already pitched two innings, and it would be better to have someone hit who would at least be in better practice (relief pitchers almost never get at bats). That left starting pitchers. More to the point, that left Jon Lieber.

In 2001, Lieber became a darling of the Cubs fans. He was leading the pitching staff, putting together a twenty-win season. He pitched quickly, threw strikes, and was generally good for at least seven innings.[16] In this marathon game, he seemed like the fairy tale prince. Here was the pitcher who had ended losing streaks all season; maybe he could win us a game with his bat. When Cubs manager Don Baylor, out of players and lacking any real option, sent Jon Lieber to the plate, the crowd reacted as if their prayers had been answered.

Lieber's appearance was a triggering action for an already buzzing and tightly wound crowd. August was late enough in the season that even a casual fan would have known Lieber's name, even if his profile could not begin to rival that of then-superstars Sosa or Wood.[17] The fans knowledgeable enough to know that there was no one else on the bench recognized the desperation move, and they stood behind their team fiercely, cuing any fans who felt uncertain. The crowd, chanting for their hero, was once more in a state of unified consciousness.

How extensible is this idea of a three-fold requirement (i.e., anticipation, knowledge, and triggering action) for collective effervescence? I suspect further investigation would find the model widely applicable. I find it works for almost every scenario I have encountered, and certainly for every moment of effervescence I have found at the ballpark. I also suspect that an anticipatory crowd that has some reason to be disappointed will create scenarios that promote effervescence, often seeking triggering actions that may lead to violence rather than more predictable releases of energy.[18] I again follow Durkheim as well as anthropologist Victor Turner (1974) in my ideas here; much effervescent energy is spent in ritualized action, and such action requires a crowd that "knows the rules," so to speak.

"Let's get some runs!"—
An Example of Ritualized Effervescence

When Harry Caray became the Cubs play-by-play man in 1982, he also imported his tradition of leading the ballpark crowd in the singing of "Take Me Out to the Ballgame" during the seventh-inning stretch.[19] WGN television made a point of broadcasting this event every game, cutting into potential advertising time to show the Wrigley faithful rising and singing with Harry. By the time of Caray's death in 1998, his seventh-inning stretch had become so much a Wrigley tradition that younger fans could not imagine that there was a time when people didn't sing with Harry. The Cubs decided that no one could fill the void, and the idea of playing a recording of Harry was roundly criticized in the media, so they opted to have "guest conductors," visitors to the ballpark who would come expressly to lead the singing for a game.

One consequence of broadcasting the sing-along has been the wedding of "Take Me Out to the Ballgame" to Wrigley Field tradition. While many fans who attend a game might be oblivious to the finer points of baseball, it is hard to find someone who does not know that s/he will sing in the seventh inning stretch. The importance of the tradition is such that during blowout games or games marred by uncomfortable weather, most fans will stay until after the song is sung—and then a visible mass exodus will begin. Here we have a known ritual, anticipated by the crowd, triggered by the first chord of the song played on the organ. For some fans, it is the whole point of going to the game, perhaps not an extreme kind of effervescence, but certainly a warm-glow moment of sharing an experience and an emotion with a large group of people.

The regulars usually sing along. They've cynically changed the words ("If they don't win it's a shame" has become, "If they don't win it's the same") and often offer critiques of the singers (sometimes on grounds of legitimacy, other times for the quality of the singing, and on occasion simply because the on-air interview with each day's singer distracts from the broadcast). They do sing, though, and they also know the correct placement of the cry, "Let's get some runs."

Harry Caray used to yell that phrase at the end of singing if the Cubs were losing or tied in the seventh. In 1997, during a Cubs loss in Shea Stadium, Linda from Centerfield leaned over to me to say, "At this point, a generation of Cubs fans thinks the last four words of 'Take Me Out to the Ballgame' are 'Let's get some runs.'" The joke—that the Cubs had been losing so often that Caray was always saying it—was particularly poignant in '97.

These observations aside, the seventh-inning stretch is almost a sideshow to the regulars. Respecters of tradition, they would not demand it be abolished, although a particularly bad choice of singer will prompt grumbling that it is time for the guest conductor nonsense to end. Is it an effervescent moment? Certainly. It is also routine, and such routine effervescence becomes assumed. Regulars are more likely to throw themselves into the stretch, abandoning critique in favor of the mass celebration, when the Cubs are wildly ahead or on a day of some kind of ritual significance like Opening Day. Otherwise, their performances are often perfunctory when compared to other fans. At the same time, if something goes *wrong* with the stretch, they will be among the vocal complainants.

The example of the stretch highlights the ways in which effervescence does not have to be entirely spontaneous. A triggering event can be routinized, and while a crowd might have very different relationships to the effervescent experience, the reliability of the triggering action is something everyone may come to count on. The apparent contradiction of routinized effervescence is easily resolved by my model of effervescence, and on careful consideration, it is clear that such routinized effervescence is more the rule than the exception. Examples from outside the realm of my case study include the striking of midnight on New Year's Eve or the American tradition of celebrating twenty-first birthdays. These often effervescent moments rely on the anticipation of their arrival, a knowledge of their significance and accepted modes of effervescent reaction, and the existence of a moment in which ordinary rules will be suspended (i.e., a triggering action).

Is Effervescence Necessary to Community?

I have already mentioned that effervescence is not uniform for all people who experience it; or rather, that it is the reflection back on the effervescence that matters, and this will vary dramatically within the same crowd. I want to extend this idea and examine Durkheim's contention that effervescence is essential to social cohesion (1995).

In the first place, effervescence does not *guarantee* community. Quite the contrary. While the sense of connection in the moment of energy may be very real, the reflection back on the moment might serve to highlight insurmountable differences between people who shared the moment. As an example, when fans flood out of the ballpark after the seventh-inning stretch, the dispersing fans are regarded with contempt by the regulars. Clearly, those fans came only for the singing; they have no respect for the *game,* and by extension, the team. For the regulars, this disrespect of the team with which they identify so closely is felt as disrespect toward the regulars. The ways in which this difference of experience are used to establish boundaries are discussed in detail in chapter 5, but for the moment, it is enough to realize this difference exists.

The next question to consider is whether effervescence is always positive, and if negative, does it contribute to community? This is easily answered through consideration of the bleacher regulars' reaction to one of the most painful phrases in current circulation: "Five more outs!"

In 2003, the Cubs had made it to the second round of the playoffs, the National League Championship Series (NLCS), for the first time since the institution of divisional playoffs in 1995. On October 14, the Cubs were playing the Marlins in game 6 of the best-of-seven series. The Cubs had already won three games. They had to win only one more to go to the World Series, an event the Cubs had not participated in since 1945 and had last won in 1908.

On October 14, 2003, the Cubs were leading 3–0 at the end of the seventh inning. I was watching the game on a television at a bar two blocks from the ballpark, my ritual vantage point during the playoffs for those days when the Cubs were away or I had no ticket. Like many Cubs fans, I was looking at the score and began to picture the champagne. A buzz of excitement filled the bar.

The eighth inning started. Mark Prior got Mike Mordecai to fly out. Then the chanting started. "Five more outs! Five more outs!" I thought at the time it was just at the bar. At game 7 the next night, I learned from the regulars who had been there that the same chant was going in the stands, that in fact it may have started in the bar because those close enough to hear the television picked it up. I was chanting with everyone else. We were so close to a World Series.

Then the Marlins' Juan Pierre came up and hit a double. The bar groaned and quieted for a moment, but it was Juan Pierre. We almost never got Juan Pierre out. Juan Pierre was FAST. He could successfully bunt for a base hit with the infield drawn in and the first and third basemen charging down his throat. I'd seen him do it. The energy of the crowd was undiminished; his hit was nothing against a three-run lead. Let him hang out at second. We'd get the next guy.

The chanting began again. "Five more outs!"

Luis Castillo hit a foul ball to leftfield. It was just barely foul, and Moises Alou made a leap like he really honestly and truly could catch it for out number two. He came down with an empty glove. The ball had been deflected by a fan reaching for a souvenir. Alou stomped his feet and pointed up to the stands, claiming fan interference. The dozens of television cameras at the ballpark zoomed in and isolated the offender—a stunned looking Steve Bartman.[20]

The wheels promptly came off for the Cubs. They gave up eight runs in the eighth and lost the game 8–3. The next night they lost game 7. The season was suddenly, painfully over.

Fast-forward a year and a half. On June 29, 2005, Cubs pitcher Kerry Wood made his first return appearance after an injury that had put him on the disabled list early in May. The start was much anticipated; Wood had been a favorite son of Chicago since he struck out twenty batters on May 6, 1998. His career had been injury plagued, and many hopeful predictions for various Cubs seasons had included the proviso, "If Wood stays healthy . . ."

He was healthy this day, and he threw his first pitch for a strike to enthusiastic applause. His next pitch was grounded to the first baseman, and the first out of the game was recorded. In centerfield, Norb turned from his seat at the end of the row 13 and said, "Twenty-six more."[21] Judy, a row above him, shot back, "Wait until there are five more outs." A collective groan answered her, as she knew it would.

The theme was revisited five innings later, when Wood was still pitching beautifully but approaching his pitch count for the day.[22] Norb once more offered comment on Wood's pitching: "He hasn't had a bad inning like he usually does."

This time I objected loudly, "NORB!" and Judy followed quickly with "FIVE MORE OUTS!" We were both reacting from the same impulse, and Judy's invocation of "Five more outs," made that clear. The mere mention of good fortune could potentially be enough to make that good fortune go away, a topic I discuss further in chapter 8.

Norb's response, though, is more interesting. He looked back at Judy with a sober expression. "That's worse," he said, referring to the invocation of "Five more outs." "That's a *mortal* sin."

Judy instantly picked up the theme: "That was the worst. It was worse than '69, worse than '84 . . ."

As it happens, I was present for two other conversations where "five more outs" was quoted on June 29. The first was beside the fireplug outside gate N before the gates opened, and involved a couple of leftfield regulars. The second was in rightfield about an hour before game time. In each case, the pleasure-turned-pain of game 6 was distilled into three words, instantly understandable by any regular. The effervescence of one night in October had swept through all of Cubdom, but for the regulars it had a particular resonance. In the thrill of the moment, in the raw excitement of being within hailing distance of a place the Cubs had not been since before many of them were born, they forgot to be cautious with their optimism. The lessons of years, decades, *generations* of heartbreak, usually strong enough to withstand any temptation to count victories before the final out, were forgotten for two at bats. When regulars say, "Five more outs," to one another, they know they are hitting a nerve among other regulars that hurts each of them in the same way.

This collective pain is not unique to regulars. Many Cubs fans who participated in those chants during game 6 of the NLCS might also have a wincing reaction to hearing them repeated. For the regulars, though, the chants represent a departure from their normal state in a relatively similar degree. "Fall[ing] back to [their] ordinary level . . . [they] can then take the full measure of how far above ourselves [they] were" (Durkheim 1995: 212), and regulars recognize and identify to one another that they were collectively out of character. The invocation of "five more outs" serves to signal a community that shares values and believes in the same things.

Here it is clear how collective effervescence is useful to a community. The ability to understand and react appropriately to a particular catch phrase based in a moment of effervescence has become one quality of all regulars. Regulars are saying to one another, "I feel your pain," and meaning it literally. More to the point, each regular is *certain* that the other means it literally. But is such effervescence *necessary* to a community?

Anthropologist Claude Lévi-Strauss, arguing explicitly against Durkheim, claims that people in communities are there because the community is what they are used to (1963: 70–71). In his argument, people feel connections because they share the experience of doing things the way they always have been done. Community for Lévi-Strauss, then, is almost exclusively based in *habit*. He appears actively appalled at the notion that community could be based in effervescence, and claims the emotions of a community only get aroused, "when the custom, in itself indifferent, is violated" (ibid., 70).

Clearly, the example of the regulars refutes the absoluteness of Lévi-Strauss's claim. The otherwise innocuous phrase, "Five more outs," has been heavily invested with symbolic meaning and can act in conjunction with other measures as a gatekeeper for the community, as discussed in chapter 5. At the same time, it is easy enough to envision other self-identified communities that do not have such clear and obvious moments of effervescence. A neighborhood block club comes to mind, or an office coffee klatch. Nonetheless, even these groups have regular gatherings, a potential for shared emotion. I submit that part of what makes a community, even one based on habit, is a belief in shared values, and shared values bring with them a shared emotional investment.

At this point, I am persuaded that a community must *believe* it has the *potential* for such effervescence. Lévi-Strauss's objection that emotion might only be felt when custom is violated does not dismiss the importance of effervescence. Rather it demonstrates the need for its potential. A group for whom some violation of habit brought *no* collective emotional response *at all* would *not* be a community. That group would show it had no affective investment in the things and events that bring it together.

This brings us, then, to another question of community, that of a shared moral universe or system of values. To argue which comes first, the effervescence or the values, is a chicken and egg exercise. However, where a belief in the *potential* for effervescence may be enough for a community, the belief in *actual* shared values is essential, as we shall see in the practices of boundary making in the next chapter.

5

Boundaries
and Gatekeeping

My first experience in how ballpark friendships form came from Linda from Centerfield during our games at Shea Stadium. As I described in the introduction to this book, Linda and I began meeting at Shea for Cubs games in 1996. I learned then that among bleacher regulars, vague plans and promises have more weight than they appear to, and reliable patterns can set in with astounding swiftness. By the end of the season, our joint appearances for Cubs' series in New York was so consistent that the ushers in our usual section began to comment on it.[1]

At that time, I was not able to recognize the replicability of the experience. I was, I confess, rather in awe of Linda. Her stories of her bleacher friends in Chicago captured my imagination. She seemed to have inside knowledge of the team, of Wrigley Field, of baseball in general. My awe of her only increased in 1997 when she made it possible for me to make my first visit to the bleachers.

When the home opener (hereafter Opening Day) rolled around in April 1997, I was determined to sit in the Wrigley Field bleachers. I had booked a flight to Chicago from New York, combining the Opening Day trip with a prospective student event at the University of Chicago. I called some college buddies still living in Chicago and pitched my plan. In February, I began dialing the Cubs ticket line the day single tickets went on sale. Unfortunately, and astonishingly to me, by the time I got through, the bleachers were sold out.

Disappointed, I secured four tickets to the upper deck for my friends and me, consoling myself that I would still be at Wrigley with friends on Opening Day. I also called Linda to let her know how my plan had worked out. I learned she would also be in Chicago for Opening Day (I did not know then that it was a high holy day of obligation), and she sympathized with my inability to get bleacher tickets. I hazily remember that she may have even had an extra that she offered to me, but as I was bringing my friends, I regretfully declined.

So it was that on April 8, 1997, I pushed and prodded my friends out into freezing weather and had them in the upper deck in time for the first pitch. It was not the joyous day I anticipated. The Cubs had yet to win a game (they had lost six in a row). An icy wind off Lake Michigan pierced layers of clothing and blankets, and in the absence of any reason to cheer (the Cubs managed to lose their seventh game of the season that day), all that was left to do was shiver.

However, I had a plan. Or rather, I was the object of a plan. Prior to the game, Linda had asked me where I was sitting and had told me to watch for a particular beer company representative around the third inning.[2] My friends later reported the extreme strangeness of the moment when the representative showed. He leaned over toward my seat and asked, "Holly?"

"Are you Beer Company Joe?" I asked, and at his nod, I turned to my friends with a promise to return and followed him from the seating area. Beer Company Joe took me to an elevator down from the upper deck and led me around underneath Wrigley Field, nodding to other vendors and ballpark workers as if it were the most natural thing in the world to escort a random fan around the "backstage" area of the ballpark. He unerringly found Linda and handed me off, promising to be back in a few innings.

It seemed incredible to me that Linda could make such a thing happen. She seemed to have effortlessly pulled strings, letting me circumvent the rules that usually bound fans (it remains impossible to get into the bleachers with a grandstand ticket). And I was only an acquaintance! Clearly, she was secure enough and well enough known at the ballpark that this bit of sneaking around was not much of a risk, or, if it was a risk, it fell on the shoulders of Beer Company Joe, who was willing to go through with the plan.

I understand now that Linda's scheme was an example of ongoing boundary-marking work on the part of the bleacher regulars. While most regulars would not acknowledge it in those terms, such boundary-marking is one of the crucial aspects of maintaining community. It is also an often neglected aspect of what the warm-fuzziness of community requires: a "them" to contrast to "us." From observing the regulars, we can see the nuances of such definition through opposition and understand its benefits and potential pitfalls.

Let's start by continuing my Opening Day story. It was the seventh inning before I was returned to the upper deck on Opening Day, giving up a warmer and companionable seat in the centerfield bleachers with the excuse that my friends would be missing me.[3] They had been missing me, in fact, inventing speculative stories about a secret life during my absence and huddling together for warmth. They tolerantly stuck with me until the end of the game and joined me for a single postgame drink at the Wrigleyville Tap,[4] although they abandoned me to my new baseball friends fairly quickly after that. I flew back to New York the next morning, still a touch buzzed, wearing my Cubs hat with fake ivy woven around it, grinning crazily at the world. I had decided to move back to Chicago for graduate school, and, more importantly, I knew I would be back in the bleachers.

I was not yet a regular, though, or anything even close. It took another two and a half years for me to become a regular. During those two and a half years, I was subject to a fairly subtle exercise of gatekeeping. Such gatekeeping is one sign of the boundaries that define community; without such boundaries, there would be no way to claim an us or a them.

So what was my status? I was a guest, tentatively approved and invited to return. Linda had vouched for me, and I had presented myself much as she had described me. I had also shown by my return to the grandstand that I cared about my friends. Within two weeks, I would also demonstrate that my loyalty to the Cubs was sincere.

In mid-April, ten days after I met the regulars, the Cubs limped into New York. They had lost their first twelve games, already done for the season before it had begun, but Linda and I were undeterred. We took our usual seats at Shea Stadium, armed with signs to hold up between innings. We were going to find a way to make the Cubs win.

The media coverage of the Cubs was getting painful; were the Cubs poised to take on the 1988 Baltimore Orioles' record for futility, a season that opened with twenty-one consecutive losses? Certainly, the regulars in Chicago had thought it possible; some among them predicted an 0–23 start after the Cubs lost the home opener. It had been my first taste of undistilled Cubs fan pessimism, startling to me in my young, hope-springs-eternal phase of Cubdom. I was still in the process of learning how to inure myself to losing streaks.

We had some cause for hope that weekend in New York. The first game of the series had been rained out. That meant a doubleheader on Sunday, and after the Cubs lost the first game, Linda and I reminded each other that doubleheaders are usually split.[5] We stayed for the second game, modifying our signs to reflect the changed Cubs record, cheering for every good Cub play and every Cub hit. We were very visible, fewer than twenty rows back from the field, close to the third-base camera pit.

We were also each holding our breath as the Cubs took a 4–1 lead into the bottom of the ninth. The Mets had their final licks, and the lead began to crumble. It was 4–2, then 4–3, and the Mets had a runner a second with two outs when Turk Wendell finally got the last out. The Cubs won, as the *Chicago Tribune* headline pointed out the next morning, "barely" (Sullivan 1997).

That story proved significant for Linda and me. We were among the last to leave Shea Stadium that night, and the next morning we were back for batting practice. The first couple of people who mentioned seeing us on television or in the papers made no impression on us. Linda discounted the observation by pointing out Arne Harris, then the director of Cubs baseball broadcasts, was adept at picking Cubs fans from the crowd at road ballparks. I for my part figured there had been pictures of Cubs fans in the paper and that people were lumping us into a category. It wasn't until Linda checked her voice mail that we learned that we were the faces of the Cubs' first win of the season. A color photo of us, compliments of the Associated Press, had graced the front page of the *Chicago Tribune* sports section, and that image was picked up by dozens of newspapers following the story of the Cubs' long losing streak.

The various pictures and footage of Linda and me at a game on April 20, 1997, gave us a brief moment of celebrity at Shea, but it also showed to the regulars that we were precisely where two Cubs fans living in New York should have been for the Cubs' first victory of the season: at the ballpark. Moreover, it gave me an excuse to begin corresponding with the regulars back in Chicago, so when I reappeared in the Wrigley Field bleachers in August of 1997, I was remembered.

I only made it to eight games in the bleachers that fall, and the regulars knew me as "Linda's friend from New York." Whenever I appeared in centerfield, everyone asked after Linda, a pattern that would continue into the 1999 season. I understood later that the regulars' apparent acceptance of me was hospitality offered on Linda's behalf.

If we trace back through my introduction to the regulars, we can begin to see a series of gatekeeping functions at work. The regulars, like any community, have boundaries. There are limits to who can participate. Jeff from

Centerfield captured this well: "Even the fans who are here who don't know what's going on are part of the community. They give us something to talk about." More seriously, he claimed that the oblivious fans "give us a way to know who we are and something to compare ourselves to. We gather together so we're not surrounded by idiots."

And who are the idiots? As noted in my demographic review of the regulars, it is not any particular race, class, or gender that suffers the disdain of the regulars. Rather, anyone could *potentially* be a regular, provided they meet the criteria laid out by *Bleacher Banter* columnist Ken Devoe in 2000: "It's time for the real Cubs fans to take back Wrigley Field, starting with the Bleachers. So, dilettantes, Sammy groupies, beer-party revelers and yuppie-scum, beware. If the Cubs are gonna be for real this year, then Wrigley and the Bleachers have to be for real Cubs fans only!" (12).

From Jeff and Devoe we see the same sentiment: there's us, and then there's them. This opposition is accompanied by a self-consciousness of its importance and a quality of intolerance that I contend is common in community. I am not alone in this idea. In his 1922 work, *Group Psychology and the Ego,* Sigmund Freud argued that any tight-knit community must necessarily be hostile to people perceived to be outside that community, with increased intolerance going hand in hand with increased community bonds.

In contrast to Freud, I am not convinced that the us-them of community has to result in intense and unthinking group hatreds. However, a community that feels challenged or threatened is more likely to strictly police its boundaries. Such a challenge to the community of regulars has emerged in recent decades as Wrigley Field has developed a reputation for its social scene. Jeff's continued comments reflect this challenge: "It's like circling the wagons. We're circling our wagons against marauding college kids and others who see the game as just a background to their party."

One consequence of Wrigley's popularity has been a pervading image of the bleachers as a site of drunken revelry. On June 1, 2004, the front page of the daily Chicago tabloid *Red Eye* featured a full-page cover photo of bleacher fans holding beers into the air, the words "BEER NUTS" superimposed over the centerfield scoreboard rising over their heads. The subtitle was "The chaos of game day in Wrigleyville."[6] The regulars, many of whom date back to the days when you could "count the house" at Wrigley Field, are no longer visible as the few faithful.

Some theorists, including Richard Sennett, would anticipate that the social change enveloping Wrigley would lead to a desire for "purified identity," a model of community that demands homogeneity and conformity from its members. Such community is made possible by abundance and affluence, according to Sennett, which "opens up an avenue by which men can easily conceive of their social relatedness in terms of their similarity rather than their need for one each other" (1970: 49). Interestingly, despite the clear us-them line established by the regulars, the community does not demand this kind of homogeneity.

The problem with this basis of community was implied in chapter 1: community based on a taken-for-granted assumption that everyone in it is the same is actually operating to *minimize* people's involvement with one another rather than deepening connections. As it happens, while the regulars do define themselves in some degree in opposition to the party crowd, it would not be impossible for a Wrigley party animal to eventually become a regular. What ultimately proves the line between a regular and a nonregular is a set of nonspecific behaviors that reveal what might be considered a moral quality: a capacity to take care.

The Principle of Taking Care

Robert Putnam points out: "The touchstone of social capital is the principle of generalized reciprocity—I'll do this for you now, without expecting anything immediately in return and perhaps without even knowing you, confident that down the road you or someone else will return the favor" (2000: 134). My objections to the language of capital notwithstanding, the idea of a community as an environment in which people can be trusted is an important one. Putnam acknowledges that sometimes the deferred rewards of generalized reciprocity are so nebulous that they give individual actions the appearance of altruism (135). I would extend this further in the case of the bleachers, and arguably any community. Sometimes such apparent altruism is geared not toward the benefit of a single individual, nor toward the vague idea of a future benefit to the person performing a given action. Rather, a person can take action with an eye toward the overall well-being of the *group*. Such an attention to the group's well-being does not confine itself to interpersonal relationships. Stephanie from Leftfield, explaining how much caring is a part of what makes a regular, pointed out succinctly: "When I say we care it's not just about people but also about their surroundings. We don't throw trash on the field or curse when kids are around. You can be yourself, but we want people to pay attention to what's going on around them. We want people to talk well about us and to come back. We're a part of something that's irreplaceable. I never thought I'd be a part of something like this, but here it is."

In Stephanie's words we can see the idea of *taking care*. Regulars recognize their community as something "irreplaceable," requiring respect and maintenance. A regular, by definition, is someone who understands the need for respect and contributes to community maintenance. In other words, a regular is someone who knows how to take care. Each regular can be *trusted*, not so much in interpersonal dealings as in terms of their responsibility to the larger community. Yet such trust must be earned. This presents an instrumental basis for limiting the size of community; membership can extend only so far as the limits of trust.

If the limits of trust are dictated internally by a perception of shared values, they are marked externally by the idea of distinction. As noted, the regulars seek to distinguish themselves from the party crowd. This is arguably a necessary move for people in a society that values individuality and freedom, as the United States does. If we buy into the Enlightenment idea of a universal brotherhood of man, something Americans are widely encouraged to do, the things that distinguish people exist as a thin veneer. When social groupings and upbringing and status markers are stripped away, people's individuality likewise disappears.

If, as philosopher Georg Simmel (1971) pointed out in 1908, such individuality hinges on our distinct social ties and experiences, the ability to form communities is very much a part of the psychological health of twenty-first-century humans. In essence, one is simultaneously defined by one's membership in a community and defines the nature of that community. The social grouping of the regulars is defined and bounded by the regulars, but being a member of the community also contributes to the identity of every regular. For the regulars, the trust to take care of the community is also a trust to maintain a particular identity. This identity is determined by a shared desire to form a particular relationship with the Cubs and Wrigley Field.

It is important to regulars that they be perceived as a particular kind of fan—a *trustworthy* fan. This desire is evidenced in the delight voiced in an issue of the *Bleacher Banter* upon reporting this exchange between two members of Wrigley Field's security personnel: "These are the regulars, they have their own system" (Roundtripper 1998: 5).

It makes sense that the regulars would care about the external perceptions of the community, given how the community serves as a component of each regular's identity. However, the stakes of external perception are higher than simply reputation; to some degree the perception of outsiders is crucial to the existence of the community *at all*. Sociologist Pierre Bourdieu articulated this basic idea in terms of socioeconomic class in France, stating: "A class is defined as much by its *being-perceived* as by its *being*" (1984: 483). When Wrigley Field security personnel acknowledge the regulars, they affirm qualities that the regulars perceive in themselves. For example, the regulars are bleacher fans who would never throw anything on the field,[7] distinguishing them from a body of fans in the bleachers who would (and do). While there may be many nonregulars in the bleachers who would also never throw anything on the field, they do not enjoy the same trust of that fact that any regular, as a known member of a known community, enjoys. Boundary maintenance by regulars "creates a sense of belonging, of identity—and, by the same token, of difference from others" (Cohen 1985: 53), and it helps ensure that other people at Wrigley Field can perceive that difference. The next question, then, is *how* the regulars maintain such boundaries.

Gatekeeping

When I first met Linda at Shea, it was as a member of the Cubs Nation. Any professional sports team has its faithful followers, and the shared emotion following a win or a loss can cross innumerable boundaries. When the emotion of a game is heightened by being in a hostile stadium, it is not surprising that the fans of the visiting team would find one another, deliberately seeking one another out against the general ebullience or misery of the home fans.

The experience of meeting a fellow Cubs fan bears similarity to the experience Margaret Mead described when Americans meet abroad. The shared national origin of Americans tends to manifest in conversations about hometowns and stories of growing up. Mead notes: "Americans establish . . . ties by finding common points on the road that all are expected to have traveled" (2000: 17). When Americans discover that their paths have crossed, a "potential intimacy" is produced.

As two Cubs fans in New York, Linda and I had discovered a "potential intimacy," and as we talked, we realized we both shared a more-than-common devotion to the Cubs. We had both cleared our schedules for any date the Cubs were in town. This assured us that we both took the Cubs very seriously, and it made us confident that at any game, there would be at least one other dedicated Cubs fan in the stands. We were in some way the same kind of people, not simply because we followed the same team, but because of the *way* we followed the team. This quality of devotion to the Cubs, win or lose, is one of the hallmarks of any regular. While anecdotally evident in the way regulars use the pronoun "we" to refer to the team, I decided to test this apparent identification with the team using a survey developed in sports psychology, Wann and Branscombe's "Sport Spectator Identification Scale" (in Wann et al. 2001: 6). This survey asks respondents to answer a series of seven questions on a scale of one to eight, and as Daniel Wann explains, "scores of greater than 35 suggest a high level of identification [with a team]" (5). I surveyed roughly 20 percent of the regulars, and every survey I did produced a score well over 35 points. The only significant variation in responses came in identifying the Cubs' biggest rival, which split nearly evenly between the St. Louis Cardinals and the Chicago White Sox.

Beyond such close identification and devotion, another quality that Linda and I shared came clear during our games at Shea: we both *knew* the game of baseball. We had both grown up with it, Linda at Wrigley, me listening to Vin Scully on the radio with my dad. Even as we chatted, we watched every play, periodically yelling encouragement (or critique) to the players on the field. It not only mattered if the Cubs won or lost; *how* they won or lost made a difference as well. While not every regular has the same level of game attentiveness, any regular can easily assume the role of an armchair manager. Bill Veeck Jr., talking at a time when the bleacher seats were the cheapest in the ballpark, once said, "I have discovered, in twenty years of moving around a ball park, that the knowledge of the game is usually in inverse proportion to the price of the seats" (Quotes 2003). The regulars, who shared their bleachers with Veeck for years before he died,[8] take pride in Veeck's comment even as they express their frustration at the party crowd that has come to dominate the bleachers (notably no longer the cheapest seats at Wrigley).

So the first criteria for being a bleacher regular are knowledge of the game of baseball and a dedication to the Cubs. These qualities manifest in thousands, if not millions, of fans in the United States. Thus, in addition to dedication and knowledge of the sport and the team, a regular must demonstrate dedication to and knowledge of the *bleachers*.

My own membership among the regulars hinged on all three of these elements (connection to the sport, the team, and the bleachers). A key moment in my transition from guest to member happened late in the 1999 season. The Cubs were down by two in the fourth inning, and Sammy Sosa was at the plate. Sosa was in the middle of putting together a sixty-three–home run season, a follow up to his sixty-six home runs in 1998.[9] One of the older regulars, gazing out at the field, said, "Now he's going to hit his dinger; there's nobody on base."

I watched Sosa swing at a ball low and outside and corrected my elder: "No, he's going to save that dinger for the bottom of the ninth when we're down by three and there is one man on."

My answer was cynical in the extreme, founded on the observation of a home run–driven season that had nevertheless left the Cubs struggling to stay out of the cellar of the division. Far too often, Sosa's home runs came with the bases empty, or when the game was clearly lost or already handily won—that is, they were what baseball fans call "meaningless home runs." Even more, the comment I offered reflected the steady diet of one-run losses that were part of being a Cubs fan in 1999.

What makes this particular scenario at all memorable to me is the reaction of Norb sitting further down the bench. No sooner was my prediction out of my mouth than he turned and looked at me. "You belong here," he approved.

While it would be too much to claim those words signaled formal acceptance into the bleacher regular community, it did make an impression on me. Had I been an established regular, such an approval would have made no sense. Of course a regular belongs in the bleachers. Despite my increasing presence in the bleachers over three seasons, I was still ultimately a guest. That explained why everyone asked after Linda whenever I appeared at a game. Even though I no longer lived in New York, my connection to Linda and her willingness to claim me as a friend and a good baseball fan were the most solid evidence the regulars had that I might be regular material. I *should* know how Linda was doing and what she was up to as her friend, regardless of where I was living or what I was doing. Part of being accepted as a regular, as it turns out, is the ability to be a friend, to commit and invest in the community—to *take care*, as discussed above.

In hindsight, I do not know why I was surprised to realize I was still a guest. By the start of September 1999, I had attended about fifty games in the bleachers over three years,[10] squeezing them in as my schedule allowed. I was an intermittent presence at best until the end of 1998, my reliability largely untested. My increased presence in late 1998, while increasing my credibility, also opened the question of whether I might be a bandwagon fan. The Cubs made the playoffs in 1998, and Cubs fever had gripped Chicago. I had formed close relationships with a couple of the centerfield regulars, but my natural reticence had left me relatively unknown outside of centerfield, and in the flood of fair weather fans, my loyalty was hard to gauge.

Nonetheless, it was in the fall of 1998 that I began to show my developing commitment to the bleachers for the longue durée. A gap between my just-ended summer job and the early October start of the academic year left me with time to go to more games. I made my first road trip with the regulars, going to Milwaukee.[11] I was invited to my first bleacher wedding, which united two of my bleacher friends who had met at the ballpark.

That wedding, late in the season while the Cubs were on the road, was tinged with the excitement of the Cubs' wildcard chase. Judy from Centerfield tried to subtly listen to the game through an earphone during the ceremony; Tammy, the bride, paused on the way down the aisle to check the score. While the happy couple went to Wrigley Field to get their photos taken, the regulars in attendance found a nearby bar to watch the end of the game, won by the Cubs when a Houston player managed to get called out for running outside the baseline. The reception was a fantastic party, and the traditional wedding dances were supplemented by anthems like "Go Cubs Go!" It was a time of high emotion and many shared experiences, and it was as a participant in both that I started to demonstrate my *ability* to belong.

My presence in 1999 was far more steady, although I still had not reached my eventual level of forty to fifty games a season.[12] I made another road trip, and I began to get together with other regulars when the Cubs were out of town. I had arrived at gate with consistency and saved seats when I was asked to, garnered attention for my elaborate scorecards, and, more to the point, was still showing up with regularity in September after the Cubs went 6 and 24 in August.[13] My appropriately timed comment on Sosa's home runs was not so much my ticket to entry as it was an embodied moment of being in the right place at the right time, knowing precisely what the moment meant and making that knowledge clear.

While I have less detailed accounts of other people's experiences of becoming members of the bleacher regulars, the general outlines I've collected show similar contours. Jonathon from Leftfield began sitting the bleachers in 1998, trying various fields before settling in on the edge of what was then section 153, the primary territory of the leftfield regulars. After he had sat there for several games, the leader of leftfield started talking to him. Over the course of the next two years, he cemented his relationship with the leftfield regulars, eventually taking responsibility for saving sections of seats and racing up the ramp at gate opening. His experience in leftfield has led him to write about the internal hierarchies of the group and the leftfield regulars' efforts to counter the image of the bleachers as a rowdy party zone, and among his findings is that it seems to take about two years to integrate into the group (personal communication).

As Jonathon's account demonstrates, an introduction by a regular is not a requisite to becoming a regular. As often as not, regulars become regulars because they have been in the bleachers long enough to attract the attention of the existing regulars. I met one regular in July of 2005 as he was unpacking an elaborate picnic for the rightfield regulars, including burgers and grilled shrimp and a range of side dishes. He had been sitting in the bleachers since 1990, and he noted that the regulars had noticed him there game after game and invited him to sit with them. He and his fiancée often come to games together, and he shares the sentiment that the rightfield regulars are like an "extended family—they adopted me." In fact, these stories demonstrate that while there are boundaries to the regular community, they are porous. Many regulars, like Bill from Centerfield, would describe themselves as extroverts, willing to introduce themselves to new people and to open the door to them to join the group.

That said, the criteria for membership remain. New regulars are as responsible as any regulars for taking care, for contributing to the community, for policing their own and others' behavior. Bill from Centerfield, asked why the bleachers work as a community, replied, "*We* make it work. We could all come to the ballpark and be strangers to each other, but we're not that way."

The Excommunication

I have described the existence of boundaries and the gatekeeping efforts that the regulars make to ensure that the members have demonstrated their trustworthiness. While the basic principles of community membership are evident from this account, the question of community policing needs further attention. What, after all, is being policed? And given the simplicity of such ideas like taking care and respecting the community, the ballpark, and the team, how is that the regulars are not a much larger group? What makes a regular evident to another regular?

The first thing to understand is the idea of the regular "family." In nearly every formal interview I've done with bleacher regulars, the word "family" has entered the conversation (for more on this, see chapter 9). One of the notable features of the bleacher regulars is that once a person is accepted as a regular, that status lasts for life—a quality that begins to explain the long gatekeeping interval. Because membership includes a judgment of trustworthiness, it is not extended lightly. The relative smallness of the community means that many regulars are known to one another by face, if not by name. A regular can assert his or her status to another regular and affirm his or her claim by a knowledge of family dynamics, as was discussed in chapter 2.

There are, at the same time, tacit rules for members. The most stringent attach to tickets, the source of the only excommunication I have personally witnessed in the bleachers. As tickets to the bleachers are increasingly difficult to come by, regulars are understandably anxious to ensure they can get into the ballpark. Not every regular has a season ticket (or a share of one), and the priority for any extra ticket is that it get offered to family first. This stricture is not so firmly enforced that people are forced to sell to the family or not at all; if it is established that the family is taken care of, regulars may dispose of extras as they see fit.

In the early 2000s, T began to sit in centerfield. He had a long history of sitting in the bleachers and had a season ticket, and he knew the game and the Cubs. He had his quirks, including an almost compulsive need to get every Cubs giveaway item he could, but all regulars have their quirks. Things began to go amiss when, over the course of several conversations, it became clear that T had at least seven season tickets. The Cubs by this point had decided not to issue any additional bleacher season tickets, and while they allowed existing season ticket holders to continue their accounts, once a season ticket lapsed, it could not be renewed. In this environment, T had an embarrassment of riches. Puzzlingly, he also always seemed willing to buy other people's extras, allowing them to abide the rule of keeping tickets in the family and ensuring that they would not have to eat the cost of games they could not attend. It was not long before the question arose, what was he doing with his extras?

One answer came when he was seen pacing the streets in the vicinity of the ballpark, missing gate in order to scalp his tickets on the street. Rumor floated that he had been busted for scalping at some point in the past, and some of his extra tickets were in the names of family members from a time when he was denied the right to have a ticket of his own. Anxiety began to surface among people who had sold T their extras. Season tickets have numbers on them that identify their owners. If T was scalping them, there was a risk he would be caught selling the ticket of another regular, and that could easily cost the regular his or her season ticket. Whispered advice spread among the regulars: whatever you do, don't let T have your extras.

This uneasiness, though, was ameliorated by plausible explanations. T had been accepted as a regular; surely he would not do wrong by the family. Likely, he had a circle of friends he was keeping in tickets—a not unheard of practice among the regulars—and he occasionally overbought. It could happen to anyone. Everyone had a friend or two who had asked to come to a game and then backed out. In that situation, a person did what he or she had to do to avoid a complete loss on the ticket.

The seeds were sown, though, and regulars became cagier around T. People remembered the dates they had sold to him, and regulars began to ask him if he had x date or y date. T would regretfully report he did not have an extra for that day, and an increasing number of regulars revealed that he had denied having tickets they *knew* he had.

The death knell came in 2003 as the Cubs began to assemble a winning season and management established new rules for reselling tickets. Two centerfield regulars, looking for a ticket to a game, walked into the office of a ticket broker by the Addison El station.[14] Inside, they found T, sitting on the broker side of a desk and starting guiltily upon being caught. The report flew back to the bleachers, the hottest topic of conversation over a number of weeks, and when T next appeared in the bleachers, he found himself pointedly ignored by many regulars, particularly in centerfield. Any regular who engaged him in conversation would be pulled aside at the first available opportunity and filled in. Some were skeptical and went to check themselves, each time coming back with another sighting of T at his desk in the ticket broker's office.

It was, without exception, the coldest cold shoulder I had ever seen (or participated in). After a few games of being completely unacknowledged in centerfield, T drifted away. He was perceived as having betrayed the community, not only refusing to take care of family but actively putting people's season ticket status at risk. He had abused the trust he had been extended.

T's story is unusual. While regulars are capable of seriously irritating one another, and I have seen several on nonspeaking terms at various times, even the most grating are grudgingly acknowledged. My own inclination to disown a particularly noisy and celebrity-driven fan was gently reproved by Mary Ellen from Leftfield: "He's been out here for forty years," she reminded me. "He's one of ours." In short, much will be tolerated by the regulars, but betrayal cannot be countenanced.

"Yuppie on the Phone!"

While the story of T shows how the community boundary can become hard and unforgiving, it does less to reveal the day-to-day rules of being a regular. There is a good reason: such rules would be difficult at best to articulate beyond vague generalities. Anthony Cohen gives us a sense of what that would be, describing community as a place where people learn to be and practice being social. He notes, "[community] boundaries are symbolic receptacles filled with the meanings that members impute to and perceive in them" (1985: 19).

In other words, community boundaries are not maintained by hard and fast rules, but rather suggest the outlines of what is acceptable or not. Being on the inside of the boundary verifies that a person understands the boundary exists and has demonstrated a shared respect of the shared symbols of the community—*even if that respect is not constructed on the same basis of every other regular.* "To put this another way," Cohen writes, "the boundary as the community's public face is symbolically simple; but, as the object of internal discourse it is symbolically complex" (1985: 74).

Regulars watch the game religiously—except when they don't. Regulars never fight in the stands—except when they do. Regulars love the Cubs— except when they hate them. In short, almost every particular rule that the regulars might point to to distinguish themselves from nonregulars has been broken at some point by a regular. The circumstances might have been extreme, such as a regular defending his wife from a boorish fan, or innocuous, such as throwing an opponent's home run ball back onto the field of play (see n. 7), but the rules have been broken.

How is this reconciled? Turning to Cohen one more time, "The norm is the boundary: its reversal, a symbolic means of recognizing and stating it" (1985: 69). When rules are broken, regulars take note of the fact and devise responses that show their recognition of the rule.

A classic example of this is the issue of using cell phones in the ballpark. When cell phones were first popularized in the 1990s, members of the bleacher party-crowd were among the conspicuous consumers of the new technology. They would bring out their phones with a flourish, apparently calling every friend they knew to say, "Hey, dude, I'm in the bleachers of Wrigley Field." Such loud cell phone abusers often stationed themselves just above the seating areas, directly behind almost every group of regulars.

The use of cell phones was quickly deemed one of the noxious traits of the "yuppies," the crowd of twenty-somethings who seemed to view the bleachers as a place to relive their fraternity and sorority party days. The habits of drinking too much, ignoring the game, and talking on a cell phone became the standard media image of the bleachers, an image picked up by White Sox fans as a point of ridicule against their Northside rivals.

Even at this point, a few regulars carried cell phones. As noted in chapter 3, Tom the Fireman in Centerfield, for instance, always had one on his belt, but it was hard to begrudge an emergency services worker one of the tools of his trade. Over time, however, as cell phones became more generally ubiquitous, regulars began to acquire them. They were sheepishly revealed on occasion, but many steadfastly refused to even turn them on at the ballpark.

Eventually, the rule softened; they would not turn them on unless there was a *really good reason*. Such reasons usually involved children or other family members not at the game, checking in on people who were supposed to be at the game but had not appeared, or calling friends to let them know a ticket for the day's game had become available and did they want to come?

At present, it is not at all unusual to find a regular talking on his or her cell phone during pregame. However, bringing out a cell phone at the ballpark immediately brings notice from other regulars in the area, who gleefully yell out, "YUPPIE ON THE PHONE!" Unless someone intervenes to reveal a serious reason to be on the phone, this call might be repeated any number of times, drawing attention to the fact that the regular has "broken" a rule that serves to symbolically distinguish regulars from the yuppies. One of the more entertaining examples of this phenomenon occurred during a night game in 2005. Colleen from Centerfield was calling to check in on her children, and Howard, the blind man sitting a row in front of her, picked up the conversational pattern of phone use. He paused in his discussion of what was happening on the field to announce loudly, "Yuppie on the phone!" Howard successfully marked his membership as a regular, and the rest of the regulars burst out laughing. Colleen finished her call amid the noise of the regular crowd with a half-hearted glare, but also she joined the laughter.

A final example will hopefully make the point here clear. Among the qualities of the party crowd is an unseemly (to the regulars) effort to get on camera. They wave wildly whenever a camera points in their direction, oblivious to whether the camera is actually recording or not. In fact, it seems this is part of the regulars' objection; the yuppies are so unobservant that they have not noticed that a live camera shows a red light. The problem, as the regulars would explain it, is that when fans are tracking the cameras, they are clearly not paying sufficient attention to the game. Unaware of the action on the field, they stand and wave inappropriately during game play, putting their own self-promotion ahead of any kind of respect for their surroundings.

Regulars term such behavior and related efforts to get media attention being a "media whore." It reflects a lack of perspective on a story and one's part within it and a tendency toward self-aggrandizement. However, by virtue of their regular attendance at games and their clear self-identification as Cubs fans, regulars can often become the focus of media attention. When a regular is singled out by the media for some reason or another, s/he will be subject to taunts at the ballpark for being a media whore. It is part of the affected regular's responsibility to take such jibes with good grace, accepting the label and acknowledging the breach.

In the governing of their boundaries, the regulars establish criteria of membership that require time and commitment to satisfy. A potential new member is held against the field of other bleacher fans, compared on terms that they may come in with (like knowledge of the game), and studied for their ability to measure up to the responsibilities of being in a community. Is the new person someone who can take care? Who can live within the standards and expectations of a regular without bringing embarrassment (or at least, not too much embarrassment) to the community? Will this new member recognize the symbolic boundaries and be able to accept the ribbing that will necessarily accompany the violation of a rule? These are the qualities of membership that matter, ill-defined as they are, and when these qualities have been demonstrated to the satisfaction of enough of the community, a new regular is truly a regular.

What we have seen in this chapter is that being a member of the regular community appears to be about who one *is*, but *becoming* a member of the community hinges crucially on how one *behaves*. I submit that this is an increasing determinant of community formation in the twenty-first-century United States, particularly as professional and personal mobility become necessary components for competing on the job market and discrimination becomes less socially acceptable. A shared affinity opens the opportunity for community, and it is not surprising that sports spectatorship is up, or that more television shows seem to be developing cult followings. As James Oliver Robertson observed of American sports in 1980:

> The games and their teams are not only sources of activity and entertainment, their rituals provide opportunities for communication among townspeople who would not otherwise have had any relationships at all. The teams, and participation in the rituals, are avenues by which newcomers are included in communities; individuals can win social approval. . . . In general, American team-sport rituals aim at the creation and maintenance of the ideals of community in the midst of the fragmenting forces of urban life. (252–53)

Through their shared experience as Cubs fans in the Wrigley Field bleachers, the regulars have established a belief in a set of shared values, a symbolically marked collection of attitudes and behaviors that distinguish them from the raucous bleacher crowds and the larger Cubs Nation. Our next task, then, is to look on the inside of the regular community. How do they organize and hierarchize themselves, and how important is such organization to the community? I will investigate this in the next chapter.

6

Organization and Hierarchies

One of the classic ideas of community is that it is an egalitarian social grouping. It gets contrasted to the dog-eat-dog scramble for the top of the pile scenario that seems to characterize contemporary American society. This contrast produces the image of a group of warm relationships where everyone has the same power. The fact that every community has fairly clear roles and hierarchies tends to be elided in this fantasy of what community should be.

As we shall see in this chapter, a community might not formally institutionalize its hierarchies, but we can see clearly that real roles and rules are important to community maintenance. The need for organization is perhaps more obvious than the means by which organization comes into being and is negotiated. By looking at three distinct cases of leadership and organization in the bleachers, we can get an idea of some of these means. The first case I'll consider is the story of Ron from Leftfield.

Ron first experienced the bleachers in the late 1970s, but did not discover the existence of a group of regulars until late in the 1980 season. He grew up in Chicago and had been to Cubs games earlier in his life, but "there's a difference between going to a game and being in the bleachers," he explained.

So it was that in 1980, he began attending games in the bleachers with some fellow Northwestern students.

Ron quickly (and "accidentally") discovered that there were a lot of people in the bleachers who were there day after day, doing the same thing he was. He met Robyn from Leftfield, who was already established as a regular, and learned that there was a little knot of twenty-somethings residing daily near field level in the leftfield corner. Ron settled in with this group. In 1981, a year split by a players' strike, Ron attended almost twenty games.

It was during 1982, Ron's first uninterrupted year as a regular, that Ron began coming earlier to the ballpark, and that was when he learned how the section was saved for each game. Ron quickly began to participate in the daily seat-saving ritual. This was a significant moment. Ron is now the leader of leftfield and an important figure for all regulars. That started, though, because his concern about seats got him involved in coordinating leftfield.

By 1983 Ron's quest was to find a way to get the regulars seated together on Opening Day. At that time, the usually general admission bleachers were reserved seating for Opening Day, and the standard practices of seat saving were not possible. Ron investigated and learned about Ticketmaster, at that time a new ticketing service starting in the city. For their inaugural event, Ticketmaster was handling tickets for the Cubs and Sox home openers. Ron did a lot of legwork before tickets went on sale, getting in touch with the Ticketmaster folks and making arrangements so he was the first Ticketmaster customer at a sporting goods store the day sales opened.

His legwork paid off. He was able to get the regulars together, but the first five rows of the bleachers weren't sold through the ticketing system that Ticketmaster ran. This led Ron to explore additional meetings with the Cubs front office network.[1] He discovered a very helpful atmosphere and was able to meet with several people in the front office, including then general manager Dallas Green. "In fact," he noted, "in 1983, I was able to convince Dallas Green that a season pass to the bleachers was a good idea." The idea was not realized until the early 1990s, but it clearly made an impression.

In 1984 Ron was able to set up arrangements for the regulars for the playoffs. At this point in his bleacher history, the Cubs organization knew Ron was legitimate, both because of his earlier dealings with them regarding the bleachers and because he had dealt with them as a member of the community organization working to prevent lights from being added to Wrigley Field. In August the Cubs had told him to put together a list of people who should get playoff tickets. "It was the first time a definitive list had been made of the regulars, complete with last names and addresses," he pointed out. The day after the Cubs clinched the division, he got a phone call from the Cubs front office. He pointed to this as an example of how helpful the Cubs organization can be. "When they want to be good to us, they can be." He continued the story: "The Cubs clinched on Monday, I got the call from the Cubs on Tuesday and they said, 'Give us this much money by Friday.' People were wiring me money, driving it to me, and somehow I got it all together and took the money to the ticket office on Friday and was handed a wad of tickets to [what was then] section 153."

Ron's success with the playoff tickets and his ability to get along with Cubs management has done much to cement Ron's position as a bleacher leader. He is an organizer by nature, the kind of person willing to put time and energy into making sure things he cares about continue to happen and thrive. He organizes the annual halfway to Opening Day party every winter and a barbecue late in the season every year. He maintains lists of who among the regulars needs tickets for which games, and many regulars go to him first when they discover they cannot use their tickets. When the Wrigleyville Tap closed at the end of the 1999 season,[2] he went around the neighborhood seeking an arrangement with a bar that could accommodate the regulars and help fill the void left by the Tap's absence. As people began using email more, he established a Listserv for the regulars. In short, he will perceive a need and act upon it.

First and foremost, though, Ron continues to organize the activity that worried him in the first place. He saves seats. He has an easier time of it now that bleacher tickets are sold in advance rather than exclusively day of game, a change the Cubs instituted after the 1984 season. "I would leave the game on Friday in 1984 and just sit down at the front of the line to wait for Saturday's game," he recalled. His job then was to buy one ticket and run in and save seats. Back then, "Everyone got their butt in line before the gate opened, because if they didn't, they weren't getting in."

Now, the challenge is saving enough seats for the regulars when the bleachers are regularly sold out. This has become something of a science, and Ron explained, "I've always saved a little more territory than I expect to need so we can be selective about who sits around us. Our group provides an anchor for the left field bleachers." In addition, controlling territory "allows us to bring new people into the group."

Ron is not an elected leader or an appointed spokesperson. Rather, his willingness to take on some burden of responsibility made that responsibility his. For a time, he worried that people were taking his efforts for granted. When he felt particularly put upon, "I would sometimes miss a game unannounced," he revealed, letting the resulting confusion in leftfield remind people of how much work he does. He doesn't skip games anymore. "Now I just take a beer. I'm pretty unabashed about taking a beer tax."

Most regulars are happy enough to pay their beer tax, particularly in leftfield, where section 303 thrives.[3] A certain percentage of leftfielders also accept informal deputizing. Ron cannot arrive at gate for every game, nor can his wife, Karen (also a regular), cover every day he must miss. However, someone has to be there at gate N with the familiar bag of blankets and towels. "Because of where we're located," Ron pointed out, "BP [batting practice] is more active than centerfield,[4] so when the gates open, someone has to get their butt up there. It only takes two to three people to nail down the territory."

"Nailing down the territory" consists of spreading blankets and towels across the seats in section 303 and stationing regulars at strategic points on and behind the benches. The system that Ron has devised with the other regulars is now a settled thing, and people take their roles in accordance to their pregame habits and predilections. The upper rows of section 303 are patrolled by the ball hawk regulars, people who arrive early in order to shag batting practice home runs.[5] They range far past the edges of section, and in between catches, they are an advance guard. They watch the size and disposition of groups who might try to join the regulars in their seating area.

"The oldest trick in the book is to send two attractive females with six big dudes hiding in the bushes, so I'm always careful to check how many," Ron noted. The ball hawks contribute to this information network. "I look to make sure we're going to get somebody who's not going to cause trouble or throw stuff on the field," Ron continued. "Security knows they can count on our group be their eyes and ears, as well as to give them usually one full section that they don't have to worry about."

For years, before the renovation of the bleachers, the smokers relegated to the back rows of the section served as checkpoints.[6] "We look for families, groups with little kids who don't want a bunch of drunken crazies around them," Mary Ellen from Leftfield explained to me. "When the rest of the bleachers starts throwing stuff on the field, you can look over at the field in front of our section. It's clean. We don't let people get away with that kind of thing. If we make a mistake and get someone in our section who throws something, we'll rat them out right away. We've got no problem getting someone tossed for behaving badly."

The pride the leftfield regulars have in their system is part of what maintains it. Section 303 polices itself, and the regulars take delight when security recognizes it. A column by the leftfield regulars in the *Bleacher Banter,* the regulars' newsletter, made a point of quoting an overheard remark from a bleacher security member to an obvious rookie: "These are the regulars. They have their own system" (Roundtripper 1998: 5).

The regulars in the back row keep a sharp eye both on the batting practice balls and on the seats of their section. On one summer day in 2005, for example, a man wandered down and plunked himself down squarely in the midst of the saved seats, and Donna from Rightfield[7] shot a meaningful glance at Mary Ellen. "Do you know that guy?" she asked under her breath. When Mary Ellen said yes, she visibly relaxed and returned to the usual pregame chat. A few minutes later, Tim from Leftfield called down from his ball-hawking position to Gary from Leftfield, anchoring a row three rows into the section. "Gary, have you got room for four?" Gary looked back, offering a secondary assessment of the group that had been talking to Tim. "Yeah," he called back, shifting over and making obvious the seats they would sit in. A little later, a largish group worked down the aisle and along row 3. They were watched intensely until they had traveled beyond the edge of 303, and then another anchoring regular pointedly stationed himself at the boundary between sections 303 and 304.

What we see in leftfield are two things that merit further discussion: an established leader and a smoothly efficient organization, complete with a fairly well-defined division of labor. The leftfield regulars have runners to claim the section, ball hawks to monitor the people heading toward their section, back row inhabitants to assess the visitors looking for seats, and seat watchers in the section to challenge people who try to take a seat without clearing the other checkpoints. In addition, we see leftfield using these methods to identify new potential regulars, such as we saw with Jonathon from Leftfield in chapter 5.

Leftfield is by far the most obviously organized of the groups of regulars, but there are systems of organization at work in all three fields, as we shall see later in this chapter. Using leftfield as an example, however, allows us to consider the importance of leadership and organization to the development and maintenance of community.[8]

Leadership

From Ron's own account, it is clear that the community of bleacher regulars existed before he discovered it. A similar pattern is visible when Stephanie from Leftfield describes how she started the *Bleacher Banter*. Stephanie was sitting regularly in centerfield, and she always heard people saying, "Whatever happened to so and so?" She asked the other regulars, "Don't you guys have some sort of newsletter?" Some of them had thought about it, she told me, but it had never really gotten off the ground. It planted the seed for Stephanie.

Wilma, the women's room matron at Wrigley,[9] was there at the time, and she was "like a mother confessor to the group," Stephanie told me. Wilma had been working for the Cubs for thirty-three years. Stephanie wrote to Cubs management and said, "'Why don't you have a Wilma Fields Day? It could be a way to honor all long-term employees.' The Cubs answered, 'Well if we do it for Wilma, we'll have to do it for everyone else, yadda yadda yadda,'" Stephanie recalled.

Stephanie, however, was determined. "I'm going to honor you, Wilma," she said, and she put out a flyer in February 1991 about starting a newsletter. She wanted it to be a fan's newsletter, where they could vent or share happiness or sadness or keep in touch if they were moving. "Like a community newsletter," she explained.

She got no response from the flyer.

Still undeterred, Stephanie started her newsletter anyway. That spring, she wrote up the whole *Bleacher Banter,* which was only the front of one page then, and she printed it up and handed it out for free. She did everything for the first four or five issues, and she was writing one for every home stand. At first, she "had to beg for addresses to which to send copies of the next issue, but before long, I began to receive verbal and written input when fans realized they would actually see their name in print." Then Rich Harris at the *Chicago Sun-Times* suggested to Bob Herguth that he contact her for a then-regular feature, the Chicago Profile. When Bob contacted Stephanie, she agreed to be profiled, and, "I went over to the *Sun-Times* and we did this whole thing. My photo was on the same page as Barbara Streisand, and I was in color and she was in black and white," Stephanie described. In the profile, she said to people if they sent their name and address, she would send them a copy of the Opening Day issue.

This time, the response was overwhelming. "I got over six hundred letters, and I answered every one," Stephanie told me.

In both Stephanie's and Ron's cases, we see people who saw a need or had a concern and acted on it. From the rest of the regulars we see initial caution, followed by gradual acceptance, and eventual enthusiasm. Because of their vocal presence and their willingness to negotiate relationships between the regulars and the Cubs organization, Ron and Stephanie are relatively high profile, and as a consequence, they fill the role of leaders. Or is it the other way around? If we take their willingness to do what needs to be done as the source of their leadership, Ron and Stephanie both exercise what Max Weber calls charismatic authority. As he explains, "Charisma is self-determined and sets its own limits. Its bearer seizes the task for which he is destined and demands that others obey and follow him by virtue of his mission. If those to whom he feels sent do not recognize him, his claim collapses; if they recognize it, he is their master as long as he "proves" himself" (1978: 1112–13). The basis of leadership here is precisely what we saw with Ron's developing organization in leftfield and in Stephanie's establishing of the *Banter*. There are differences, though, in what each of their stories tells us. Let us leave Stephanie's case aside for a moment and focus on Ron's leadership.

Ron took on the tasks to which he felt destined—the coordination of the regulars and the protection of a section of leftfield—and so long as he continues to succeed in those tasks, he will hold his leadership position. While his connection to daily life in center- and rightfields is more tenuous, he maintains importance to both sections because of his ability to negotiate playoff seating and, to a lesser degree, because of his ability to connect people looking to buy or sell tickets.

Likewise, the reason many regulars go along with Ron's organization seems to be the virtue of his mission: they share a desire for the protection of their community status in the bleachers and are willing to turn their energies to that end. However, their contributions to the community vary widely, and while some "obey," many only do so on their own terms. While clearly the ball hawks and the seating anchors in section 303 are actively participating in Ron's work to maintain and police the section, Ron freely admits that there is a "bit of a divide between the front and back rows." In addition, the system operates whether Ron is in attendance or not, and the extent to which another regular appears "deputized" has a lot to do with how reliable they are in ensuring that leftfield regulars are able to sit in their section when Ron is absent.

This is in its own way further evidence of charismatic leadership. As Weber points out: "The leader, generally, [has] his agents. There is no such thing as appointment or dismissal, no career, no promotion. There is only a call at the instance of the leader on the basis of the charismatic qualification of those he summons. There is no hierarchy; the leader merely intervenes in general or in individual cases when he considers the members of his staff lacking in charismatic qualification for a given task" (1978: 243). However, there is a complication in using this model of leadership to explain what is going on in leftfield. In point of fact, certain qualities of leftfield's organization are reminiscent of systems in both right- and centerfield, although Ron is not involved in coordinating either field. In addition, while it is rarely explicitly discussed, there is a hierarchy and a set of status relationships at play in all bleacher interactions.

Ron's authority is built in large part on his skills as an organizer, on his ability to routinize and rationalize patterns of behavior and bring them in line with the needs of the group as a whole. By way of illustrating both the rational organization he employs and of clarifying a distinction between leadership and organization in community, I turn to the day that is, by Ron's own account, one of the most important of his leadership each year. This is the first day of individual game ticket sales.

Despite the fact that the Cubs play eighty-one home dates in a ballpark with a capacity of 39,538, ticket day has a frenzy comparable to the hottest limited engagement concert. In 2005, twenty thousand wristbands were prepared for distribution the week before tickets went on sale. Each wristband was printed with a number (mine was 13399), and at the end of the week, one of those numbers was drawn by Cubs management (explained below). The line to get wristbands stretched at least a block throughout the week in which wristbands were handed out.[10] The wristband scheme was devised to prevent people from camping out, and I still saw people in sleeping bags in front of Wrigley at 6:30 am on the Monday wristbands were first being offered.

Many people elect to go with a wristband because trying to get tickets via phone or Internet or an off-site vendor is a study in frustration. Most attempts to get through on the phone during the first few hours of sales bring the phone company's three-tone signal that the lines are overloaded, and it feels like a triumph on the rare occasion when a busy signal sounds instead. Virtual online waiting rooms keep internet browsers occupied with promises that in ten minutes there is a chance of placing an order. Invariably, the ten-minute window seems to refresh rather than processing any further. When the press seems to lessen in the afternoon, it is only because prime dates and seats are sold out

The frenzy after the 2003 season was extreme, and in four of the five years since, the bleachers have been reported as sold out for every home date within a week of individual ticket sales beginning. Prime dates—like Opening Day, Cardinal and White Sox games, and rare interleague matchups—disappeared in hours, if not minutes. Within this context, it makes sense that in 2005, Ron put the word out: regulars needed to get wristbands and work together. By the time ticket day dawned, he had a group of forty people he was coordinating, all wearing their numbered wristbands, all waiting for news of whether they'd won the wristband lottery.

On the morning of Friday, February 25, the Cubs drew one of the wristband numbers and announced it on WGN Radio at 6 am. The person who had the number (or the next closest number above that number) was the first person in line at 8 am. The next highest numbered wristband would get the next opportunity for tickets, and so on. Phone lines and online sales opened at 10 am. Each person had a forty-ticket limit, and bleachers were limited to four per person per date to discourage scalpers.

Two of the forty people in Ron's group had good numbers. This made the whole enterprise a success; between the two, they were able to get eighty tickets, and that in turn translated to at least one prime ticket for everyone in the group. In addition, Ron was speed dialing and working online to secure more tickets. He had stationed himself in a local tavern, and that site was a nerve center of activity rivaling a trading floor. The regulars would be taken care of.

However, not every regular was participating in the group of forty. Centerfield had a less organized system; everyone drew a wristband, and anyone who got a good number was instructed to get Opening Day and Red Sox games[11] (this would cover sixteen of their allotment) and encouraged to use their best judgment on the rest of the dates. Two good numbers supplied the group admirably, and a flurry of emails plus an evening at a local bar ensured the distribution of tickets among centerfield regulars. The negotiation was fairly amicable, with each regular explaining what they felt they needed and what they would like to have but could live without. Absent and out-of-town regulars were taken into account, and a loose hierarchy, explained later in this chapter, served to expedite the process.

In the distribution of tickets in 2005, we can see a clear distinction between organizational styles in left- and centerfields, and this returns to the issue of leadership. Centerfield, section 311,[12] does not see the daily benefits of Ron's system of organization. The perception in center is generally that Ron's priorities lie, understandably, with leftfield. To participate in Ron's ticket purchasing plan would be to cede control of any tickets gained to leftfield rather than allowing a person to exercise magnanimity among the centerfield regulars with whom he or she sat every day. Further, it could potentially disrupt centerfield's own organizational scheme and the resulting social order that allowed the ticket distribution to proceed so amicably. In the case of issues that deal with the daily running of centerfield, Ron is not thought of as someone with a basis for giving orders to (or bestowing order upon) section 311.

At the same time, however, Ron's leadership is acknowledged as essential for *extraordinary* needs—that is, the assurance that regulars will be able to sit in their accustomed seats for playoff games. In this we see how precisely Ron's leadership fits Weber's definition of charismatic authority (1978: 1111).

Many of the regulars are season ticket holders, and through 2003, a season ticket to the bleachers included the opportunity to buy two tickets for every playoff game at Wrigley. Before 2003, season ticket holders could also order additional playoff tickets before they went on sale to the general public. As a rule, then, most regulars were assured of seeing at least some playoff game should the Cubs play any. The problem was that their general admission tickets became reserved seats for the playoffs, and without someone telling them, the Cubs organization had no way of knowing *which* bleacher seats a given regular wanted.[13] Ron, with his gift for organization and his recognition by Cubs management, was perfectly placed to get the needed seat information to the Cubs front office. In early August in potential playoff years, Ron visits all fields and compiles a list of regular season ticket holders and their seat requests. He passes this information along, and when regulars get their playoff tickets, they are printed with assignments of the seats where they usually sit.

Obviously, the problem of playoff seating has not been one that comes up often. The situation has been further complicated because the Cubs have opted to redesign the playoff packages for bleacher season ticket holders, offering only one ticket to each playoff game per season ticket held. In order to offset the ticket crunches this produced, many regulars took advantage of a one-time only deal in 2006 that allowed each existing season ticket holder to add another season ticket to their package. This has produced new networks of ticket relationships and new patterns of leadership, but the issues of seating for playoffs remains.

In the postseason situation, we can see a distinction between Ron's leadership in special circumstances and his everyday leadership in the bleachers. I have already mentioned the perception of his bias in favor of leftfield, and I submit that in this case, leftfield is *allowing* him to take on a leadership role rather than necessarily *following* him. As I noted above, there is a clear division of labor involved in the protection of section 303, a set of fairly clearly defined roles. With the exception of crowd control members and vendors who have been integrated into the community, though, the roles are flexible. *Any* regular could potentially fill any of the roles, and in practice, people do trade roles with a fair bit of frequency. While in leftfield, as in center and right, there are regulars who do *not* take part in pregame seat saving, this is either excused as a product of their circumstances (for example, family and work obligations can consistently cause people to arrive late, even after the first pitch) or simply a quirk of personality that is accepted—provided it is not accompanied by demands or complaints about those who are saving seats.

While leftfield has a more formalized pattern of organization than other fields, there are similarities between the fields. Seat saving in center and right, where most regulars sit along the back row, has a less urgent feel than in left. Ron correctly pointed out (see above) that batting practice is far more active in left than in center, and unlike center- and rightfield regulars, leftfielders extend their territory all the way to the baskets.[14] Since most early-arriving bleacher fans rush to the baskets to beg for player autographs and to snag balls tossed into the stands, center- and rightfield regulars, who tend to spread along the back rows, do not need to send their fastest runner up first. Nor do they need to defend their territories as fiercely, since it usually takes about an hour after gates open for there to be any serious encroachment attempts by nonregulars. In addition, regulars in right and center tend to scatter into smaller groups.

What is most notable, though, is that there are people who will put down towels to save seats and people who will take responsibility for guarding those seats in all sections. The jobs get distributed to whoever is available, and a process of constant negotiation ensures that there is always someone to save seats or an alternate plan if, by some fluke, a regular finds him- or herself seated alone. In essence, the division of labor we witness in leftfield is a product of necessity, emerging from a relationship that leftfield regulars have to their space. A less ornate division of labor is visible in the other sections, but in neither case is it the kind of division of labor that sociologists have long observed as being key to large-scale societies.

This difference may lend credibility to the claim that community does not host divisions and hierarchy. However, as anthropologist Marshall Sahlins pointed out, it is important not to fall prey to "confusion between an open system and a lack of system" (1985: viii). While small-scale communities may lack the formalized and transparent structures that are a given in larger societies, they are emphatically *not* structureless. Rather the structures are so implicitly understood that they rarely require articulation in the abstract.

William Foote Whyte, in his famous study of an Italian slum, *Street Corner Society,* keenly observed the various kinds of organization at work among "corner gangs": "The daily activities of the corner boys determined the relative position of members and allocated responsibilities and obligations within the group. They judged a man's capacities according to the way he acted in his personal relations" (1993: 96). While the regulars produce a less explicitly hierarchical structure than Whyte describes among groups like the Nortons

(3–51), they too use daily activities and personal relations to develop internal status distinctions. I submit that some sort of informal organization is essential to a community, and that there must also be potential leaders possessed of enough charisma to address crises that threaten the community.

Organization and Status

From the outside, the regulars do appear egalitarian. No strict status rules prevent lower-ranking people from disagreeing with those in higher ranks, and on issues of baseball, seniority does not automatically produce better insights. In many ways, argument is part of the life's blood of the regulars. However, there is a rough status system at play among the regulars that emerges in all fields from a combination of seniority and organizational roles.

The point of such organization, and such organizational roles, is well articulated by anthropologist Raymond Firth: "There is no doubt that for any society to work effectively, and to have what may be called a coherent structure, its members must have some idea of what to expect. Without some pattern of expectations and a scheme of ideas about what they think other people ought to do, they would not be able to order their lives" (1961: 30). In leftfield, regulars know what to do and what to expect. The gate opens, and they follow routines of organization with minimal discussion, integrating those routines into their usual behavior. Those who do not arrive at gate appear in section 303 knowing the regulars will be there. The realities governing what must be done to ensure this predictability operate with equal force in the other fields, and this in part explains the similarity of organizational structure between leftfield and the other two pockets of regulars.

As noted in chapter 2, the regular community begins with proximity in the ballpark. During the 1960s and '70s, such proximity was easy to find or avoid; the bleachers were sparsely populated, and indeed, games at Wrigley were often so poorly attended that tickets to the upper deck were not sold and the ramps going up were closed off. "You could count the house," Marv told me.

By 1985 the bleachers were a different place altogether. Tickets were available in advance, and the "fun in the sun" marketing of the bleachers had had its effect. Regulars who knew each other from standing in line day of game, who ran into each other in the restrooms and hailed each other across rows of empty seats, now had to contend with throngs of newcomers who didn't know bleacher rules. Some, disgusted and disgruntled, abandoned the bleachers. The others, for the most part, began to sit together in various groupings. If the bleachers as a whole could not be maintained as they had in the old days, at least some portion would be.

Regulars who date back to the 1970s or earlier have a certain indisputable senior status. This is a first axis of status determination in the bleachers, a hierarchy that rarely gets invoked save for times of scarce resources (like playoff tickets or seats on standing-room-only days) or, implicitly, in certain daily activities. For instance, the stories of senior regulars (senior in terms of years in the bleachers, not strictly age) about the old days have pride of place, and questions of tradition are directed toward them. As they get older, they are forgiven more idiosyncrasies, and the most senior are exempted from organizational duties. A general case study of centerfield organization helps illustrate the way this works.

Among the centerfield regulars, Norb from Centerfield is a member of long standing. Now retired and living in Indiana, he lives for music festivals, working in his garden, and hot, sunny days, all of which he enjoys with obvious relish. He hates night games in principle and refuses to attend them (although I learned he did attend the first night game at Wrigley). His objection to night games has been so vociferously pronounced that he is frequently teased when the lights come on at Wrigley, as they do often on overcast days. "You have to leave, Norb," someone will say as soon as the lights are noticed.

In the time I have known him, Norb's attendance at games has depended on the weather. He doesn't do cold weather, or rain. In recent years, his disgust with high ticket prices and "crybaby" players has cut down on the number of games he's attended, so his formerly predictable pattern of appearance on any glorious summer day has fallen by the boards. No one is entirely certain on what days he'll saunter in, shortly before game time, often with fresh basil or tomatoes to share. However, it is certain where he will sit: the seat on the aisle in front of the death seat.

Norb himself doesn't save seats. A casual observer might mistake aspects of his arrival as rude, wondering why he can simply appear and sit in the spot that other regulars had already announced was saved for Howard from Centerfield. However, this misses two things. The first is that Norb usually arrives shortly before Howard, who is blind. Norb ensures there is space for both of them, shifting people around as necessary, and as soon as he spies Howard at the concession stand, he walks over to guide him to his seat. Howard scoots over from his accustomed spot on the aisle without complaint, and the pair chat companionably throughout the game. The rest of the regulars, meanwhile, greet Norb with a healthy dose of welcoming abuse, returned with quick wit and laughter all around. This is the second, and perhaps more important, point: senior regulars like Norb are felt to have paid their dues, and just as the centerfield regulars routinely left the death seat for Marv, they adjust their patterns for the days when Norb appears. Seniority has its privileges, granted as a matter of course.

Norb's senior status is different from the middle generation of seniority, a broad swath of the regulars who may have a few decades in the bleachers but cannot date their attendance back into the 1950s or earlier. It is in this generation that responsibility status is more keenly felt, and positions continuously change. Regulars in this seniority bracket have a minimal obligation of letting the rest of their section know their schedules and the size of the parties they are bringing; failure to do so will generally result in grumbling and the real possibility of not getting a seat, depending on the relative social responsibility status of the offender, his or her seniority, and the nearness to game time.

Responsibility status crosscuts seniority, then, in particular ways. This kind of status, rather than being determined by the organization of the bleachers, is determined by the contributions of a given regular to recreating the organization at each game. It is the manifestation of what Marshall Sahlins would call a "performative" structure. Ron from Leftfield's position in the bleacher hierarchy is based first on such a performative structure; he fills the role of primary organizer in leftfield. As the person who formalized and routinized the organization, he is relatively assured of his status, which is reinforced by his leadership in ticket concerns and further developed by his increasing seniority within the group. Norb's status, in contrast, comes from a "prescriptive" structure that grants status based on longevity. As Sahlins explains, "The performative orders tend to assimilate themselves to contingent circumstances; whereas, the prescriptive rather assimilate the circumstances to themselves" (1985: xii).

These two crosscutting axes of status are important for the general smoothness of community relations. They are means for creating personal differentiation, a pattern anthropologist Raymond Firth recognized among the Tikopia. The balancing of different axes of personal status defines relationships in "a consistent, interconnected system, by which every member of the . . . community finds his social obligations and privileges defined" (1961: 53–54).

Similarly, the regulars find their social obligations and privileges defined by their positions on the axes of seniority and social responsibility. At this point, it is worth considering the organizational structure of centerfield. Centerfield regulars distribute themselves on either side of the aisle dividing section 311. During my first years in the bleachers, these sides were referred to as the light side and the dark side, and the light side also included a subset of regulars who had winter and summer seats.[15] I sat (and still sit) on the dark side, the side closer to the batter's eye in straightaway centerfield. Marv, seconded by Tom from Centerfield, anchored the dark side, and Streamwood Linda anchored the light side.[16] Bill from Centerfield led (and still leads) the seasonal migrants.

Anchoring a section in centerfield is a status conferred by reliability. The person who a) consistently arrives at gate and b) attends the most games becomes the anchor. He or she is the person who keeps tabs on how many regulars will be in attendance at any given game and when they can be expected. Anchors direct seat-saving activities. When there is some question about whether a seat needs to be saved, the anchor's opinion is sought. If an unexpected regular appears, the anchor negotiates whether he or she can take over a seat that had been saved for someone else. This demonstrates the four principles that Firth identifies as crucial to social organization: coordination, foresight, responsibility, and compensation (1961: 75–78).

The way such coordination and foresight operates and depends upon status as marked by seniority and social responsibility is clearest when seen in practice. Before her retirement in 2004, Judy from Centerfield, a teacher, was obliged to come to the ballpark after the end of the school day during spring and fall games. Judy, with thirty years in the bleachers, had a high level of seniority. She also could be counted on to arrive at gate on days when she was not teaching, and most years, she attended at least a few innings of every one of the eighty-one games of the Cubs home season, which conferred a high level of status on the responsibility scale. On days when Judy was teaching, everyone knew to save her seat, and Marv would remind people to do it (coordinating and exhibiting foresight). As the section filled in, regulars would sprawl, making sure space was maintained for anyone who was expected. By first pitch, though, the pressure of late arriving fans to find seating generally persuaded the regulars to make decisions on anyone who wasn't there. Empty stretches of towel would get pointed to. "Who's there?" Tom would ask. "Connie? She'll be here. Marv, is Norb coming, do you think?" The section would contract to make room for a couple from out-of-town who seemed okay, or a dad with his daughter, based upon the assessment of who was unforgivably late (a determination made by their status). Judy's seat, however, was always jealously guarded (compensation granted to high status). Centerfield regulars would sit spread-kneed and refuse to budge— even for another regular.

Most of the regulars who would sit in centerfield understood this seat protection, although even that was subject to assessment. On one occasion, when I arrived late without advance notice, I was allowed to "keep Judy's seat warm" until she arrived. At other times I witnessed other regulars, with less responsibility status, refused even that much consideration. More to the point, there had only been one occasion in my experience where anyone asked any further questions about the seat after another regular told them it was for Judy.[17] The seat was left open without complaint, even by those regulars forced to stand.

Judy, since her retirement, has become the anchor of the dark side. Tom's move to Florida and Marv's decision to stop attending games, combined with her own organizational skills, have made her the section leader. She now coordinates seat saving and deputizes the next rank of regulars, conferring status with responsibility.

In addition to the anchors, each group in centerfield has a scatter of people who are predictably available to help protect seats and either relieve the anchor or keep him or her company. This is a role I fall into, one that grants me a responsibility status significantly higher than my seniority. Such a layer of organization is important to the continuity of a section, as we learned to our sorrow in 2004. At the end of the 2003 season, Streamwood Linda suffered a severe illness after losing her job earlier in the year. The light side, already depleted of members by increasing ticket prices and various developments in people's lives outside the bleachers, lacked a strong secondary layer. Linda, unemployed and in poor health, was compelled to leave Chicago. The light side as such has since ceased to exist. For a time, Jan from Centerfield sought to maintain it, but she is among the out-of-town fans, unable to make every home stand. No steady anchor remained, and regulars who used to sit there drifted to new sections. Without a reliable cadre of regulars to join her when she was in town, Jan found the light side lonely and eventually crossed the aisle. On cold days, Bill from Centerfield's wintering group gives the light side a semblance of life, but the dark side/light side distinction has lost its meaning.[18]

The loss of the light side demonstrates both the organizational necessities of the community as well as its contingencies. The continuation of a section depends on the participation of its members in the maintenance of the community space. It also requires an understood, default order of responsibility. If the anchor is unable to attend a game, if no one else can step in to cover, there is a real risk that regulars arriving too close to game time will be unable to find a place to sit at all, let alone with people he or she knows in his or her accustomed seat. When Judy cannot make gate, responsibility falls to me (nonschool weekdays) or Fred (weekends) or Jan or Linda (if either is in town) or Connie or Jeff (if they are not working that day). In an absolute worst-case scenario, centerfield has reciprocity with rightfield, and either a rightfield regular will be persuaded to hold centerfield until someone comes to relieve him or her, or lost centerfielders will be invited to rightfield for a new angle on the game.[19]

What must be remembered is that, in terms of privileges, the status distinctions I have pointed out only manifest when resources are scarce. They emerge when there is a seat shortage, or tickets are hard to come by. They operate to prevent or settle disputes, and thus help create an outward face of deep social solidarity. Nor is that social solidarity false, but rather than being based on the uniformity of members and a pure egalitarianism, it is based upon established and known hierarchies and routines that tell regulars what should happen in almost any eventuality. These systems in turn reflect and produce a set of values that can be regarded as moral, such as we'll see in chapter 7.

Because of the crosscutting hierarchies of seniority and responsibility, and the contingency of the organization, it is difficult to state a rule of thumb for determining the status of any given regular (although in practice, any regular could assert his or her status in action and be supported). Thus, it is easy to see how the regulars, or any similarly constituted community, could be regarded by outsiders as uniform and internally undifferentiated.

Nonetheless, there remain those instances of leadership that extend beyond the capacities of the organizational network. I have already explained Ron's role in these instances; it remains to discuss Stephanie's *Bleacher Banter*. Her case makes up my third case study.

The *Bleacher Banter* and Community Representation

When Stephanie from Leftfield started the *Bleacher Banter*, she, like Ron with the playoff tickets, was starting something apparently unprecedented. Much in the way that Ron established the first list of regulars (see above), Stephanie established a means for the bleacher regulars to represent themselves to themselves. She also created a means for old regulars to maintain ties and for new regulars to begin to form connections. I have already mentioned the place of the *Banter* in my early bleacher years. The newsletter played a similar role for Linda from Centerfield.

Linda first met the regulars at the Wrigleyville Tap, when Tom from Centerfield saw her there, sitting by herself and reading a book. The incongruity of seeing someone reading there in the bar prompted Tom to chat with Linda and to tell her stories about his bleacher life. The next day, Marv from Centerfield saw her sitting on a bench outside of Murphy's Bleachers, a bar across the street from gate N. They struck up a conversation, and Marv invited her to come sit with him and the rest of the centerfield regulars. She accepted the invitation.

The next day, the 1994–95 baseball strike began.

"How did you ever get established as a regular with that start?" I asked her when I learned this story in 2004.

"I got the *Banter*," she told me, "and I kept in touch that way. And when baseball started again, I was back."

In many ways, Linda's perseverance through the strike helped cement her position as a regular fairly quickly. Her correspondence with Stephanie, always faithfully reported in the *Bleacher Banter*, helped bridge the gap between her appearances in the bleachers and in fact gave her a way to connect with the community when appearances in the bleachers were impossible. The printed page created a community-by-proxy. It is a process similar to what political scientist Benedict Anderson hypothesizes for newspaper readers. As Anderson noted, the newspaper allows the reader to imagine a world to which s/he belongs, and knowing others are reading the same paper helps cement the idea that the imagined world is real and grounded in everyday life (1991: 35–36).

For some *Banter* readers, the world of the bleachers is as Anderson suggests it is imagined: they share the community with others reading the newsletter. There are odd degrees of separation involved here. When Harry Caray was alive, he would occasionally read the *Banter* on the air. "He would be in the middle of the broadcast and suddenly say, 'Hey did you see this in the *Banter*?' and read out parts," Stephanie remembered fondly. Mark Grace, longtime Cubs first baseman, used to take copies to the Cubs clubhouse, and corrections would occasionally come from the Cubs front office. The public figures around whom the regulars had built their community were in this way brought in, not just as objects of discussion, but also as potential participants. The *Banter* provided vicarious reports for those who were unable to attend games or who might be too shy to chat up players or who might wonder what was going on out there beyond the outfield.

Stephanie provides the glue that holds it together. She publishes the *Banter* bimonthly, charging $4.50 per issue to cover expenses (subscriptions are offered at a discount from the cover price). The decision to charge for the newsletter did not come easily. "I told people if they wrote to me, I'd put their name in the Banter," she said. "By this point the Banter was already up to about four pages, and then suddenly it grew to ten. That was getting hard, getting it out every home stand, and I had to start charging for it. Seventy-five people subscribed right away."

More would follow, as did regular columnists and occasional contributors. For the regulars who subscribed, they found themselves reading a material representation of their lives in a particular moment in time. For this group, the Banter is another layer in the community rather than its full representation, but it still has an effect.

When the Banter first started appearing in 1991, Stephanie was still sitting in centerfield. A leftfield regular approached her with a hint of disapproval, noting, "He might've known it was a person from centerfield who started the Bleacher Banter," Stephanie remembered. His complaint was that everything reported in it dealt with centerfield, and she shot back, "You want something in about leftfield, you gotta write."

The result was the "Inside Bitch" column,[20] and the Banter was on its way to being a uniting force between fields. The various pockets of regulars had always been aware of each other's existence, but several regulars have confirmed that people didn't really start hanging out across fields until the 1984 season. Participation in the Banter gave regulars another line of connection, emphasizing the shared values and relationships that partially overrode the geographic distinctions that regulars still invest with meaning.

In establishing the Bleacher Banter, Stephanie showed many of the qualities of charismatic leadership discussed above, although it was not exactly the same kind of extraordinary circumstances that spurred her to action or the community to follow her. The response that she received after her spotlight in the Chicago Sun-Times suggests that the Banter serves not so much a need of the regulars at the ballpark every day, although it is a valued part of the community. Instead, the Banter primarily provides a venue for participation for regulars no longer able to attend games or for could-be regulars to get a sense of the values of the community. For this latter group, though, the best the Banter can give is a snapshot. As we shall see in the next chapter, those values are continuously negotiated and demonstrated in practice and in the small rituals of everyday life.

7

Ballpark Rituals

Over the last five chapters, I have been laying out a set of relations to the world that allow the bleacher regulars to feel a sense of community. Throughout, I have been relying on their own reports and practices as evidence of how space, time, effervescence, boundary keeping, and social organization serve to identify the regulars as a community. In this chapter and those that follow, I focus explicitly on the practices themselves and how they create a moral community. To do this I follow anthropologist Edmund Leach, who, in his work on highland Burma, pointed out that every functional action includes "aesthetic frills" specific to the local context. He claimed those "frills" reveal the ethics of a place and a people (1965: 12). While Leach's claim regarding the link between aesthetics and ethics may raise some eyebrows,[1] he does pick up on something important. The little local quirks that attend ceremonies of greeting, gathering, and planning speak as much about the things that a given community values as anything the community members might say. With that in mind, allow me to unpack the ethics attached to standard repeated practices, the rituals of the bleacher regulars. I offer analysis of a typical ten minutes prior to gate at any given game.

Gathering Outside the Gate

I have already discussed the importance of arriving in time to "make gate." Functionally, regulars need to have at least some members in position to enter the ballpark early and save seats. However, the location where the gathering occurs has various levels of meaning.

Before 2006, the regulars entered the ballpark through gate N, known within the bleachers as the "main gate." Rather than lining up against the wall of the ballpark or assembling at the gate itself,[2] the regulars would station themselves about forty feet away from the gate at the fireplug on Sheffield Avenue. There was usually a blue sawhorse or two, property of the Chicago Police Department, sitting by the fireplug, and regulars lounged against them and stood around, clustered in groups of three to five and arrayed in a rough circle.

This was a luxury.

Until the renovation of the bleachers, the Cubs policy was to allow season ticket holders to cut to the front of the bleacher line. After the renovation, a new gate was created for bleacher season ticket holders (gate L), but the effect is the same. Unlike the single ticket holder, season ticket holders are not obliged to arrive at the crack of dawn to hold down a spot at the front of the bleacher line. Because most regulars have a share in a season ticket or can claim to be entering with a friend who is a season ticket holder, the season ticket gate is effectively the regulars' gate. Simply by congregating, the regulars demonstrate to others that they have a particular, privileged relationship to Wrigley Field and the Cubs and that they value that relationship and wish it to be known.

An additional effect of gathering in a preset and set apart location is that it makes the regulars especially visible to one another. The corner of Waveland and Sheffield is particularly open and visible from any angle of approach, and the location of gate L at the join of the bleachers and the grandstand gives it special prominence when approaching down Kenmore Avenue, a common route for regulars. Regulars can arrive at the gathering place and assess even from a distance the size of the regular crowd. They can also discover who is already there and anticipate who might be running late and require a seat. Prompt appearance at the gate becomes an acknowledgment of responsibility to one another and a means of physically reassuring oneself of the continued regular presence at the ballpark. This is particularly important when we consider that once in the ballpark, regulars immediately rush to their territories, and those territories are scattered throughout the bleachers. The *wholeness* of the community beyond the individual fields and seating preferences is made evident by the daily gathering before the gates open. The self-consciousness described in chapter 1 is reinforced by this experience of being complete and separate, and contributes to a sense of what makes us us.

Greetings

One August day in 2005, Tom from Centerfield appeared for only the second time all season. As noted earlier, he and his wife, Tammy, had left Chicago, moving first to Green Bay, Wisconsin, and then to Florida. When I saw him at the fireplug outside gate N, I greeted him with exaggerated shock. I stopped in my tracks and clutched at my heart as if I had seen a ghost. After my display of theatrics, Tom offered a sarcastic remark on my lack of tan and we settled into companionable conversation.

My overdramatized reaction was in keeping with standard greeting practices among the regulars. It makes sense that there should be some kind of greeting exchanged between friends meeting on a street corner, this being standard in American culture. It is even common sense that such a greeting would be more effusive than usual to mark how long it had been since I had seen Tom. Note, however, the assumed values: people should be greeted, and that the passage of time should be marked. Bleacher greetings are in fact often pointedly distinct, even when regulars have seen each other daily.[3]

The greeting rituals are particularly marked because regulars are gathering in crowds. The area around Wrigley Field and the space in the ballpark itself are filled with thousands of people, many of them complete strangers. Greetings take on a larger aspect by asserting connection in a throng that is simultaneously familiar and unknown. Even if regulars refrain from physically demonstrative greetings, the words exchanged frequently index how often the regulars see one another, as in the often said, "Well, here we are again."

This brings me back to Tom's long absence and my shock at seeing him. In truth, I was not at all shocked by Tom's presence. Even if I had forgotten in that moment that he would be there, he has an established pattern of being in town that week in August. His request for tickets circulate among the regulars for months in advance as we seek to ensure he can attend at least some games whenever he is in town.

There were two elements to my reaction. The first is that given Tom had been a steady regular for years, my greeting needed to reflect both his period of absence *and* his known commitment to the bleacher family. The second is that Tom is in my direct bleacher ancestry (see chapter 9 for more on this concept). Linda from Centerfield, who introduced me to everyone, considers Tom the person who introduced *her* to everyone, and Tom in turn was regarded as "Marv Jr."[4] From the start of our relationship, Tom razzed me about everything in a classic joking relationship, which I will explain in more depth in the next section. Given this background, it was not only appropriate but expected that I would remark upon Tom's presence with a certain irreverence and in a way that marked the event as out of the ordinary.[5] In doing so, I acknowledged both Tom's and my place in the bleacher social order and reinforced a sense of its existence in our lives. I also bore witness through my action to the value that the regulars put on relationships.

Waiting in Line—The Updates

Regulars are involved in one another's lives in very particular ways. While someone's job may not be common knowledge, it is fairly common for people to share stories of their relationships, their families, their hobbies, their home improvement projects—in short, anything about which they care deeply. The principle of *taking care* discussed in chapter 5 includes a sense of trust, an idea that regulars are the people with whom any regular can reveal the things that are most important to them. As Judy from Centerfield is fond of saying, "There are no secrets in the bleachers!"[6]

The pattern of greeting among regulars is followed by a series of check-in questions reflecting developments in regulars' lives. Even in the middle of a home stand in July, when everyone in line has seen each other every day for a week, regulars will ask, "How's your mom?" or "How'd Nick's game go?" For regulars who sit together, awareness of what's going on in one another's lives is an obligation that they reaffirm with every query. The answers to these update questions are often brief, accompanied by promises that details will be offered "when we get inside." The conversation that fills the hours before the first pitch is often set on the street by the answers to update questions.

When regulars have not seen each other in a while, update questions become demands that regulars come prepared to meet. Regulars routinely bring new photos of their children and grandchildren to the ballpark on Opening Day as part of the community renewal symbolized by that high holy day of obligation. They also bring photos of home improvements, souvenirs from vacations, and newspaper clippings about events in their lives. When I was writing my dissertation, I was asked every game for an update on "that paper you're still working on." Part of my obligation as a regular was to respond politely to such inquiries and recognize them for evidence that the regulars cared about this project that I cared so much about, even if I was experiencing personal frustration at a particular moment of writer's block. Since 2005, the repeated question for me has been, "What's the news on the book?"

Security Checks

Since September 11, 2001, bag searches have become standard operating procedure at many entertainment venues, including Wrigley Field. Between seat-saving supplies and various all-weather gear, the regulars tend to carry more and larger bags than most fans do and are often able to cite precisely the limits on what will be allowed in the ballpark. While the threat of a terrorist attack remains background to these regulations,[7] the security questions asked of fans address more pedestrian concerns. Crowd control personnel ask, "Any cans or glass bottles? Any alcohol?"

As noted above, the regulars know these rules, and so the questions are perfunctorily asked by bleacher security personnel. Regulars begin opening their bags when they see the check starting. They hold them out toward the security personnel, continuing conversations as they wait their turns. They joke with the people who search their bags.

"What kind of sandwich is that?" a checker will ask, threatening to confiscate it for lunch. The regulars know most of the security personnel and are friendly with them, and the casualness of these exchanges demonstrates the special relationship that the regulars have with Wrigley and the people who work there. The unconcern of the security personnel validates the regulars' sense of ownership of Wrigley Field and demonstrates that Wrigley personnel understand and respect the regular principle of taking care. The regulars, meanwhile, do not begrudge the bag checks, recognizing that security has to do its job, even though everyone on both sides of the interaction *knows* that no regular would do anything to "disrespect" Wrigley Field.[8]

What results, then, is a *performed* bag check. It is a ritual rather than an actual security measure. Everyone knows how it will play out, and this produces a certain playfulness that marks it as ritual.

This ritual is most remarked upon when it is missed. With the advent of the season ticket gate, bag checks have become even more perfunctory for regulars at gate L, but most regulars are no longer recognized at gate N. Where the gate L crew recognizes the familiar sweatshirts, rain ponchos, and snack bundles in the baseball bags of the regulars, gate N personnel are likely to insist that bags be completely unpacked for inspection. More than once, a disheveled regular has appeared in his or her section saying only, "I had to come through the main gate" as an explanation.

There is usually a tone of hurt and irritation that accompanies the experience of being processed through the main gate. While intellectually the regulars understand the bag check policy, the implication that a regular would ever consider doing harm to Wrigley Field or its denizens is an affront. The community takes pride in being recognized for its upstandingness, to the point of upbraiding members who put that reputation in any kind of jeopardy. When a regular is not recognized as a regular, the absence of recognition is keenly felt as a moral comment.

Ritual and Social Order

As we can see in the analysis above, even the smallest actions have flourishes and elaborations that are particular to the regulars and shed light on their values and organizational structure. As Leach points out, actions such as these comment on the individuals and their place within a community (1965: 13). We have seen glimmers of this point in the material I presented above. Every ritual not only reflects the values of the community but also captures the ways in which each regular is embedded in the community. The regulars understand the rituals and position themselves within them, taking particular roles and playing particular parts, maybe consistently, but maybe only "for the time being" (11).

When we consider the temporariness implied by "the time being," we also have a new lens for thinking about the relationship between the structures of the community and how people use those structures to produce values that get reproduced in actions. In short, there is a semiotics—a sign system—of community belonging, and each community will have its own semiological values. This idea comes from French literary critic and semiotician Roland Barthes, who points out that there are systems that underlie how people use symbols, and these systems require agreement by their members. Such systems are usually elaborated by "a deciding group" (1967: 31).

In the case of the bleachers, the regulars are a deciding group, and the system of values that they are tapping into has been decided through long practice. Each ritual taps into this system—a system I have been describing throughout this book—as we saw in the previous section. This system is to some degree "imposed upon" the regulars, as we saw in chapter 5 in the ways that boundaries are created and maintained. There is a requirement, an obligation, to behave in ways that reflect the values of the regulars. This is what Barthes calls a "signifying contract" (1967: 32). The regulars have an implicit agreement to both abide by a certain set of values and to accept that certain behaviors are reflections of those values. Thus, when we see me react to Tom's presence with exaggerated shock, we see a) my relationship to Tom as a senior member of the regulars relative to my position, and b) the "joking" nature of the relationship between Tom and me.

One of the qualities of being a regular is the ability to "take a joke." Joking in the bleachers is continuous and can sound cruel or even vicious to the uninitiated. When security leads Bobby from Centerfield, one of the blind regulars, up to section 311, someone will invariably yell, "Spin him around!" Amid disapproving looks from other fans, a regular might take hold of Bobby's shoulders and gently urge him to turn 360 degrees before leading him down the second row to his seat two or three down from the aisle.

Bobby greets everyone by name when he hears their voices, and he periodically cues new rounds of teasing. Eventually, he will make some passing reference to food, and I've seen him grin as he does it, waiting for the next line: "Bobby, all you ever think about is food. Geez!"

On one occasion, this beginning led to the following exchange:

"How much do you weigh now, Bobby?"

"Two hundred and twelve," Bobby answered. "They just weighed me today. They wanted me to ride the bike, but I hid from them."

Judy from Centerfield spluttered with laughter. "Bobby, that's almost as good as getting out of swimming because the chlorine hurts your eyes!"

The conversation continues like this, teasingly rude, throughout the game. Periodically, Bobby will say something that prompts someone in the row behind him to whack him on the back of his head with a scorecard. Out of context, it looks for all the world like the regulars accept Bobby just to have someone to pick on. While all this is going on, however, regulars keep a careful eye out for Bobby's welfare. They warn him every time someone comes down the aisle trying to climb over him. Anyone from another row caught climbing through to cross in front of Bobby is berated, warned to "go down your own aisle" in the future. "So you came all the way over here to crawl over the blind?" someone will remark in loud, sarcastic tones.

Regulars check with Bobby when they make runs to the concession stand and make a point of getting him safely to transportation after games. In recent years, when bleacher prices increased enough to prevent Bobby from coming to many games, regulars made a point of periodically setting aside a ticket specifically for Bobby, each given freely so Bobby could still participate in the world outside the group home where he lives.

Bobby is also a precious resource for the scorecard keepers—at any missed play or double switch or pinch runner, someone will yell, "Bobby, what happened there?" He will raise his ear from his transistor radio and tell everyone, and if he is unable to answer, he catches grief: "Geez, Bobby, pay attention to the game!"

What is noteworthy here, though, gets lost when I have already revealed that Bobby is blind. While his disability affects the content of the joking that is part of his relationship to the regulars, the interaction between Bobby and the rest of the regulars is *fundamentally equal* to that of any other regular's interactions within the group. *No* regular is spared from merciless teasing. Such teasing, in point of fact, is a signal of regulars' solidarity with one another.

This was evident on one summer day when I arrived at the ballpark with freshly skinned knees and elbows. I had been rollerblading to the ballpark and had not seen a hose stretched across the street. I tripped and fell, and, mortified, got up quickly and skated the final miles to the ballpark without tending to the resulting scrapes.

The initial reaction of the regulars when I appeared with blood dripping down my limbs was concern. I was ordered to clean up and supervised as I did so while someone found one of the medics on call. It quickly became clear I wasn't badly hurt. The road rash looked dramatic—and was too extensive to bandage—but it was only road rash. I was given some antibiotic ointment and allowed to settle into my seat, but then all bets were off.

Tom from Centerfield was among the instigators. "Rug burns!" he exclaimed. "Who were you with that you didn't notice the pain?"

Tom got points for his zinger, and he simultaneously cemented both his and my place within the bleacher regular community. He demonstrated he knew me well enough to make a relatively crude remark without me taking offense, and the other regulars, in appreciating his comment, acknowledged his knowledge of me—and their own. They were certain the comment would not harm me, was not made to damage my reputation, and would inspire little more from me than some very entertaining embarrassment. The joking also served to diffuse what tension might have arisen out of genuine concern that I might be hurt. Every time I stood up for the balance of the game, someone would yell, "Holly, don't trip!" and mocking hands would be raised around me protectively. That I could smile and object and roll my eyes all acted as reassurance that I was fine.

This kind of joking, with its hint of cruelty, is both a ritual and an index of belonging among the bleacher regulars. Any regular is a potential target of rude remarks and mockery. The ability to get in a good "zinger" at someone else's expense is well rewarded, and the victim is expected to go along good-naturedly with the joke. The give and take of this joking is so valued that sometimes, as we saw with Bobby, a regular will level an opening volley on him- or herself to get the ball rolling.

Joking relationships were initially recognized and analyzed by anthropologist A. R. Radcliffe-Brown in the 1950s. Pointing out their "peculiar combination of friendliness and antagonism" (1952: 90–91), Radcliffe-Brown notes such relationships work to both call to mind and dismiss the issues that always threaten to disrupt the relationship between any two people. This seems to make a fair amount of sense: by joking about Bobby's blindness, the regulars act to mitigate any threat that blindness might pose to Bobby's inclusion as a regular.

However, there is more to these joking relationships than Radcliffe-Brown would allow. Radcliffe-Brown focuses on the structural relationships (i.e., man to mother-in-law) in which joking relationships serve some function in keeping a society going. He starts with the assumption that because people occupy certain roles, they must engage in joking relationships. I propose something opposite: the joking relationship ritually signals that a person has successfully occupied a certain social role. It is as Leach noted; this ritual action "serves to express the individual's status as a social being in the structural system in which he finds himself *for the time being*" (1965: 11, emphasis added).

The joking relationship in the bleachers is a signal of inclusion, and jokes will frequently be used to test the potential of a bleacher visitor. In one pregame exchange, Marv from Centerfield began chatting with a group of men who had taken over the other half of the regular bench along the rail. At some point in the conversation, Marv's age came up, and one of the guys remarked that Marv looked good for someone in his seventies. Marv gave a short laugh, took the cigar from his mouth, and said to the heaviest of the men, "Heh. Well, you'll appreciate this. Ever see wrinkles on a balloon?"

The heavyset man seemed to bristle for a moment, asking, "What's that supposed to mean?"

"I'm just sayin," Marv continued, backing down. The other man began to laugh, but he laughed too late. The regulars tolerated the group of men with easy camaraderie, but they were not included in the joking that continued through the game.

They were equally excluded from a mode of joking that is crucial to the regulars—the digs at the team on the field. Regulars are expected to be able to make biting commentary about the Cubs, always well-grounded in observation. Other fans are rarely allowed such license—for a nonregular to rag on the Cubs is to bring out every defensive instinct in a regular. The exception is when the nonregular is able to back up their complaint, to demonstrate a competence and baseball knowledge equivalent to that of a regular.

The right to rag a player is *earned* in the world of the bleachers. Although the relationship is one-sided, it parallels the joking relationship that exists between the regulars. The parallel suggests a special relationship between the team and the regulars, that the team *belongs* to the regulars as much as the regulars feel a sense of belonging with respect to one another. The joking relationships serve a pragmatic purpose, both marking the boundaries of the group and ritually establishing their right of ownership of the team (see chapters 2 and 4). Anthropologist Evan Hanover expressed this well to me in an email exchange about the regulars:

> This leads to the next point, which is easily the most fun for me to consider as a fan: the proprietary relationship (and right or obligations therein) which fans feel they have with their team. What's being contested is whether or not one is a true fan and therefore not whether they are capable of operating humor's semiotic machinery, but whether they have what it takes to inhabit a social role. Ah footing. It makes all the difference as to whether the bleacher bum will say "Yes that was a funny comment you made about the bullpen," or whether there will be indignation: "Don't even go there you cell phone toting yuppie scum!!!" (August 15, 2000).

Hanover's invocation of "footing" above is useful to us here. He is building from Erving Goffman's idea of interactions being shaped not only by the people present and the words spoken and the gestures made, but also by the implicit and understood relationships of all those people to one another (1981: 137). This kind of analysis, sorting out who relates to whom and in what ways, shows how even very subtle practices get ritually encoded and charged with meaning to show insiders and outsiders. So it was that my already discussed jab at Sammy Sosa one day in 1999 and the response of another regular signaled a change in my footing, a move into the role of a full regular rather than a guest.

Anthropologist Victor Turner pointed out, "Symbols instigate social action" (1974: 55). Each ritual action produces a kind of symbol, exists within a semiological field. Bobby's blindness, my skinned knees, or the Cubs poor defense all serve as triggers to ritualized responses, to social actions that help concretize the relationships the regulars share.

Rituals of Parting and Farewell

In addition to the rituals of greeting and participation outlined above, the regulars are also periodically confronted with loss. I will deal with the loss of friends and loved ones in chapter 9, but here I would like to spend some time discussing *institutional* loss.

What I mean by institutional loss is the loss of some place or activity that cannot be regained, a loss that signals a change for the entire community that is not manageable within the standard practices for handling change. As an example, for the period of 1984 to 1999, the bleacher regulars gathered before and after games at Jimmy and Tai's Wrigleyville Tap. The Tap was very much a neighborhood tavern, nestled in next to the Metro, a concert venue specializing in alternative and punk music, and two blocks from gate N. Jimmy, the bar's owner, was adopted into the regulars and always welcome in any section, although his duties at the bar often prevented him from attending games.

On game days, I could rollerblade to the ballpark and stop at the Tap. The burglar bars across the door would be unlocked at 10:30 am, even though they were still pulled closed and would not be pulled to the side until the bar opened at 11:00. I would push aside the burglar bars and close them behind me, entering the bar to stow my blades in the break room and get a big glass of water. Linda from Centerfield would stop by the Tap when she came directly from O'Hare, stashing her suitcases in the break room to pick up after the game. Regulars departing the ballpark would take their leave by saying, "See you at the Tap?" knowing everyone would stop by for at least one drink or a burger. At the end of every season, Jimmy would put roasters out back in the alley and have a pig roast for the regulars to celebrate another year together.

On Opening Day 1999, though, the rumors began. Someone had bought the building that housed the Tap. Jimmy's lease might not be renewed. By midseason, it was a certainty. The Tap would close in October.

The regulars responded in a few different ways, all of which have been repeated in similar situations. One response was a deliberate statement, "I don't want to think about it." The Tap closing would come up, and someone would shudder and announce their desire to leave the topic alone. This is one phase of what anthropologist Victor Turner calls a "social drama" (1974: 37). The impending closing of the Tap represented a *breach*, a breaking of "regular, norm-governed social relations" (37) through the elimination of the venue that supported those relations.

Turner's model tends to assume that the breach that gives rise to social drama is motivated from within a community. In this case, the change was externally imposed and unexpected, but it would have a real impact on everyday interaction. No longer would Marv be able to walk into the Tap to find his Leinenkugel Red already being poured and the pepper shaker sitting on the bar next to it.[9] No longer would Tom and Tammy, then still Chicago residents, be guaranteed a kid-friendly tavern where their children could practice shooting hoops at the game in the back room and play hide-and-seek among the pool tables. No longer would Ron be able to send a runner ahead to hold a couple of tables at the Tap, knowing they would be filled with regulars within minutes of the end of the game. The closing of the Tap would signal the end of dozens of ritualized practices that could not easily be relocated. A crisis was brewing (see Turner 1974: 38).

The regulars did think about it, though, worrying their anxiety like a sore. Plans were sprouted to find Jimmy another location on Clark Street, to boycott the new bar that would be where the Tap had been for fifteen years.[10] These "redressive actions" (Turner 1974: 39) were starting points toward eventual acceptance of the truth; the Tap was going away, and it would not be back. This realization produced a new set of redressive actions.

In October, Jimmy and Tai's Wrigleyville Tap had its "last call." I still have the black T-shirt from that night, printed by Jimmy to commemorate the occasion and sold out before the real last call. The dates stand out starkly: "The Last Call, Wrigleyville Tap, Chicago, 1984–1999." The T-shirt was the regulars' mourning garb.

I came and went early on that day. It was a warmish day for October, and the Tap was crowded, so the doors were open. I vividly remember a stray autumn leaf scuttling in across the floor, so evocative of endings and never-agains that I cried, and I hugged other people who were crying, too, trying to swallow tears and party hard and leave with good memories.

Later that night, long after I left, the people who stayed began the process of demolishing the Tap. I heard reports of toilets being removed and hauled off to new homes. Large markers were passed around, and the bar covered by graffiti. This was not behavior Jimmy had encouraged or even condoned, but it was an outpouring of frustration and grief. People wanted to keep a piece of the Tap. They wanted to break with the place, to sever the relationship by visibly not making it the Tap anymore before they left. It was not only bleacher regulars involved, but other regulars of the Tap as well.

The reactions of the regulars to the night's ending were mixed. People worried that Jimmy would suffer some negative consequence for the actions of the frenzied crowd that finally had to acknowledge they would not be back tomorrow. The impulse, though, was generally understood. When everything was going to change, a bacchanal seemed as good an answer as any.

For a few years after the Tap closed, the old "Jimmy and Tai's Wrigleyville Tap" sign was bolted to the fence behind the building that had once housed it. Regulars made pilgrimages; I have photos of Linda from Centerfield kissing the sign. The community continues, although no postgame watering hole has emerged to fill the gap left by the Tap. Instead, new patterns have emerged, "reintegrat[ing] . . . the disturbed social group" (Turner 1974: 41).

This kind of social drama intersects in obvious ways with the daily rituals that establish values and moral judgment among the regulars. Rituals that mark change acknowledge the events that occasion such change and help reorganize daily rituals into a form that fits the changed conditions. This pattern repeated itself with the 2006 bleacher renovation. The destruction of the old bleachers was avidly documented on bleedcubbieblue.com.[11] Several regulars spent days in lawn chairs set up on the corner of Kenmore and Waveland, watching the demolition unfold in a self-described "wake." To this day, regulars wear T-shirts to the ballpark emblazoned with the logo, "These Old Bleachers, 1937–2005," a physical reminder of the space that once was.

Nonetheless, the regulars endure. The ability to handle such changes is part of what ensures the continuity of the community, as such changes occur with more frequency than bleacher narratives might suggest. They are, however, of a different tenor than the rituals developed specifically to create change, to provoke interventions by the baseball gods into the games that are a focus point of the community. We shall see how this plays out in the next chapter.

8

Baseball Gods

On June 1, 2008, the ESPN Web site's RSS feed featured the following head-line: "Cubs top MLB on June 1 for first time since 1908." The next day, a group email was sent around by Mary Ellen from Leftfield, citing the June 1 convergence and adding, "Ok, we all know that. But did you know how many games the 1908 Cubs were up on this date? 2 1/2 games; just like the 2008 Cubs. Getting spooky, isn't it? :)"

In 1908, the Cubs won their second World Series. They returned to the playoffs fairly regularly throughout the 1920s and 1930s, but they didn't win another championship, and after 1945, they did not even make it to the World Series again. As of this writing, they still haven't.

Mary Ellen's comment about the spookiness of the Cubs' winning ways in 2008 reflected a kind of magical thinking that infected Cubs Nation that year. Wouldn't it be poetic, the reasoning went, if the Cubs won their next World Series one hundred years after their last World Series win? It seemed likely they would, and each win they added increased the certainty that 2008 would be *the* year. The Cubs finished the regular season with the best record in the National League. In the previous four seasons, other teams that had suffered long championship droughts had seen them end: the Red Sox broke their eighty-six-year streak in 2004, and the White Sox broke their eighty-eight-year streak in 2005. It seemed like it had to be the Cubs' turn. Both the performance of the team and the mystical signs suggested that 2008 would be the year the Cubs won it all. It wasn't. Instead, it became yet another reminder of a curse the Cubs had hoped they could beat.

I initially learned about the curse at the ballpark. From what I was told, the pivotal moment happened during the 1945 World Series. There at the turnstiles, the entry point to Wrigley Field, there stood the owner of the Billy Goat Tavern—and his goat. Apparently, the goat had accompanied the tavern owner to Wrigley Field throughout the 1945 season, so he had some grounds for assuming the goat would sit next to him for the World Series. Except, of course, it was the World Series. The oral version of the legend does not offer a particular reason for why the goat was not to be allowed in, but the rules were apparently firm. The tavern owner could enter, but his goat—alas!—could not.

The tavern owner was irate. He cursed mightily. Or more to the point, he issued a curse. From my understanding, it was uttered right there at the gate, although the exact words are lost to time. Which, really, is a blessing, because it was a singularly effective curse. This is the gist of it: a World Series game would never again be played in Wrigley Field.

There is a reason the curse is remembered; the events surrounding the goat and its eventual ejection from the ballpark (it did gain entry, as it turns out) were reported in both the *Chicago Times* and the *Chicago Tribune* (Gatto 2004: 3).[1] Nonetheless, there was nothing at the time to suggest that the curse had any real meaning. The Cubs were so frequently among the top finishers in their league that fans remained confident that they would win again. A glimpse of that confidence is witnessed in the signature line of one Cubs fan, writing online under the avatar "flyingdonut": "'Don't worry, Joey. We'll go next year. They're in the World Series all the time' —My grandfather to my sick father, October 10, 1945."[2] October 10 was, poignantly, the day the Cubs lost game 7 of what would be their last World Series appearance for at least sixty-five years.

There are more logical explanations for the Cubs' long drought than the curse. By the 1940s, the team built by William Wrigley was becoming the team built by his son, Philip, a man who had no great love for baseball and who was more interested in the profitability of the Cubs than their won-loss record (Golenbock 1996: 265–80). P. K. Wrigley owned the team until his death in 1977, and four years later, in 1981, the Cubs were sold to the Tribune Company.

It takes time to resurrect a ball club, but the Tribune Company appeared to be making a good faith effort. In 1984 they fielded a Cubs team that took over first place in the National League East for keeps on the first of August. They even won the first two playoff games they played against San Diego and were only one game away from going to the World Series.

The side effect of this impressive run was that Cubs fever seemed to grip the entire nation. The romance of the Cubs as perennial underdogs captured American imaginations, and the bandwagon following was huge. The crowds at Wrigley swelled, even though it would be five more years before the Cubs would make the playoffs again. With each successive year of losing baseball, however, the grumblings grew in intensity: why should the Tribune field a winning team when the "lovable losers" were selling so well? This exchange from the 2000 season, when the Cubs were en route to losing over ninety games *again*,[3] captures the sentiment well.

It was a June day before gate, and the regulars were gathered around the fireplug outside gate N, discussing the possibilities of trading Sammy Sosa and bemoaning the poor trading skills of then Cubs general manager Ed Lynch.[4] Gradually, the conversation shifted to the popular topic of the Cubs ongoing mediocrity. Crowd control was preparing to open the gate for season ticket holders, so the regulars began to move toward their spots inside the red tensor barricades. As Marv got up from the hydrant and moved toward his place, he commented, "It's still the same problem. Even when they're lousy, the Tribune knows there are idiots who will still buy tickets and fill this place up. And," he added wryly, "I'm one of them."

Other regulars in the line chuckled, and replies came fast from all directions. "Well, that's honest."

"Heh. Yeah, I guess I'm one of 'em, too."

"We're all just part of the problem," a fourth person added with a mock sigh of tragedy.

Then finally, an explanation for this "idiocy" was offered: "I'm telling you, it's a disease."

In the end of this exchange, the regulars crossed over from rational explanation to something more in keeping with the odd system of belief that manifests in the bleachers. Being a Cubs fan is *in the blood,* and regardless of what one may wish, the regulars are tied to their cursed franchise. Part of being a regular is acquiescing to and occasionally bargaining with powers beyond human control, as we shall see.

Do the regulars believe in the curse? It is hard not to, not so much because of the Cubs' generally miserable performances, but because of the events surrounding the rare occasions when the Cubs were really good. The 1969 team, for instance, won eleven of their first twelve games, claiming and retaining first place in the National League East through September 9. The collapse of the 1969 Cubs and the rise of the "miracle Mets" loom large in Cubs fan memories; the New York Mets remain among the most hated rivals for regulars old enough to remember 1969.

I have listened to several regulars explain that if the Cubs had only played .500 ball in September, they would have won the division. I have heard the explanation that the Cubs were tired; manager Leo Durocher apparently followed the principle of "dance with the one who brought you there," playing his regulars without rest. The day in, day out grind of the season simply caught up with the Cubs, and then there were the Mets and their incredible September winning streaks (they had two long ones, ten games and nine games respectively). Startlingly, 1969 was the first year the New York Mets had ever won more games than they had lost in a season; indeed, from 1962 to 1968, they had lost more than a hundred games five times. In 1969, they *won* one hundred games. There were lots of improbabilities involved in the second place finish of the 1969 Cubs, and then there was this event, recalled by one of the editors of *The Week* magazine:

> On the afternoon of Sept. 9, 1969, during a crucial game between the Chicago Cubs and the New York Mets, a black cat appeared on the field at Shea Stadium. From my seat in the upper deck, I watched the mysterious cat circle Cubs third baseman Ron Santo, awaiting his turn at bat. As 56,000 people began to point and cheer, the cat padded directly up to the Cubs' dugout steps. There it stopped, and seemed to fix its gaze on manager Leo Durocher. A roar of exultation filled the stadium. The game stopped, as the players all stopped to look at the black cat looking at Leo. It was just a cat, of course, but after that none of us doubted that the first-place Cubs were doomed. The Mets beat the poor cursed Cubbies that day, and the next. The Cubs fell out of first place for good, as the Mets, with fairy dust on their spikes, went on to win the World Series.
>
> Any statistician would tell you that omens and curses have nothing to do with baseball games. But you don't have to believe in witchcraft to see that baseball isn't wholly governed by the laws of probability (Editorial 2003).

Was the black cat a manifestation or reinforcement of the Billy Goat Curse? Many regulars reject this idea, but a certain fatalism took root in 1969 that has made it hard to ignore the possible power of the curse. The idea of the curse was reinforced in 1984, when the Cubs were once again a solid team, this time in the playoffs. They had already won two games in a best of five series and went to San Diego in high spirits, convinced they were going to win. Many regulars traveled to San Diego to watch the Cubs win the pennant and make it to the World Series for the first time in thirty-nine years. Everyone was *sure* it was going to happen. Judy from Centerfield has told me that they booked their flights around the idea that they would be partying in wild celebration of the Cubs' pennant.

The Cubs lost all three games in San Diego. The first had been no cause for alarm; the Padres won it easily, but a postseason sweep seemed almost unsporting. Game 4, though, the Cubs fans thought they would win. The game was tied 5–5 in the ninth when Steve Garvey, already 3 for 4, hit a home run and gave the Padres the win. Everything boiled down to game 5, and for the first five and a half innings, the Cubs led easily, 3–0. The Padres scored two in the sixth, but it was the seventh that spelled the Cubs' doom. In the seventh, with one out and one runner on, first baseman Leon Durham misplayed a grounder by Tim Flannery. The ball rolled between Durham's legs,[5] the tying run scored, and soon the Cubs were losing.

"That was the quietest plane I've ever been on," Judy reported. The Cubs fans flew back to Chicago in misery, unable to savor having been within one game of being in the World Series for the pain of losing the chance. Back at home, Robyn from Leftfield described leaving the bar after the Cubs lost the last game, and "walking around the ballpark with the rest of the Cubs fans, crying."

The memories of 1989 are far less painful. Perhaps more cautiously optimistic than in 1984, the regulars rarely tell stories of 1989. The rare specific mention of '89 is a vague regret that the Cubs did not clinch their first-place finish in Wrigley Field. But the curse held firm; the Cubs were eliminated during the playoffs. They were also eliminated in 1998, a season that tends to be regarded more as a gift than as a tantalizing glimpse of what could be.

This brings me to 2003. I have already described the raw agony of game 6 of the National League Championship Series (see chapter 4). The Cubs were *five outs* away from the World Series, and people believed the curse was over. Among the marketing giveaways for fans in Wrigleyville for the playoffs were cardboard cutouts of a goat's face with the words "We forgive you" printed on them. It is the one archival item I have managed to misplace . . . deliberately.

In truth, there have been more efforts to lift the goat curse than I can fully recount here. As early as 1950, P. K. Wrigley wrote a letter of apology to William Sianis—the tavern owner who originated the curse—and asked for it to be lifted (Gatto 2004: 16). In April 1969, Sianis finally agreed and lifted the curse (20)—or at least tried to. Since then, goats have been brought to the ballpark, grazed in right field, been photographed with fans, appeared on *The Tonight Show,* and become a hot marketing item. Sianis's Billy Goat Tavern, which remains in operation, became the inspiration for the popular "Cheezborger" *Saturday Night Live* skit featuring John Belushi and Dan Aykroyd.

There were also gestures that were less of the "make amends" camp. One Wrigleyville restaurant prominently featured goat on its menu on Opening Day 2004. In 2007, when the Cubs made the playoffs, someone hung a whole skinned goat from the Harry Caray statue in front of Wrigley Field. That particular moment was captured on YouTube.[6]

Perhaps the most interesting effort to deal with the goat's curse was the scheme of three Cubs fans (Bill, Dave, and Jim) in 2003, inspired by WGN radio host John Williams. By mid-September 2003, the Cubs had managed to climb over the St. Louis Cardinals in the standings, but Houston was staying stubbornly in first place. John Williams had a brainstorm. The goat curse could be *transferred.* All that was needed was a goat, a ticket for the goat, and someone to try to get it into a Houston Astros game at Minute Maid Park. A group of listeners, enthralled by the idea, bought four tickets to the September 22 Houston home game (one for each fan plus one for the goat), flew to Houston, bought a goat, and headed to the game. Bill called the John Williams show as they headed to the ballpark, and the audio of the effort to get the goat, "Virgil Homer," into Minute Maid Park is archived on the WGN radio Web site. Despite having a ticket, Virgil Homer was not allowed into the ballpark, and there outside the turnstiles, Bill said:

> Two years shy of 60 cursed,
> For all this times, the Cubs were worst.
>
> Armed with goat and mystic verse,
> We hereby Reverse The Curse!
>
> You had your chance to let him in,
> But now no more will the Astros win.
>
> We'll take our goat and leave this place,
> Along with your hopes in this pennant race!
> (Gatto 2004: 68–69)

The Astros lost the game on September 22, and when the Cubs won the following day, the Astros fell out of first place. They ended up not making the playoffs. This made the power of the goat seem difficult to dispute, although the fact that the Astros went to the World Series in 2005 could be regarded as evidence that the curse is transfer resistant.

At this point, I should clarify that the goat is not really important. Nor, for that matter, is the curse. What *is* important is a system of beliefs that make a curse *seem* plausible, a shared means of making sense out of an often incomprehensible universe. The bleacher regulars are savvy baseball fans; they can analyze any baseball situation to its finest qualities. They are *specialists* in Cubs knowledge, and as anthropologist Tanya Luhrmann explained about specialists: "The specialist learns a new way of paying attention to, making sense of and commenting upon her world [and] sees coherence where the non-specialist sees only chaos" (1989: 115–16).

If you ask a regular about what really happened on October 14, 2003, when the Cubs were only five outs away from the World Series, he or she will point out without hesitation that it was not Steve Bartman who cost us the game. The problem with the Bartman play was not that a fan interfered with a ball Moises Alou could have caught. In fact, the regular will note that Steve Bartman saved Alex Gonzalez from years of notoriety for blowing the Cubs' playoff chances. Gonzalez, after all, was the Cubs shortstop who mishandled a sure double-play ball that would have gotten the Cubs out of the disastrous eighth inning of the Bartman game. Regulars will also point out that Mark Prior, the pitcher that night, was clearly unsettled by the events down the leftfield line and Alou's dramatic reaction to losing the ball. Dusty Baker should have sent someone out to talk to Prior, or even talked to Prior himself, to settle the kid down. No matter how much poise Prior had shown through his first two seasons, he was still a twenty-three-year-old in a high-pressure game.

During game 6 of the NLCS, the wheels fell off. The uncharitable would claim the Cubs choked. There are dozens of plausible explanations. However, it doesn't take long to get below the surface to the secretly nurtured *truth* that the regulars will reveal, a truth that many Cubs fans share. Somehow, impossible as it sounds, the fiasco on the field in the Bartman game was the fault of every Cubs fan who, for even a second, believed we had the game won. Our *hubris* cost us the game; we had affronted the baseball gods. I will have more to say about such hubris later in this chapter, and the ways in which a specialist Cubs fan can see evidence of it, but first I must explain the baseball gods.

The Baseball Gods

The baseball gods are familiar figures to anyone who has more than a passing interest in the sport. They are also difficult to explain to someone who does not know them. In a sense, the baseball gods are a metaphor. They account for the freakish, inexplicable events on the baseball diamond. When Henry Blanco changes his number from 9 to 24 midseason and promptly goes on a hitting tear, as he did in 2005, he has pleased the baseball gods.[7] If a game has multiple rain delays, someone might say the baseball gods don't want the teams to get the game in. When the Yankees win yet another championship, opposing teams' fans shake their head and wonder what they've done that makes the baseball gods smile upon them so much. For some fans, a reference to the baseball gods is a turn of phrase, a bit of poetic license. For the regulars, and for Cubs fans generally, the caprice of the baseball gods has been too often directed against the Cubs. The baseball gods may still be metaphorical, but the supernatural forces they represent are not to be trifled with.

Following historian Johan Huizinga's explanation of personification in religion, "the baseball gods" is a shorthand for "those forces in the universe that surpass human understanding and yet seem to have a vested interest in meddling in our affairs, operating against all probability and producing results that seem to be the direct action of will" (1950: 136). These are the forces that prompt superstition, familiar to anyone who has ever felt compelled to "knock on wood" when announcing some positive happening. The power of the curse, for instance, requires that some force both heard it and decided to act upon it. While the regulars and other baseball fans might not articulate the existence of that force in so many words, they are cognizant of its necessity, and to the extent that they take seriously such forces, they will express them to one another in terms of willful beings: the baseball gods.

The baseball gods are capricious and whimsical, but above all, they are determined to remind the followers of the game of their power. I can think of no clearer example than the playoffs of 2003.

In the Bartman game, all of Wrigleyville was chanting, "FIVE MORE OUTS!" More than one regular—and I include myself in this list—has said that it was at precisely that moment that they began to really and truly believe it was going to happen, the Cubs were going to go to the World Series. The baseball gods, their attention drawn by the delirious chanting, sensed their opportunity to indulge their taste for cruelty. In reaction to overconfidence, to Cubs fans counting on a victory before the game was over, the baseball gods chose to issue a reminder of their power. They took the win away.

Irrational? Perhaps. By the end of game 6, Wrigley Field was deathly silent. The crowd filed out into the streets in shock. One Cubs official described the scene to me as surreal: "It was like watching people come out of church. There was no cheering or booing, just silence." How many of those fans were remembering how much they believed in 1984, when they were sure they were going to the World Series? They had learned not to predict the win until the game was underway, but now they had relearned what they had already known: "It ain't over till it's over."[8] More to the point, they had been reminded forcefully that the universe was subject to controls beyond those of human will and desire. Frankly, the lesson was that the universe was not nearly as rational as we wanted to believe it was. Ironically, this lesson did not prevent the magical thinking of 2008, although the Cubs playoff losses that season will leave their mark.

From this perspective, is belief in the baseball gods by otherwise apparently rational twenty-first-century Americans so crazy? Common sense and experience says that teams leading baseball games after the seventh inning are going to win 80 to 90 percent of the time. It also dictates that teams that are down three games to one, as the Marlins were at one point during the 2003 National League Championship Series, rarely come back to win the series. And while low probability events are not impossible, and while a succession of low probability events through history can happen to the same team, it is not surprising that at a certain point a string of bad luck looks a lot like a malicious influence. As the editor of *The Week* properly noted, "you don't have to believe in witchcraft to see that baseball isn't wholly governed by the laws of probability" (Editorial 2003).

There are some parallels between witchcraft and the kinds of superstition and belief that emerge from the improbable events that are the mainstay of being a Cubs fan. And as anthropologist E. E. Evans-Pritchard pointed out in explaining the belief in witchcraft among the Azande, such beliefs fit perfectly with the idea of a rationally ordered universe (1976: 30). If a person has done everything according to the rules and still fails, an American would blame luck, but is it so much of a stretch to imagine some force behind that kind of luck? Whether it's called witchcraft or the baseball gods—or freak chance—it is hard for humans not to seek an explanation for things *not* going according to plan.

So, if the regulars express their consistent encounters with flukish and irrational happenings in baseball as a belief in the baseball gods, what does this have to do with their sense of community? I have already mentioned Luhrmann's observations on the specialist's knowledge, and I return to her work to note her observation that people *systematically* depart from the rational ideal. The regulars, among other things already identified in previous chapters, share "interpretative techniques [that] depend on things which might seem irrelevant" (1989: 13).

Take, for example, a September night game against the Montreal Expos in 2004. Colleen from Centerfield was looking over her scorecard and player stats before the first pitch. "Let's see, Downs's ERA is 7.22?"[9] she noted of the opposing pitcher, Scott Downs. "Well, he'll look like Cy Young against us."[10] There were general murmurs of assent as a sense of fatalism began to take hold. On paper, the Cubs should have had the upper hand. They were sending veteran pitcher Greg Maddux, a three-hundred-game winner with an ERA of 3.70, out against Downs. The mismatch should have caused the Expos to roll over and take their defeat—or at least that's what the statistics and the records would have indicated. However, Colleen was reacting to a curiously consistent improbability in 2004. Starting pitchers with ERAs over 7 seemed to dominate the Cubs, almost without fail. The idea that this was inevitable developed legs in May of 2004, when Casey Daigle of the Arizona Diamondbacks, ERA 8.55, held the Cubs scoreless for six innings (the D'backs won the game, 2–0). At later games, we referred in disgust to "Cy Daigle." For a time, the magic ERA was thought to be over 8, but over the 2004 season, the number was revised down.

As it happens, Scott Downs pitched a five-hit shut-out against the Cubs that night in September, prompting Judy from Centerfield to remark, "There was a time I never thought I'd criticize a Cub team playing .500, but I'm so mad at this team."

Throughout the Expos improbable win, the regulars in centerfield were interpreting the experience through many apparent irrelevancies. Most strikingly, the Expos broke the game open in the eighth inning. Up until that point, they had been winning 1–0. Then, *with five outs left,* they scored five runs to lead (and eventually win) 6–0. It was as if the baseball gods were reminding the regulars of their folly of the previous fall. No regular, upon noting this quirk of the game, could ignore its significance, even if he or she desired to minimize it.

What is of even more importance than the shared interpretive frame that the regulars have produced, though, is the common idea of *appropriate action* within that frame. There are behaviors that a regular must engage in in relation to the baseball gods, and these behaviors have a ritualistic quality somewhat different from that discussed in chapter 7. Every regular has a repertoire of negative and positive rites that he or she performs as needed to appease or evade the baseball gods. Some are shared, others are idiosyncratic, but all are acknowledged and respected for what they are. And while the function of such rites is to some degree transparent—they are designed to bring wins—there is also this observation from China by way of A. R. Radcliffe-Brown: "For the most part the question of the efficacy of rites was not considered. What was thought important was the social function of the rites, i.e. their effects in producing and maintaining an orderly human society" (1952: 158).

This claim about the maintenance of orderly society via magical and religious rites is not as self-evident as the similar role played by the daily rituals discussed in chapter 7. However, these rites are worth exploring further to see precisely how they bring the bleacher regulars together.

The Negative Rites

There are two different types of game-related rites performed by bleacher regulars. The first are more universally practiced and follow a pattern described by Emile Durkheim as a "negative cult," a set of prohibitions against certain actions (1995: 303–4). As the word *cult* has somewhat different connotations today than it did at the turn of the twentieth century, I have modified his phrase, calling such actions "negative rites." Negative rites, however, are not rites at all in a certain sense. Rather, they are abstinences, deliberate refusals to do or say something.

I have already discussed the 2003 Bartman game far more than any Cubs fan would wish, and I content myself with this final, promised discussion of the hubris of the "five more outs" chant. As this is easiest to explain in the logic of the supernatural, I will use that metaphor, although it should be understood that it would be extremely unlikely to get this exact explanation from any regular.

In essence, the curse, maintained by the baseball gods' whim, made it highly improbable that the Cubs would go to the World Series. However, the curse was reaching a point where it might have lost its power to entertain said baseball gods. If they could be induced to allow "normal" probability to assert itself—that is, the kind of probability that would operate in absence of the curse—then the Cubs would have a chance. Effectively, the baseball gods were giving Cubs fans a gift by looking the other way as they approached the World Series.

Before game 6 of the National League Championship Series and the "five

more outs" debacle, there had been eager attention paid for signs of supernatural intervention. There was Virgil Homer, the goat, and his Houston
adventure, discussed above. More importantly, there was Ron Santo's jersey.
Ron Santo, the Cubs color commentator on the radio side and a member
of the 1969 team, fell ill shortly before the end of the 2003 season and was
unable to broadcast any playoff games or accompany the team. His number
(10) was retired on Closing Day in an emotional ceremony, and it was clear
that he enjoyed a special relationship with the 2003 team.

Throughout the playoffs, a Cubs jersey featuring Santo's number hung
prominently in the Cubs dugout. Surely, the regulars felt, the baseball gods
could let the Cubs win for Ron Santo. During game 3 of the NLCS, which
I watched in a local bar with a number of the regulars, the television cameras kept panning into the dugout and showing the jersey. The game was
a nail-biter. The Cubs went up 2–1 in the second inning, then there was
no scoring until the seventh, when the Marlins went up 3–2 and chased
starting pitcher Kerry Wood from the game. The Cubs got two back in the
top of the eighth, but the Marlins tied it in the bottom of the inning, and
the game went extra innings.

The intent silence in the bar was palpable. People were sitting with their
hands over their eyes and peering through their fingers. I could hear everyone
gasping and holding their breath on every pitch. And at one point during
that agonizing pitch-by-pitch experience, the camera panned again to the
dugout and Kerry Wood, as much a spectator as any of us by that point in the
game. Wood was sitting on the dugout bench, his arms stretched out across
the back of it. From somewhere in the bar, a hoarse whisper said in a tone
of awe, "He's touching it."

It was true. Kerry Wood's outstretched fingers were twined in the hem of
Ron Santo's number 10 jersey.

The Cubs won the game in the eleventh.

There was evidence, then, that some forces were working in favor of the
Cubs. A true cynic would claim the baseball gods were toying with us. But
contrast the crowd in the bar for game 3, braced for disaster, with the crowd
in the same bar for game 6,[11] chanting (like everyone in the ballpark, and,
indeed, the neighborhood), "Five more outs!" The game 6 crowd had forgotten that their potential victory was a gift; they were taking for granted that
the baseball gods would give them this one. Perhaps even more galling (if
we consider this from the point of view of the baseball gods), people were
beginning to believe all that curse talk was just silly, and really, a team with
a good pitching staff and a good manager would clearly prevail. In fact, the

overconfident Cubs fans were so sure the game was in the bag, they were *rubbing the Marlins' faces in it*. The "five more outs" chant was a manifestation of "overweening pride" (the definition of hubris), and the baseball gods recognized that it was time to put the ungrateful and neglectful Cubs fans in their place.

Despite the fact that no regular would describe events in exactly these terms, most would likely agree wholeheartedly with the proposition that we lost because we drew the attention of the baseball gods to what was about to happen. We *gloated* prematurely, and the baseball gods don't like that. We broke the most important taboo; we spoke of what we wished would happen. We not only spoke of it, we *counted* on it. We *chanted* it. By a curious logic, we got what we deserved.

This kind of fatalism may well be specific to Cubs fans, but the taboo they broke is widely familiar in baseball. It is almost universal in one instance to my knowledge: no-hitters. A baseball game in which a pitcher is able to prevent all the batters he faces from hitting safely is a rarity, and entire seasons have gone by without any pitcher achieving the feat.[12] Throughout baseball, though, if a pitcher gets into the fifth inning without giving up a hit, the rule is firm. No one is to mention that there is a potential no-hitter in progress. Television broadcasts delight in showing a pitcher en route to a no-hitter in the dugout—alone. Not only will his fellow players not talk to him beyond what is necessary to play the game, they will not even sit near him. No one knows what baffles opposing bats on such occasions, whether it is something in the pitcher's mental makeup that day, or some lucky streak where every ground ball finds an infielder and every fly ball stays in the yard, or some unknown problem weighing down the opposing team. Ballplayers apparently would rather avoid the successful pitcher than risk doing or saying anything that will interfere with what is working.

Fans, with decidedly less ability to affect the game, take the same superstition to heart. Whatever else happens, no one can mention the fact that a no-hitter is underway. The logic in play is much like that involved in the Cubs' lost playoff hopes: if the attention of the baseball gods is drawn to what is going on, they will take the no-hitter away. The most spectacular destruction of a no-hitter I have ever witnessed was a game between the Cubs and the Cardinals on September 20, 1999. It was a bitter cold night game with the wind blowing straight in—comparatively good pitching conditions. Jon Lieber was pitching for the Cubs, locked in a scoreless tie with the Cardinals' Mark Thompson. Lieber, however, had not given up a single hit. He had not walked a batter, nor hit one. The defense had played almost perfectly behind him. No one had reached base. In short, Lieber was pitching not just a no-hitter, but a perfect game.

The regulars were in rare form at the end of a losing season. Someone commented that we would "be paroled in six more games," a reference to the number of home games remaining on the season. A no-hitter at the end of a miserable year would at least take some of the sting away. Throughout centerfield, everyone was scrupulously NOT talking about what was happening on the field, even though every out was being cheered wildly. The crowd *knew* what was going on, but everyone also knew not to talk about a no-hitter in progress. In the top of the seventh, Lieber got Edgar Renteria to ground out to the first baseman. Then he got Adam Kennedy to ground out to the first baseman. Then Mark McGwire . . .

Mark McGwire hit a home run deep into center field. Good-bye perfect game. Good-bye no-hitter. Good-bye shutout. Good-bye *lead*; McGwire's home run made the score 1–0 Cardinals. And that was only the beginning.

Ray Lankford, up next, hit a single. Then Thomas Howard homered, making the score 3–0 Cardinals. Fernando Tatis singled. J. D. Drew homered. Marcus Jensen, hitting a measly .200 at the start of the game, singled. Cubs manager Jim Riggleman must have sensed a trend; he pulled Lieber out before he gave up another homer. By the end of the inning, six runs had been charged to Lieber (the relief pitcher gave up one more to make it 7–0 Cardinals). In total disgust, the regulars decided that someone in the broadcast booth had said something about the no-hitter. It wasn't anyone on the radio side; that we would have heard. It must have been one of the television guys. The notion that Lieber might have finally gotten too tired to strike out McGwire again (he had done so twice earlier in the evening) or that there were easily a half-dozen explanations why the no-hitter had ended did not enter into the conversation.[13] The no-hitter ended because some television broadcaster had broken the taboo, had failed to abide the widely known and understood negative rite of no-hitters. There were even some half-hearted efforts over the next few days to verify the villain by consulting with people who had watched the game on television—a welcome diversion until the Cubs managed a meaningless win streak against the Pirates to close out the home season.

The negative rite of no-hitters is simple: no one is to mention it. For the regulars, most negative rites take the same form, but their applications go far beyond no-hitters and playoff games. Any positive or potentially positive occurrence can be subject to a negative rite. In centerfield, it is taboo to mention the relative pace of the game if it is going quickly. It is a casual enough observation of a kind that would normally establish baseball competence. A person can glance back at the clock on the centerfield scoreboard, see what inning the game is in, and say, "Wow, this game is moving quick." It takes a certain amount of experience to recognize how the pace of the game compares to the average, and the observation of swiftness, if accurate, shows an attention to detail normally applauded by the regulars. However, if the person making the comment is a regular, the reaction of the rest of the section ranges from scandalized shouts of the regular's name to librarian-worthy "Shhhh!"s or silent dirty looks.

Here, then, is where we can see how the rite reinforces the community. The offending regular will generally know *exactly* what his or her offense was. If there is any confusion, a quick glance toward the clock by any regular will render the problem clear. Without any mention of the broken taboo, since such mention will only compound the error, a regular who has mentioned the quickness of the game will know s/he is obliged to offer an apology, or perhaps even a moment of self-approbation, acknowledging his or her transgression. Both the acknowledgment of the taboo and the understanding that the reaction of the regulars was appropriate signals membership in the community and respect for the interpretive frame through which it views the universe. Even regulars from right- or leftfields, regardless of whether they shared the taboo, would recognize the negative rite. The rite simultaneously marks the boundaries of the community, as discussed in chapter 5, and establishes rules of behavior. A similar function is filled by positive rites.

Positive Rites

While this "baseball gods" explanation for Cubs failings serves as a rationale for negative rites, a somewhat more complicated logic governs positive rites. I define such rites as actions regulars deliberately take to influence the outcome of games. Contrasted to negative rites, where the objective is to avoid particular actions, the positive rites demand some ritualized behavior, a self-consciousness of intent. They are activities toward a purpose, and notably a purpose in which the fans have relatively little ability to influence outcomes. This will be clearer with an example, so I offer the "tomato inning" in rightfield. The tomato inning is explained in Al from Rightfield's blog, "Bleed Cubbie Blue," in his entry for July 1, 2005:

> I have decided to bring back the Tomato Inning on a full-time basis after its crashing success on Wednesday. If you are arriving late at this discussion,

the Tomato Inning was invented by accident last year. Howard had brought me a Jimmy John's sandwich, and while I was eating it a piece of tomato accidentally fell onto my scorecard.

The Cubs scored ten runs in that inning. (Yes, they won the game, smartass. Scroll down to the Thursday, June 10, 2004 listing in that link for details.) So we decided to make it a ritual. We did it nearly every day, and the Cubs would always score in that inning—they didn't always win, but the tomato did seem to have the power to generate offense.

With Mark's proclamation and gift tomato the other day, I decided to bring it back. Yesterday, Howard didn't get to the game till after game time, and that is one of the ritual rules—the tomato must be dropped *before* the lineups are written. I ask Jeff, or Mike, to hold the scorecard, move it around a little, while I drop the tomato piece.

Today, it landed on the sixth inning.

Bingo! D-Lee home run. Bingo! Todd Hollandsworth home run.

Do *NOT* underestimate the power of the tomato (Yellon 2005a).

By mid-July, the tomato had apparently lost some of its power, but while it was capable of inducing offense from the Cubs, the ritual was obligatory. And regardless of whether a regular truly believes his or her rituals have anything to do with the outcome of the game, once such a ritual is instituted, most will concede it is not worth the risk of assuming it does not matter.

It is worth reiterating that the magic rituals—and I do believe they can be regarded as a form of magic—performed by regulars at various points of any season are *acts*. They are, as Jean and John Comaroff point out, "persuasive practices that enjoin a reality and an authority stretching far beyond the immediacies of the present" (1993: xvii). The immediate, rational world could see no relationship between a tomato and the Cubs offense. However, in the specialist imagination of the regulars, the baseball gods were sufficiently amused by the besmirching of Al's usually pristine scorecard to grant offense during the inning in which the tomato would make it hardest to record said offense. Lemons had become lemonade, and the trick should be repeated for as long as it continued to amuse. Such rites, after all, represent the height of a regular's power.

I have been a participant in such positive rites. On Memorial Day 2008, I arrived at the ballpark without my hat. It was a sunny day, and after my first pregame hour in the stands, I knew I could not go the whole game without a hat. I swallowed my pride and went down to the concession stand at the base of bleacher ramps to buy a hat. Pat, who had worked the stand for years and from whom I always bought my scorecard, openly gaped at me. How could I, a regular, have come to a game so unprepared?

I took her ribbing for a few minutes, then asked her to pick me out a hat. She did so, and I wore it while the Cubs won. The other regulars, knowing the story, insisted I had to wear that hat until the Cubs lost. I did, and the Cubs won again and again and again. It was fourteen games before the Cubs lost a game while I was wearing the hat. The hat was a winner.

I was experiencing something anthropologist Bronislaw Malinowski had observed: in a situation in which I had little power, I was ready to seize on any evidence that I could make a difference. I was unwilling to believe that the only thing I could offer the Cubs was "passive inaction" (1954: 79), even though rationally, I knew my personal impact on any given game is probably nonexistent. My hat and its magic gave me an illusion of power. If I continued to wear the hat—a positive rite—I could make the Cubs win.

In short, positive rites emerge as a way to counteract the sense of impotence that the regulars feel in influencing the game. The shared experience and witnessing of positive rites, including the limits of their effectiveness, serves to create and reinforce the concept of the baseball gods and their whims, which in turn becomes a mutually understood interpretive frame for understanding baseball games.

That said, once the rite lost its efficacy, *it could be abandoned*. Some magics wear out. Others may need recharging. Some eventually bore the baseball gods, whose entertainment figures in at least a peripheral way into the effectiveness of these rites. In 2003, I began visiting rightfield an hour before the first pitch of every September game, and the Cubs began a win streak. For the rest of the season, my visits to rightfield were positive rites and were understood as such. The visits stopped bringing wins in 2004, and now they are simply social calls, ritual more in the sense presented in chapter 7. What we saw there were different kinds of *moral* standards within the community; here is something closer to religious belief.

Regulars would not describe their relationship to the baseball gods as one of worship by any stretch of the imagination, but the various rites they perform in order to affect games have a logic more like that of religious than moral sanction. Such sanctions, returning again to Radcliffe-Brown, are about purification, about addressing mistakes made in the community that reflect badly on the group as a whole (1952: 173). The religious idea of "pollution" is useful here. The question of rites is how they can heal the whole by either preventing pollution or taking action against it.

The logic of negative rites follows this most obviously; the breaking of taboo creates an impurity that in turn prevents the desired outcome. The *positive* rites, particularly in their easy abandonment once they've become ineffective, are governed by a similar idea. The key here is *sacrifice*. The Cubs continued futility suggests a condition of pollution so great that trespass offerings must be steadily and continuously offered.

The difficulty of divining the desires of the baseball gods requires a readiness to perform new tasks as they are revealed, usually when an action produces a win. Hence, the discovery of the scorecard sacrifice (or perhaps the tomato sacrifice) meant Al needed to perform that sacrifice for so long as it worked. Similarly, I had to visit rightfield in 2003, regardless of what other tasks needed doing, and I needed to wear the same hat throughout 2008. Judy from Centerfield once had to wear a yellow T-shirt with a pretzel on it (known still as "the pretzel shirt") for several games in succession when it brought the Cubs wins. She sacrificed her time, going home and laundering the shirt each night, and to some degree, she sacrificed dignity, wearing the same clothes every day in a culture where such behavior is uncommon for anyone not obliged to wear a uniform. When the Cubs finally lost, she put the pretzel shirt away expressing profound relief. "I never want to see that pretzel shirt again," she confessed.

When viewed in the context of sacrifice, the importance of the regulars' superstitions becomes much more clearly an essential element of community. To borrow from Hsun Tzu: "Sacrificial rites are the expressions of man's affectionate longing. They represent the height of altruism, faithfulness, love and reverence. They represent the completion of propriety and refinement" (quoted in Radcliffe-Brown 1952: 159). Although the sacrificial rites here all seem geared toward the winning of baseball games, they are also a gesture of commitment to a community that values the winning of those games. Inasmuch as the community is identified with the team, which, as we have seen, is quite a lot, the "altruism, faithfulness, love and reverence" that the regulars show in their rites is directed not just toward the Cubs or the baseball gods, but to the community that has invested both with meaning and life. Thus, when Fred from Centerfield leaves his seat for a moment during the game and returns to find Colleen and Judy telling him he cannot sit back down because the Cubs scored while he was away, his reaction is not anger. "I just say, 'okay' and stand behind the rail until they say I can sit down," he reveals. "I understand." His sacrifice may please the baseball gods, but it also contributes to the successful maintenance of a community and demonstrates his status as a regular.

We have seen, then, how there are both religious and moral components to membership in the bleacher regular community. We have seen the regulars produce a social space and regard that space as existing within its own kind of time. Regulars protect both their space and time with various gatekeeping behaviors. We have seen the role of leadership and organization in maintaining the community. What remains is to watch the community in operation.

What will quickly become clear is that the bleacher regulars' existence sounds eerily familiar, despite the exoticness of their community home. They use the language of family, showing the same kind of self-descriptive modes that Warren St. John observed among University of Alabama football fans in his book, *Rammer Jammer Yellowhammer* (2005). But they also show the same kinds of connection described by Ethan Watters in *Urban Tribes* (2003). Many readers will likely recognize what they read in the next chapter as part of a common experience, a way of being in a community that is recognizable even without the theoretical dimensions presented in the balance of this book. Without further ado, let us watch the regulars through their own self-descriptions.

9

Births, Weddings, and Funerals

It was St. Patrick's Day 1992, in Apache Junction, Arizona. Ellen and Tim from Leftfield stood before the judge, and he asked, "Do you want the fast or the slow service?" They didn't have to think about it. "The fast service," Ellen recalled for me thirteen years later, "we've got a ballgame to go to." So Ellen and Tim, who met in the Wrigley Field bleachers in 1991, became husband and wife and immediately headed off to a spring training game to celebrate their union. "I knew for years I always spent St. Pat's in sunny, warm Arizona; so what better place for an anniversary?" Tim confided. After all, St. Patrick's Day was right in the middle of spring training, and the Cubs were right there in Mesa, Arizona.

Ellen and Tim's story has an almost Hollywood quality. They should have met years earlier in any one of a number of contexts. "We have ticket stubs from all the same shows and the same games," Ellen told me. "There were so many times we were both at the Aragon[1] for the same show, and I was at one end of the row and Tim was at the other, with the same group of friends, and we *still* didn't meet."

The story gets more astonishing. Both Tim and Ellen started sitting in the bleachers in the 1980s. Ellen, although often out of Chicago to follow the

Grateful Dead, sat in rightfield when she was in town, "because I thought the sun was better there." Tim also began sitting in rightfield in 1984 "when everyone and their brother jumped on the Cubs bandwagon." Both sat relatively close to the field, Tim right in the baskets and Ellen a few rows back.[2] During that time, though, Tim says, "I rarely saw the same fans twice. Other than Bill Veeck, of course. I don't ever remember saying to someone 'Hey, you were here yesterday!'" So when "Hippie Jim" stopped coming out with Tim in 1985, Tim went over to leftfield.

Ellen still sat in rightfield until 1990, when one of her Deadhead friends found her there and said, "You know, Ellen, everyone you know is sitting in left." So Ellen went to leftfield and found "about twenty of my friends." Once more, Ellen and Tim were in the same field, attending the same games, and finally fate caught up with them (although even here, it wasn't until the next season that they met). "It's probably good we didn't meet in the '70s," Ellen noted. "Timing is everything, right?"

So it would seem; Ellen and Tim had been married for thirteen years and counting when I interviewed them, still attending sixty-five games a year together in leftfield. They often meet other regulars for breakfast, and "If the Cubs win that day, we will order the same food the next day!" Tim explained. "Not that we're superstitious or anything," he added quickly, not without irony.

In the story of Ellen and Tim, we can see many of the elements of the bleacher regular community. They both found their way to the bleachers after spending time at Wrigley. Ellen grew up in the neighborhood, "so it was always easy to just stroll over after school, or whenever. I thought all kids had a Wrigley in their neighborhood!! DUH!!" She started attending games in 1968 as a kid and moved to the bleachers as she got older. Tim, from the city's southeast side, did not make it to Wrigley until he was fifteen. All he remembers, "other than the Cubs winning, was looking out at all the people in the bleachers and thinking 'I wonder what that's all about?'" He continued, "Looking back, I now realize it was a defining moment in my life."

Wrigley exists as a social space for both of them in addition to a place where they have experienced the highs and lows of being Cubs fans. Ellen described in great detail the bottle of champagne Moises Alou tossed to her after the Cubs clinched the division in 2003. She still has the bottle, now adorned with a long message written in silver pen by "Mo" at the end of 2004. "I brought the bottle and waited by the player lot. Mo stopped when he saw me and said, 'You got the bottle?' Then he took it and drove into the lot and he sat there in his car for a long time, then he waved me over. I looked at security and just went right by them, and Mo had written down the whole side of the bottle. He gave me a big hug, and it reduced me to tears."

Tim remembers with equal fondness his "near-hero worship of Cubs left fielder Gary 'Sarge' Matthews." This relationship blossomed with his friendships with the other regulars in leftfield. "It was these tie-dye-shirt-wearing fans who were first to 'salaam' a player," he reported with pride, implying rightfield fans who later salaamed Andre Dawson and Sammy Sosa were only imitators.

Clearly, Tim and Ellen have experienced the effervescence of the ballpark, and they have demonstrated the commitment and respect that has allowed them to pass through the community's gatekeeping strategies. Their steady presence in leftfield gives them an organizing role, and I have seen both inspect newcomers looking for seats and call down to others sitting in 303 to check availability for a group of four or a mom with kids. They are participants in the rituals of community, and with the same breakfast for days on end during winning streaks, are well aware of the baseball gods. They usually arrive for gate and settle in to pass the time, unstintingly willing to tell stories and reminisce and to build the legends, myths, and living history that bind the community together. Valuing many of the same things and sharing so much time together, it is unsurprising that Tim and Ellen finally found one another and married.

Tim and Ellen are not the only regulars who have met and married. It happens often enough that I have chosen not to list all the couples for fear of leaving someone out. This does not mean that every regular finds a spouse in the bleachers, or even marries a baseball fan. Far from it. Take this discussion during a losing streak in August of 2005: The uninspiring play on the field prompted centerfield to turn more toward community matters. The group was relatively small—Marv, Judy, Norb, Howard, and me—and the conversation focused on regulars who were no longer coming out to the bleachers.

"Remember Mary Beth?" Judy asked. "She got married, and that was the last we saw of her."

"You see it time and time again," Norb remarked. "Someone gets in a relationship and they disappear."

"Not us, though," I threw in.

"Aren't we married to this?" Marv said, gesturing to the emptying bleachers and the ballplayers wilting in the heat.

We shared a laugh, albeit a cynical one. It was not that we were all singles (we weren't); rather, the idea of being wed to the Cubs and their fortunes felt like a particularly cruel fate that afternoon, even if it did explain why we were there witnessing a seventh consecutive loss. Marv's point, though, captures the spirit of what has emerged among the regulars: a strong sense of "family." While some regulars have cemented that relationship in law by marrying, most content themselves with a kind of "fictive" kinship.

I describe the kinship of the regulars as fictive strictly because, as anthropologist David Schneider pointed out, Americans regard kinship as being a word to describe a biogenetic (blood) relationship (1980: 23). While kinship is expanded by marriage, by its strictest definition, two people unrelated by blood are not, in American reckoning, "kin." However, Schneider's study of American kinship also presents an interesting set of complications in Americans' understanding of their "relatedness" that is relevant here.

For Americans generally (and thus the regulars), the category of "family" encompasses the union of unrelated people (husband and wife, for example) and of blood relations (mother and child, for example).[3] The first category is in what Schneider calls "the domain of kinship as a code for conduct," while the second is in "the domain for kinship as a relationship of substance." Both domains are bound by love, which Schneider defines as "diffuse, enduring solidarity" (1980: 52). He points out a few paragraphs later, "Friendship and kinship in American culture are both relationships of diffuse solidarity. What distinguishes friends from relatives, as informants tell us so clearly, is that you are born with your relatives but you can pick your friends" (53).

This final quote begs the question of why "kinship" or "family" should be a more appropriate designation for the relationships of bleacher regulars than "friendship." In part, this relates to the idea that a person has some control over who he or she chooses as friends. Bleacher friendships spring up first and foremost because the people involved are sitting in bleachers. Deep networks of solidarity form between and among regulars, but they are by no means universally shared among all members. Real animosity exists between some regulars, but once a regular is a member of the community, he or she is in for life, barring some extreme betrayal. Being a member of the bleacher regulars means also risking regular contact with regulars a person actively dislikes, because *partial membership is not an option*. I noted in chapter 5 that for almost three years, I was on a sort of probation, a guest of the regulars. When I was fully accepted by the community, I also fully accepted the community. This does not mean I have to like—or even be civil—to all other members. However, I *must* respect that a regular is a regular, as fully a part of the community as I am.

Bill from Centerfield captured this well when he explained why he felt the regulars constituted a community. He agreed that the regulars are a community, but that that was not to say that everyone in the bleachers is easy to get along with. He talked about how no matter where he's been in life, from grade school through high school and the service and work and even the bleachers, it's always been true that if it weren't for one person, everything would be perfect. He tells his son this, that that's the way the world is. "There's always one person that's hard to get along with for whatever reason. You just learn to deal with it and know it will always be true. It doesn't mean you can't be a part of things."

This begins to shed some light on the family metaphor. While one could argue that regulars *choose* to be at the ballpark, choosing to attend baseball games is not the same as choosing one's companions at said games. In this way, going to Wrigley is reminiscent of going to a job. Coworkers are rarely chosen by those who work with them, but some relationships are made necessary by virtue of the number of hours spent together. However, unlike work, which is motivated by the need to make money, going to the ballpark is voluntary. In the United States, we have a settled pattern of regarding love and money as opposing forces (cf. Zelizer 2005). In contrast to the enduring quality attached to love, money-based relationships are seen as transitory.

The American system of opposing love and money on this front ties back to my objections to the "social capital" model used by Putnam, explained in chapter 1. While the regulars might not often invoke the word *love*, they certainly use *family* nearly as often as *community* to describe their relationships. And certainly, as we have seen in earlier chapters, the regulars value relationships between persons, deeply infused with morality and sentiment. As Bill from Centerfield went on to say, "*We* make it work. We could all come to the ballpark and be strangers to each other, but we're not that way."

What the regulars have succeeded in building is a series of relationships characterized by a code of conduct similar to the type embodied in a family. The overall community obligation is toward maintained enduring, diffuse solidarity. Because regulars enter into a relationship with the *community* rather than exclusively with a few friends, some of the element of choice attached to friendship is eliminated, creating a scenario closer to that of family. The force of this idea is heightened by the propensity of Cubs fans to refer to their love of the Cubs as a disease, as something in the blood, an inheritable thing, or to claim to "Bleed Cubbie Blue."[4]

For all that, being a regular does *not* seem to run in families in the more traditional sense. With few exceptions, children, parents, and even spouses of regulars are more often guests than members of the community. Honored guests to be sure, valued because they understand enough to appreciate their loved one's involvement with the bleachers, but bleacher regular status cannot be ascribed. Regulars are tolerant of friends and family who are unwilling to invest time in the bleachers, although most demand that they be allowed to invest that time themselves. It is in fact a mark of those closest to the regulars that they fathom bleacher relationships, even if they themselves don't share in bleacher relationships. For most outsiders, however, it is difficult to understand the family aspect of the bleachers. Robyn from Leftfield explained people's reactions, noting, "After my friends stopped coming out, I started coming by myself, and people would say, 'That sucks that you have to come to games by yourself,' but I'm not by myself."

"People just don't understand," Judy from Centerfield observed. "They ask me, 'What do you do out there when you get there so early?'" Like many regulars, Judy is at a loss to explain when people don't understand we're all just talking to each other. During one particularly good game, when many regulars were in centerfield and the conversation was flowing fast, Judy suddenly threw wide her arms and announced, "My mother said she always thought I'd outgrow this!" She laughed, and we laughed with her.

Al from Rightfield remarked on how his non-ballpark friends think he's out of his mind, but at the same time, they kind of understand. "Every human being has something like that in their lives, and if they don't, they should. People accept it." He elaborated, "The Wrigley experience is unique. It gets in your soul and you don't want it to go away."

Love and Loss

The size of the regular community and the age distribution of the regulars means that any given year carries the likelihood of a wedding or a birth—or a death. This creates a social world that has a different energy than more age-graded social circles, a pattern of social connection that is more common in American society. This is another way regulars' assertion of family makes sense; American friendship tends to focus on age-mates (like college buddies or friends that meet at their children's school). The cross-generational ties most Americans experience are family ties, and there they see various quirky life-stage behaviors. Among the regulars, any number of these life-stage behaviors are in full evidence at any given game. Marv from Centerfield, for example, refuses to allow people to float him money for a game, and pays for everything as soon as he gets it, because, "If something happens to me, I don't want anyone to talk bad about me. At my age, you gotta think about these things," he adds. Old age is celebrated and elders are accorded respect. Carmella from Leftfield, six weeks shy of her 101st birthday when she passed away in December of 2002, was widely beloved, and through the 2002 season, the sight of her hot pink hat just to the leftfield side of the batters' eye was a sign that all was right in the world. People made time to talk with her and visit with her, knowing each year that it might be the last.

Even regulars who are in their prime crack jokes about death. Usually, the context is a discussion of all the various memorabilia they've collected over the years. "I feel sorry for whoever has to go through all that when I die," is a comment that is oft repeated in all fields. They know they have the sympathy of the other regulars, most of whom remember friends who will never return to the ballpark, whose memories, once embodied in collections of ticket stubs and Cubs giveaways and scorecards and box scores, are now kept alive in conversations in the bleachers.

Stephanie from Leftfield began to tear up as she remembered Ken, one such friend. Stephanie used to sit in rightfield in the late 1980s, and Ken was one of her best buddies. She described Ken as one of those guys where you'd miss him one day and say "well, I'll catch him at the next game." Then one Monday night in July of 1992, he left the game, went to bed, and never woke up. He died in the night at thirty-eight years of age. "I always thought I'd see him later," Stephanie repeated.

Stephanie dried her eyes as she talked, and as she continued her story, she began to smile at her reminiscences. Ken's father had given Stephanie Ken's tickets, and they had his family out to the bleachers the August after he died. They brought out "about fifteen bags of Ken's ashes" and sat in the stands, waiting for the end of the game so they could sprinkle them on the field. The game ended, and "I'm pretty sure the Cubs won," Stephanie remembered. "It was a day when the wind was blowing out." Stephanie gave me a significant look with this piece of information and went on: "The family all went down to the rail, and they all opened the bags at the same time. Then, just as they're going to dump the ashes, a big gust of wind came up, and . . ." she paused, making a hand gesture and beginning to laugh. "We were all white with ash," she described, chuckling. "About six guards came running up to tell us, 'You can't do that,' but it was too late."

Throughout that season, Stephanie and the rightfield regulars she sat with continued to keep Ken's memory alive. Stephanie was friends with one of the guys who flew planes over Wrigley towing banners. She talked to him about how much it cost to have a banner flown. Then she took up a collection. At the end of the season, rightfield had a banner made up that said, "'Ken

Kunce says Left Field Sucks'—because that was something he always said," Stephanie explained. On the last day of the season at Wrigley, the plane with the banner flew over Wrigley Field, and everyone craned their necks to see what the banner said. Just when it flew over left field, though, Andre Dawson hit his four hundredth home run.[5] "It was like Ken said, 'nah, let Andre have his day,'" Stephanie remembered.

Talking about Ken reminded Stephanie of another time, before Ken died, when they had seen a bunch of guards running over to their section. This time it was during the first game of a doubleheader,[6] and they looked down and the guards were laying a guy out on the bleachers. He died of a heart attack and they were there trying to revive him in the stands. During the drama, Ken leaned over to Stephanie and quietly said, "The Cubs just won the game." "What an ending to a shitty year," Stephanie remarked, shaking her head. After that, they talked about how they wanted to go when they died, how they wanted to go quickly and not from some long illness. "And that's how Ken went."

Ken's death was part of the reason Stephanie eventually shifted over to center and then to leftfield: "It just wasn't the same in rightfield," she mourned. In contrast, the death of the man whose heart attack prompted Ken's musings on how he would like to die had a different effect on Linda from Rightfield. She still sits in rightfield, surrounded by remnants of her old friends and new ones. Her new bleacher family sits farther back from the field than she sat on the day that her friend died, but they care for each other in much the same way. They sit on the back row of their section, where fan traffic is high, and she'll overhear people say, "Didn't a guy die out here once?" She turns in her seat, giving them a hard look that reminds them that it wasn't just "a guy." "Yes," she tells them. "He died in my lap." Most offenders will hurry away with an apology, but to those who will listen, Linda tells the whole story.

Les, the man who died that day, was one of a group of regulars in rightfield who attended games with Linda and her uncle Marv ("the other Marv," she noted). Uncle Marv affectionately called Les "Junior," Linda recalled, and after Uncle Marv passed in 1989, Linda watched over Les. She made him give her his home and work numbers, and if he were ever not at the game, she would check up on him. In October of 1991, the Cubs were playing a doubleheader against St. Louis, and "I think he had a premonition," Linda said. That day, Les sat directly in front of Linda instead of his usual spot a few seats to the right. In the top of the ninth of the first game, Les "suddenly stiffened up, started shaking, fell into my lap, and died."

Linda and the other rightfield regulars called for the paramedics, who tried to revive Les. "They zapped him eight times, but we knew when they carried him out that he was in complete cardiac arrest. A couple of us left, but most of us felt Les wouldn't have left so we stayed for the second game."

The following Monday, Linda had a "sinking felling that Les was lying in a morgue with a toe tag, unclaimed." She called the hospital to see if they had found his next of kin and they had not. He was still in the morgue. Not sure what else to do, Linda called Les's work, figuring they would have an emergency contact number. "They didn't know he had died; no one did at that point." They did have a contact though—Les's sister.

Linda gave Les's boss her number, and he passed it along to Les's sister. Later that day, Les's sister called Linda and thanked her for letting her know. "Then she told me she didn't know if they were going to have a funeral for Les since he didn't have much family." Linda told her to have one, "Like *Field of Dreams*—if you have it, people will come," she insisted.

And people did come. More than a dozen people came from the bleachers, including a member of Wrigley Field security and Ronnie Woo, "and we all sat on the right side of the funeral parlor." It was the first time Les's sister had met the regulars. Les and Uncle Marv had both been disheveled guys, Linda pointed out, and when Linda walked in, the first thing Les's sister said was, "Oh my dear, you're attractive!" The man who had so little family, it turned out, had a lot of people who cared about him. A *Chicago Tribune* sportswriter, Paul Sullivan, was among those who used to sit with the rightfield regulars. He wrote up an obituary for Les in the sports section, which prompted the *Tribune* to send a reporter to the funeral, too. "I guess it was a slow news day," Linda said, "because the funeral was on the first page of the *Tribune* and the wire picked up the story (see Brotman 1991). Several of the guys who sat with us served as pall bearers, and Les's sister said, 'I never realized Les had this extended family out there.' And that's what we are," Linda concluded.

Like any family, the regulars remember and memorialize the members they have lost. As noted in chapters 3 and 6, a good share of time is devoted to keeping alive the histories of the family, often in gestures less dramatic than flying an airplane over the ballpark. One off-season, the centerfield regulars came together at a bar in Wrigleyville with photo albums. Their mission was to find pictures of Maureen, who had died over the winter, and send them to her mother, who had "no pictures of her at the ballpark." Dozens of images were collected, a mix of sunny days and rain delay documenting shots, and entire seasons were recreated as the circumstances surrounding the pictures were recounted.

This recreation is an important element of community, and as tightly as the Cubs are woven into the stories of the past, the crucial point is that what people are remembering are feelings, sentiments, a shared sense of connection. The sharing of grief and the celebration of the lives of regulars who have died bind the regulars affected more tightly. The sense of obligation and care that becomes evident in regulars at such times is most familiar to Americans as family-like behavior, behavior motivated by love rather than money.

The Regulars' Two Families

As has already been hinted at, regulars are often performing a balancing act between the bleachers and life outside. For some, the bleachers are their primary community, and in times of illness or trouble, their visitors will be almost exclusively the regulars. On one occasion, when something happened to Marv from Centerfield, a cab driver who lived in his building made his way to where Connie from Centerfield worked to let her know. This prompted several regulars to visit Marv in the hospital, and Judy from Centerfield recounted the event: "We told the nurse we were his kids, and she said, 'Oh, I didn't know he had any kids,' and we said, 'Neither does he!'"

Other regulars have successfully blended their bleacher lives with their larger family worlds. Ron from Leftfield, after discovering the bleachers when he was in college, ended up living in the neighborhood of the ballpark. "I was the vice president of the no lights committee when the community was winning,"[7] he told me. "That's how I got interested in law school," he explained. "Everything comes back here [the ballpark]. I found my wife here; I found my friends here."

Most regulars, though, bring family members out only on occasion. Bea from Centerfield brings her husband on occasion, for instance, but he doesn't quite see the charm. "How can you see from out there?" he complains. He is backed up by a *Sporting News* writer, who noted, "It's hard to tell from the bleachers whether pitches are balls or strikes, and you lose sight of balls hit to the deep outfield" (Garner 2005: 14). For regulars, fiercely loyal to their seats, this objection seems ridiculous, and most will testify they can see the game better from the bleachers than from any other seat in the house. Judy from Centerfield tells how her husband, John, brought her to Wrigley on a date when they were first getting to know one another. "He got us box seats. I hated it, but I was good. He was trying."

The "I was good" comment is one oft repeated in the bleachers, an idea translatable to being well-behaved. In many ways, being "good" is in direct contrast to normal bleacher behavior. One feature of the regular family is that sharp comebacks tend to be more valued than tact. When a regular has had an exchange that seems to have invited sarcastic comment, s/he will say "I was good" if s/he let the moment pass. Sometimes a regular will even have to be "good" within the context of the bleachers, particularly when dealing with another regular that s/he doesn't care for. More often than not, though, being good becomes an issue of choosing between the bleacher family and obligations to the rest of the world. Whether such instances involve refraining from comment when someone says something about the Cubs or missing a game for a family or work function, they are reported—as are occasions of *not* being good. Judy and Colleen from Centerfield recount, with a hint of mad glee, a moment when they were unable to resist listening to a Cubs game. They pulled out a radio and each took an earbud—not in itself unusual. However, the setting was more surprising: they were at a funeral home for the visitation for Judy's mother-in-law.

The circumstances were special, as one would expect. This was near the end of the 2003 season, and the Cubs were battling the Astros for first place. While Judy and Colleen got some disapproving looks for listening to the game, there seemed to be general agreement that Judy's mother-in-law would not have minded. She understood the importance of a pennant race. Colleen remembered that moment a week later, when her own mother passed away. On October 7, 2003, Colleen appeared at the Cubs' first playoff game, her somber face contrasting with the general glee of the ballpark. "I just came from my mother's funeral," she told us. Her mother would not have wanted her to miss the game.

The point that is often raised on such occasions is that while families might not *get* what it is about the bleachers, they understand at least enough to know it is vitally important to the regulars they share their lives with. When Tom and Tammy from Centerfield got married, for instance, relatives on both sides gave long looks to the rather loud gathering of regulars in the church vestibule. Despite efforts to keep their voices down, it was hard for the regulars to muffle their excitement in seeing each other in church clothes, and everyone was trying to take pictures to document the occasion. "Those must be their bleacher friends," someone was overheard saying. The comment added to the hilarity of the regulars, but it also made it clear that Tom and Tammy's families were at least coming to terms with the *other* family represented at the wedding.

Children

Perhaps no clearer indication of the family connection between regulars can be had than the place of children in the bleachers. Children are brought out with mixed regularity, some still in infant seats and often continuing on through their high school years. Strikingly, any regular's child is automatically the responsibility of the entire section. A trust extends to the rest of the regulars in the section to keep an eye on little ones and keep tabs on the older ones. Tammy from Centerfield's daughter Emily had spent so much time in the bleachers as a toddler that when she served as a flower girl in her mother's wedding, she was temporarily distracted when she saw Judy from Centerfield in the pews. Her duty forgotten, she veered off the aisle to get a hug, to the vast amusement of the rest of the regulars in attendance.

In all sections, conversations both before the game and between pitches often turn to updates on children and grandchildren. It is de rigueur to bring updated pictures of "the kids" on Opening Day. When the children themselves show up, the sections modify their behavior to accommodate them. Norb and Tom joked that centerfield had become a nursery when both Colleen's and Tammy's toddlers were in attendance, stationed at the second bleacher bench from the top of section 311. They used the bleacher seats as tables, coloring Cubs kids' activities cards and showing off their toys, and the adults sat on all sides, creating a protected space for them to play. Leftfield, with their adamant policing of section 303, is even more consistently kid friendly, and any of the parents among the regulars can run one child down to the restrooms and trust that any other children can be left with the section.

Generally, regulars assume most children younger than ten will need to be entertained,[8] and most take turns providing entertainment. Eventually, tolerant discussion of the merits of particular toys might give over to showing a youngster how to keep score, and all but the very youngest are directed to watch the field for key players. School-age children are generally brought with a friend in tow, casually watched as they rush forward to beg balls and autographs from the players during batting practice and amply supplied with hot dogs and ice cream during the game. Evidence of baseball savvy will be reported with pride, as when Al from Rightfield blogged, "When Dusty Baker sent Jose F. Macias up to pinch-hit for Mark Prior in the bottom of the sixth inning with the score tied 3–3, my son Mark said: 'Go to the principal's office, Dusty Baker! You're being fired!'" This report was followed by an equally proud observation that after Macias surprised everyone with a two-run single, "Mark said: 'OK, Dusty Baker! You can return to the classroom!'" (Yellon 2005b). For all this, though, as much as a child's interest in the game will be widely applauded, it does not seem to be assumed that any child will turn into a regular.

This is in many ways in keeping with the regulars' community standards. A person must have the option of *choosing* to be a part of the community, even if he or she cannot choose who else is in the community. Regulars recognize that their devotion to the bleachers and the Cubs is atypical, and that their ability to partake in both is highly contingent. A child who chooses to be interested in something *else* with equal fervor would be encouraged and would find regulars who would understand the spirit of his or her passion, if not the substance. "A person needs a hobby," Judy from Centerfield is fond of saying. The passion of a hobby, when considered from the perspective of a regular, becomes a lingua franca of a circle of friends who can become a family-like support network, and for regulars, few things can be more important.

As it happens, a fair number of young people do become regulars. Many of the older regulars date their bleacher lives back to high school, and a few, like Linda from Rightfield, were steady bleacher presences from the age of five. Even the kids who do not become regulars, though, end up developing respect for the bleachers. These are kids like Adam, indifferent to baseball in his youth, who began coming to games in the bleachers more often as an adult with his father, Fred from Centerfield, and discovering the appeal of the game. Or like Kathy, the daughter of Judy from Centerfield, for whom the bleachers were a feature of her life from before she was born.

On July 26, 2005, Kathy celebrated her twentieth birthday at the ballpark, a day that proved pivotal in her becoming a regular. Kathy attended her first game when she was three days old, her infant carrier tucked under the back row bleacher in what was then section 147. As a child, she came to games fairly frequently, and she still recounts stories of Tom from Centerfield lifting her up and threatening to throw her into the garbage bins by the concession stands. In her early teens, we could count on her coming to every game that featured a Ty Beanie Baby giveaway, usually with a friend along to pass the time. When Kathy became an 'N Sync fan later in high school, Judy would come to the ballpark with stories of the latest concert, and catching a concert in another city joined seeing road games and checking out new roller coasters in the family's excuses for travel.[9] When Kathy started college, Marv from Centerfield would shake his head whenever she appeared at games. "I knew Judy and them when they were like eighteen years old. Now they've got daughters that age."

Kathy has always said she has no intention of spending entire summers at

Wrigley Field, but she still ended up spending her twentieth birthday sitting in the rain at the ballpark. Twenty years of having the Cubs as a *presence* in her family has had its effect, and among the side effects of having baseball road trips as a natural part of her summer vacations is that she was at San Francisco's PacBell Park for Greg Maddux's three hundredth win in 2004. This matters to the story of her birthday.

Judy had planned for Kathy's birthday for months, networking for extra tickets and making arrangements for birthday greetings to appear on the Cubs scoreboard. On July 26, the Cubs were playing a night game, and at 4:30 pm, it began to rain. By 5:00 pm, when the gates opened, it was pouring. All the game monitors behind the concession stands were plugged into a feed from the weather center, and for hours the radar images did not appear to change. Kathy, her father, and one of Kathy's friends dutifully appeared before what would have been game time and joined the rest of the centerfield regulars, most of whom were huddled under the overhang of the upper bleacher tier—one of only two sheltered spots in the bleachers that still allows a view of the field (the other is under the scoreboard).

The radar still hadn't changed. The birthday cake was triple-bagged in plastic grocery bags, and a corner on the concession counter was found for it. Kathy, her cheeks swollen from having her wisdom teeth removed the day before, begged people to stop making her smile, because it hurt. Al from Rightfield stopped by to say he was leaving; the rain wasn't going to stop, and he had to be up for work at 3:30 am. Another hour went by. Jonathon from Leftfield came by and said half of the leftfield contingent had claimed enough was enough and were heading for the gates. The PA announcer promised they were going to try to get the game in and said something about a window around 8:30. By 8:30 the rain had lightened a little, but it was still coming down. Judy and I were sitting in our usual seats, still under ponchos and umbrellas, turning to talk to the other regulars under the overhang and tracking a light area in the sky to the west. Colleen was visiting leftfield, where many of the regulars who had promised to leave had gotten to talking on the ramp long enough to consider it worth waiting to see what happened. There were a few other pockets of fans.

"Some birthday, huh?" someone remarked to Kathy, and she smiled (wincing a little) gamely. "At least you'll be able to tell stories about it. It's not like you'll ever forget what you were doing on your twentieth birthday." And somehow around this point, it became clear that part of the dogged determination of Kathy and her friend was about the birthday, and part of it was about Maddux. Maddux was scheduled to pitch that night, and he was entering the game with 2,998 strikeouts. Kathy had a chance to see another Maddux milestone, a birthday present that could not have been anticipated.

But the sky darkened in the west and the rain intensified again. Judy and I exchanged glances. We were in our fourth hour of rain. No one was entirely dry, even under the overhang. It was chilly. "If there's no change by nine o'clock, I think I'm calling it quits," I told Judy, not sure I meant it. Judy and I were both intensely stubborn about outlasting rain delays. Judy looked back at her family. "I want them to get it in," she said, not for the first time that evening.

The rain began to lighten again, and as if reading my thoughts, the ground crew ran out just shy of nine o'clock to pull off the tarp. A ragged cheer sounded from the sparse crowd. That sparse crowd was suspiciously larger when the game got underway forty-five minutes later. Colleen came back from leftfield to breathlessly report that a fan had taken a header in the seating area, luckily near Mary Ellen and Karen. The two nurses had tended to the man until a backboard could be brought up and paramedics carted him away. Connie returned from a trip down the ramp and said that the ballpark cleaning crew, normally scheduled to come in around 9:30 or so in order to get the ballpark tidied up for the next day, were sitting downstairs, obviously too early this night to do anything. Stephanie from Leftfield appeared to talk about details of the trip to Cooperstown that was planned to begin the following Thursday and decided to stay in centerfield for the game. Then Howard from Rightfield made his appearance, revealing he, like many of the fans streaming in by this point, had cleverly stayed home until the tarp came off. But the rest of rightfield was MIA, and could he sit with us?

By the fourth pitch of the game, Maddux had struck out his 2,999th batter, and Kathy's birthday party finally began. The 3,000th strikeout was the final out in the top of the third, and Kathy got a picture of the scoreboard with her new digital camera. She also saw her birthday wishes on the scoreboard in the middle innings. In the sixth, with the rain finally reduced to an occasional spit from the sky, the cake was cut and distributed. Had the game gone only nine innings, Kathy would have made it to the end, but tired, damp, sore, and faced with the prospect of extra innings as the clock neared midnight,[10] she decided her birthday was over and she and her friend headed home with her dad. Understandably, Kathy earned considerable admiration for her dedication.

Despite her stated intention to *not* become a regular, Kathy was still a part of the extended family of regulars. Like other family members and good friends of regulars, she was invited to join the camaraderie of the bleachers on something of a permanent guest basis. Her longstanding presence in the bleachers and her obvious understanding of the community would give her full membership at any time she chose to claim it, something she is now doing. She and her new husband, David, have become a steady presence in centerfield, and both are learning to keep score in earnest.

The attitudes of the regulars toward their children speak to the intergenerational nature of the regular community. The steady presence of people of all ages compels regulars to be cognizant of both the vagaries of age (any age) and of generational differences. A fair amount of leeway is given to the very young (not knowing the ways of the world yet) and the very old (set in their ways). Because regulars are in the habit of balancing their bleacher lives with their wider lives, they are all sensitive to the demands of those wider lives at different points in a person's life. These features, in an age when status and social groupings tend to be age-graded, help contribute to the "family" idea of the bleachers. A longtime bachelor in the bleachers will still spend some hours amusing small children, and even the most self-involved twenty-something will be compelled to slow his or her pace to match that of the elders s/he has "adopted" simply by being a member of the community.

I have left this discussion of the regulars as a family as the final piece of this study in part because the word "family" is as freighted in its own way as the word "community." At the same time, it has been less subject (sociobiology aside)[11] to the effort to entirely rationalize the affect out of the relationships it entails. The regulars gravitate toward the word family to describe their community in part because, whether outsiders accept the idea, it comes closer to what they experience than can necessarily be captured by the word *community*. This in turn is a product of a culture that, feeling nostalgia for community, has tried to market and politicize it. While it might be valid to refer to the regulars as a "community of interest" because they share a devotion to the Cubs, the implication in such a version of the word is that *all* they share is that devotion. By this point in this book, it should be very clear that they share far more.

What remains, then, is to pull the pieces together. Having seen how practices make a community, can we make more communities? Should we want to? Will we be more able to recognize the communities we already have? Or will we increase our susceptibility to people promising community if we just buy one more product or vote in new zoning laws? In the following "postgame," I return to the "so what" question and offer food for thought about what we want when we wish for community.

Postgame

The slipperiness of the word *community*, as discussed in chapter 1, is part of the reason the term is so available to manipulation. The word is conventionally understood as denoting something good, and appeals to community reach to the more affective, emotional sides of our nature. Yet the term has been stretched to mean many different things, and two people can talk about "community" and think they are on the same page while actually discussing two completely different things. This raises an important question. Given that I have argued that a community feeling itself, along with a group consciousness that the feeling is shared, is the primary basis of community, should we care that any two people have different definitions of community?

Obviously, I would say we should. In the first instance, we need to recognize that community perception does vary and abandon the premise that community is necessarily good or beneficial. We also need to acknowledge the potential dangers of politicization and marketing. From a less nefarious seeming angle, understanding community as built on practice rather than identity enables us to deal more easily with changes. Our expectations of a group will be less based in a static picture of who they are and more in a vision of the circumstances that make them work.

Is Community Lost?

The answer to that question will depend on who gets asked and in what context. I do not dispute that there are some people who feel *disconnected*, who sense they do not belong anywhere. However, to identify lost community as the source of an impending sense of crisis in the United States is a ploy. It can be a valuable ploy, and it is undoubtedly a useful one. It can serve to reframe the general contradictions upon which America is founded in a way that makes the contradictions seem answerable and fixable. It gives a name and a plan of action to an indefinable sense of *wrongness,* a sense of a world changing faster than is comfortable for a given generation or historical moment. Placing an emphasis on community gives Americans something to struggle for or against as the case may be, and the less definition that is given to the struggle, the more local initiatives can have their effects. It may well be that such struggle is precisely what some people need to create communities. However, as with any ploy, it is important to ask who is directing this sense of crisis, and to what end? If we are going along with the idea that community is failing even as we ourselves enjoy the benefits of community, we may well ask what it is we are really struggling with.

Anthropologist Arjun Appadurai has made a compelling case that the rapid changes of the late twentieth century have created a general sense of uncertainty among many populations that he calls an "anxiety of incompleteness" (2006: 8). He seeks to understand the ethnonationalist and genocidal movements that have marked the late twentieth and early twenty-first centuries, and his argument strikes a chord. He describes a world of identity politics and entitlements, of people transplanted and mobile, of national boundaries perceived as increasingly porous. What does it mean to be American, or Indian, or Bosnian or Chilean, or any other national identity? What makes someone one of "us"? Race? Ethnicity? Language? For that matter, what makes someone one of "them"? Are "they" getting better protection under the law? Or are "they" changing our quality of life? Are "they" becoming "us"? Appadurai suggests that these kinds of questions lead to scenarios where a majority group perceives a minority group as preventing consensus, community, "an unsullied national whole" (8), and what results is often violence.

Appadurai's argument explains why we need to be so clear about what community is and how the idea of community can be mobilized. In the cases Appadurai describes, the quality of "us-ness" that makes community becomes contingent on an ascribed status. The community becomes a label or identity marker, a totem, rather than set of practices. Even when practices are considered, they are thought of emblematically rather than used to form relationships. The United States, for example, is a nation that tends to base its identity in a "way of life." To illustrate, if Americans regard part of what makes them Americans is that they eat thin-crust pizza with their hands, then someone who eats thin-crust pizza with a knife and fork is potentially "un-American." It is easy to imagine such a thing said in jest. It is equally easy to find examples of Americans decrying "un-American" activities and practices in all earnestness.

To tease this out further, still following Appadurai's basic claims, if a group requires a label to be recognized, and recognition comes with some extrinsic reward, there is increasing pressure for every group to have a label. This also produces anxiety that other labeled groups are getting more or better rewards, exacerbating animosities that might initially be based on something as simple as living in different zip codes. As we have been reminded in recent years in the United States, perceived threats can be particularly powerful motivators. A savvy politician can build a substantial support network if s/he can establish an "us" that works against "them" who are threatening "our" way of life. When taken to an extreme, this can produce violence of the type witnessed in the genocide in Rwanda. Indeed, Appadurai quotes from writer Philip Gourevitch's 1998 book about Rwanda: "genocide, after all, is an exercise in community-building" (Appadurai 2006: 7).[1]

This chilling idea highlights how important it is that we understand the workings of community. It also, ironically, helps explain how a theorist like Robert Putnam came to the recent conclusion that ethnic diversity is a threat to community (2007). Remember, Putnam's definition of community hinges critically on the concept of social capital, which he helpfully recaps, "social networks and the associated norms of reciprocity and trustworthiness" (2007: 137). Based on a large statistical sample from the year 2000, Putnam argues that, controlling all other variables, living in ethnically diverse U.S. counties prompts Americans to trust everyone less than if they were living in homogenous counties.

In classic Putnam fashion, his argument proves more nuanced than he initially presents it. He observes—properly—that his study represents a snapshot in time, using categories established by the U.S. Census. The study cannot reveal how much the demographic picture of each county has changed, and even were Putnam to consult earlier census data, he does not have the correlating trust questions for earlier years. If we consider how quickly the United States has changed since the end of the cold war and the subsequent speedup of globalization, we can easily imagine the lack of trust that Putnam identifies as related to the anxieties about identity that Appadurai describes. The ethnic diversity Putnam identifies is a symptom of rapid change, a point Putnam seems to recognize when he parallels contemporary causes of diversity with the high influx of immigrants at the end of the nineteenth century (2007: 162). Rapid change promotes uncertainty; uncertainty limits trust; lack of trust triggers a feeling of disconnect and a sense of being without community. Appeals to community become all the more potent in this scenario, and if community is understood as a mix of identity markers and boundaries between them, it becomes an easy thing to sell to an anxious population.

While I have been considering the political ramifications of this scenario, it is also worth considering the market ramifications. A politician is more likely to mobilize perceived threats to community; a marketer will play toward the desire for community. So-called "lifestyle branding" is an example of how associating community with identity markers gives corporations marketing power. A lifestyle brand is presented as reflecting the values of the person who uses that brand, creating a sense of consumer agency using the same logic as consumer boycotts. If consumers have power, they not only have the power to not buy products they disapprove of, they have the power to conspicuously support products they do approve of. Consumer choices thus become statements of value. Thus, when a person sees a stranger sporting a T-shirt with a distinctive logo that is associated with fitness and environmental consciousness, s/he assumes that stranger values fitness and environmental consciousness. If the observer shares those values, then s/he might regard the stranger as a member of a community of identity. Perhaps the most striking example of lifestyle branding in recent years has been the Toyota Prius in the United States. The visual impact and message of a Prius give it power as an identity marker (see Heffner et al. 2008).

Many social movements have taken advantage of the desire for community to encourage certain purchasing patterns, and the use of consumer power to motivate corporate responsibility has generally been regarded as a good thing. However, shared consumer values do not inherently produce community any more than living in the same neighborhood or watching the same baseball team. This brings me back to the central thesis of this book: community is a set of interactions between people, NOT a set of traits. What we learn from the regulars are both the conditions that promote community and the behaviors that are characteristic of community.

Community in Practice

As this study comes to a close, the key thing to understand is that community is always actively being created. So how do people create a feeling and consciousness of group cohesiveness? The regulars teach us that communities require a number of things to develop and grow. First and foremost, they require a viable space that can be made social. It need not be exclusive space, for the regulars obviously share the bleachers with thousands of nonregulars.

They *see* the bleachers differently, attaching different significance to them than others do, which matters. It remains an open question if social space has to be physical; inasmuch as it is the shared *idea* of what Wrigley is and means that binds the regulars, it seems the same could work for cyberspace or for diasporic groups. What ultimately is needed is the capacity for gathering and reinforcing the meaning of social space.

On par with the importance of space, there is the time necessary to produce all the other elements of community. Such time, stolen from (or increasingly and ironically bought out of) its commodified status in the contemporary capitalist world, bespeaks *commitment*. Members of every community must offer more than lip service to establish and maintain the feeling that they belong, the true glue of any community. The time passed is time in which the myths and histories of a community are woven and reinvigorated. These myths and histories combine with the rituals of the group to concretize their experience, to make manifest the ties they have formed.

Time and space are not always easy to come by. In the case of the regulars, the cost and availability of game day tickets are increasingly limiting who can attend games often enough to form relationships with the regulars and renew the community. City street corners and public spaces—free gathering places—are increasingly policed against gang activity, while privately owned spaces have the right to refuse gatherings. Long commutes and long work hours combine to limit the potential time for community building. Nonetheless, people are inventive and creative. A commuter train can become a community center, for instance.

Another crucial element of a community feeling and consciousness is something that provokes *attachment* to said space and the people who occupy it. In the bleachers, it is clearly the excitement that accompanies the game that helps ensnare the regulars. They can look around and see their emotions mirrored in those around them. In other settings, the wild ecstasy of a Cubs come-from-behind win might not be the norm, but it strikes me that some indication of shared sentiment is crucial to community bonding. I am not convinced that the words, "I feel the same way," are enough; it is also the emotional force in such a statement that matters. Events that allow members of a group to see their own feelings presented on the faces of their companions also create a sense of a person being "like-minded," somehow sharing a certain sense of how the world should operate on a gut level. For this reason, it might be more appropriate to say such people are "like-hearted." The spirit of connection is not derived from an idea of what someone can do for someone else down the road, but rather from a sense that there is someone who will understand and sympathize with the ups and downs of a person's life.

This sense of connection is part of what operates in the setting of boundaries in communities. Such boundaries are as essential to communities as anything above, although their rigidity can vary wildly. The boundaries work to regulate the risk of emotional attachment, ensuring community members have a safe zone in which they can "be themselves" and be assured that their values and standards of conduct will be understood and not abused. It is worth noting here that those boundaries are formed within the context that the community operates. For the regulars, "us" and "them" relates to baseball knowledge and savvy, but "us" also is limited to the people who are drawn to Wrigley. The racial diversity of the regulars mirrors that of the ballpark: primarily white with a few Asian, Hispanic, and black faces mixed in. Other communities might show significant gender or religious skews, depending on what initially brought members together. Such unintentional exclusions are worth attention when we consider community; if we can understand when they harden into intentional, categorical exclusions, we can answer some of the concerns raised by Appadurai and Putnam as noted above.

Within the boundaries of community, there is some call for leadership and organization. Rules of thumb in dealing with different community members get encoded into interactions, and real effort is put into minimizing friction (or on occasion, increasing it to bring a festering conflict into the open). There is no set rule for how a community should be organized. Nor does a particular organization model necessarily define a community. However, the attention that community members must pay to interactions of various sorts will eventually produce patterns among those interactions. Individual skills and qualities, well known by community members, will provoke certain concessions and demands that will position different people differently, producing the effect of organization.

Habit not only establishes organizational qualities, but it also forms rituals and invests symbolic forms with deeply felt and respected meaning. The rituals and patterns of everyday interaction become the concrete manifestations of the feeling of community. Such rituals are transmittable in a more deliberate way than sentiment, and they can serve to formalize and represent the sentiments felt by community members. Less contingent than effervescence, they can contribute to the intensification of effervescence and give a recognized outlet for emotion. These are elements of community that render it articulable to its members and provide a moral structure to help guide interactions within the community.

Rituals also provide a means to articulate forces that affect the community and demonstrate the shared understanding of those forces. A community has a means for explaining and discussing the irrational and contingent events that create external pressure on the group. The sharing of this vocabulary and belief system creates a feedback loop, reinforcing the connections and the boundaries that shape the community.

So what is community? *Community* is a word that describes a set of long-term social relations that are self-consciously and regularly maintained by all participants in the relationship. Those relations are predicated on a (frequently inchoate) sense of something shared. Members of a community act within a prescribed (usually implicit) set of practices and discourses that index their membership. Community acts to establish a person in a comprehensible social role through which s/he can choose to interact with a larger, more diverse social milieu. That social role includes a set of moral presuppositions about the way people should operate within the world. It involves trust in the face of situations that entail risk, and a basis for self-understanding. The degree to which such community is felt to be "real" or "true" by its participants is contingent on an affective sense of connection between a person's "real self" and others.

Where is community? It is where people feel they belong. It could be a neighborhood. Or at Star Trek conventions. It could be among soccer moms, or caretakers gathered at the same play lot every afternoon. Perhaps it is on the 5:10 shuttle flight from O'Hare to LaGuardia. Perhaps in church. Maybe at Starbucks—the one site of community that has surprised me with the frequency with which people have mentioned it. I could go on, but my position should be clear: community is not lost in the global way that people suggest. Rather, there are groups like the regulars everywhere, springing up less in neighborhoods, where people move in and then on, chasing jobs and dreams, and more in the place where all those people stop for their morning coffee, perhaps pausing a little longer than efficiency would demand, chatting with the same commuters each day, knowing little about one another's jobs but sharing a fondness for double vanilla lattes that the barista starts when he sees them walk in. Or, as all those people move through their lives, only an email address or a blog stays stable, and friends accrue through time, sharing ideas and views and arranging meets and promising a place to stay in any town a person might visit.

It could be they all meet at a ballpark.

Closing Day at Wrigley is always a day game. It falls in either late September or early October, when the afternoon shadows are starting to stretch long by four in the afternoon. Regulars know they'll probably be shooing bees during the game, and that the ivy will be starting to turn a fiery red prior to dropping its leaves for the winter. More often than not, they'll know the year is over; in the rare years that the Cubs make the playoffs, Closing Day is greeted with a mix of enthusiasm and uncertainty. The regulars are accustomed to knowing when to make their farewells.

Some years the game is thrilling, other years it is yet another loss, and sometimes it is even a blowout marked by some huge event. In 2002, Sammy Sosa hit his 499th career home run in the first inning of Closing Day, and the rest of the game buzzed in anticipation of 500. It didn't happen, which in some ways was emblematic of the steady disappointment of that season. But usually Closing Day is a game where there are no stakes, and the full house that appears for the game is there because it is the last game of the year. The regulars, for whom the game is only slightly less important than being present for Opening Day, review the year and share off-season plans.

Eventually the game ends. The fans begin to file out. The centerfield regulars do not budge. When the crowd is thin enough, the group pictures begin, commemorating the end of another year. Security begins urging stragglers out, but the regulars drag their feet. They stand on benches or hang on the rail, staring out at the field. They will be the last people to leave the bleachers.

Former baseball commissioner A. Bartlett Giamatti once wrote, "[Baseball] breaks your heart. It is designed to break your heart. The game begins in spring, when everything else begins again, and it blossoms in the summer, filling the afternoons and evenings, and then as soon as the chill rains come, it stops and leaves you to face the fall alone" (Robson 1998:7).

On Closing Day, in that too-short stretch of time between the end of the game and the exit from the ballpark, it would be hard to find a regular who would disagree. But they know their hearts break together, and they will see each other over the off-season, and "God willing," they will be together again in the spring. Because whatever else is true, they are a community, and that is what matters.

Notes

Pregame

1. The results reported by Berliner and Biddle are from the twenty-fifth annual Gallup poll on the public's perception of public schools, and were originally reported in the 1993 *Phi Delta Kappan*. As Berliner and Biddle explain: "Only 19 percent of respondents gave the nation's schools a grade of A or B, while 21 percent gave them grades of D or F. But when these same people rated their local schools, a different picture emerged. Forty-four percent of respondents gave their local schools a grade of A or B, and only 14 percent gave them grades of D or F. Moreover, when *parents* were asked about the local school that served their children, a whopping 72 percent gave that school an A or B—while only 7 percent graded it D or F!" (1995: 112).

2. When I talk about bleacher regulars by name, I use their preferred field as a surname. In other situations, the name of the field is lowercased.

Chapter 1. Community as Experience and Practices

1. Putnam explains his use of the terms *schmoozer* and *macher:* "In Yiddish, men and women who invest lots of time in formal organizations are often termed *machers*— that is, people who make things happen in the community. By contrast, those who spend many hours in informal conversation and communion are termed *schmoozers*. . . . *Machers* are the all-around good citizens of their communities. *Schmoozers* have an active social life, but by contrast to *machers,* their engagement is less organized and purposeful, more spontaneous and flexible" (2000: 93–94).

Chapter 2. Social Space

1. Fenway Park, home of the Boston Red Sox, was built in 1912, two years before what became Wrigley Field was built.

2. Lights were installed at Wrigley in 1988. The first night game was attempted on August 8, 1988, but was rained out after three and a half innings. The first official night game was August 9, 1988.

3. The true extent of P. K. Wrigley's marketing genius is evident by exploring the Wrigley Company Web site's "About Us" section: http://www.wrigley.com/global/about-us/heritage-timeline.aspx (accessed October 2009). The link for 1944 describes how Wrigley's gum was removed from civilian circulation in favor of dedicating gum manufacturing to the support of the troops. Wrigley continued to market to its Wrigley's gum-deprived consumers by asking civilians to remember the Wrigley wrapper.

4. On summer days, the bleacher sun is relentless, and the unofficial dress code is more like a beach than anything else. It is accepted and even expected that people will be in shorts, shirtless if male, in bikini tops or tank tops if female.

5. Lee Elia, postgame press conference, April 29, 1983, copy of original audio recording, in my possession.

6. This was particularly striking in 2000, when a grandstand fan prompted the Los Angeles Dodgers to storm the stands. USA Today reported the incident as a "bleacher brawl" (Mihoces 2000: 3c). The issue of beer regulations at Wrigley was a hot news item for most of that May, but when the hype died down, the only restrictions that remained in place were those put in place in the bleachers the previous year.

7. When the pitcher throws to the batter, the ball comes at the batter against the backdrop of the stands. Because fans create a busy background, it is possible for the batter to lose sight of the ball. To avoid the risk of a batter getting hit by a ball, ballparks have established a solid color zone in centerfield where no fans sit.

8. I routinely refer to the section where I sit as centerfield, hence the preference for that term throughout this piece. "Right-center" is a more accurate description, but it also marks a regular who has been sitting in the bleachers long enough to have sat in straight-away center, the section that has been replaced by a batter's eye since 1967. An occasional regular refers to upper center as "centerfield" and uses "right-center" to distinguish the two sections, but this is relatively rare.

9. The six degrees of separation game emerges from the "small world phenomenon" described by Stanley Milgrim. Milgrim's experiments are explained in detail by Malcolm Gladwell in The Tipping Point (2002: 34–36), but the key claim from the experiment is that any person can be connected to any other person in six moves. The game is to name a famous person and challenge someone to name an acquaintance of an acquaintance of an acquaintance who personally knows the famous person. Each additional acquaintance adds a "degree of separation."

10. This is bleacher regular shorthand for arriving at the ballpark before the gates open. The expression gets formulated a couple of different ways, either "I made it for gate" or "I made gate."

11. I have seen pencil clips and adhesive mug hooks applied to the bottom of bleacher seats where regulars sit. At least a few regulars got into the ballpark in their childhood by coming in after games to put the seats up and clean between aisles, earning a ticket

to the next day's game as a result. Bleacher legend even maintains that some regulars have gone so far as to patch cement or make structural improvements in their seating areas. The truth of such rumors is far less important than the commitment to the bleachers that they demonstrate.

Chapter 3. Baseball Time

1. I freely admit a bias here, since I was among the people who stayed. Some regulars might regard it more as a mark of insanity, but the point remains that regardless of how people feel about it, they'll continue to talk about it.

2. In 1997, I bought bleacher tickets on the day of game for anywhere from $5 to $10. In 2007, I regularly spent $40 per ticket. The first year season tickets to the bleachers were offered in the early 1990s, they could be had for under $800 for the year.

3. "Tailgating" is the practice of setting up a grill and food in the parking lot before a sporting event and dining in and around your car. Pragmatically, it helps to have a pickup truck with the tailgate down that can serve as a table, although I cannot say with authority that this is how the practice got its name.

4. The most famous example is the Maya calendar, a great favorite of millenarian movements and doomsday prognosticators. There are other similar calendars, including the Chinese calendar.

5. While there are two- and four-game series, most teams play each other three games in a row before moving on to new opponents. This allows one team to claim to have "won" a series by beating their opponent two games out of three, which is the usual result of the series. The alternative is to sweep or be swept (i.e., for one team to win all three games), an infrequent enough occurrence to draw comment when it happens.

6. The actual history of the game has some mythological qualities, carefully fostered in the early years of the twentieth century. However, inasmuch as history is experienced by contemporary Americans, baseball has effectively "always been there." Very few, if any, Americans are long-lived enough to remember a time before there was a World Series.

7. I've tried, although admittedly not as hard as I could have. Groups of regulars spring up, disappear, merge, and fission, and human memory is the sole record of the how, when, what, and why. A few sections have a clearer sense of their membership over the past fifty years than others, but even those sections acquired members from other sections or have some key regular who was just always there.

8. When a team "bats around," everyone in the lineup has batted in the inning, and the player who had batted first comes to the plate again for a second opportunity. This is not exceedingly rare, but it usually does signal that one of the teams is getting trounced.

9. A pinch runner is a player who replaces a player who is standing on a base for the offense. In this case, Jose Hernandez had been brought in to run for Olmedo

Saenz, had scored a run, and was now coming up to the plate to bat for himself in Saenz's place.

10. In 1984 the Cubs went to the playoffs for the first time since 1945. They had to win three games out of five to advance to the World Series. They won the first two games easily, and everyone was sure they would win one of the next three. Needless to say, the Cubs failed to come up with the win and went home in defeat.

11. The Cubs won this game against St. Louis 12–11 in 11 innings. Cubs second baseman Ryne Sandberg went 5-for-6 and drove in 7 runs, providing most of the offense in a game that is widely regarded as the turning point of the 1984 season. Many people assert that after that game, the idea of the Cubs making the playoffs seemed realistic.

12. A prohibition against discussing a no-hitter while it is in progress keeps this discussion from beginning earlier in the game. As I have never witnessed a no-hitter, I cannot attest to what happens when a pitcher actually accomplishes the feat. More on no-hitters is in a later chapter.

13. Pappas had a perfect game through eight innings. He had gotten the first two batters out in the ninth and only needed one more out to seal the game. He had thrown one ball and two strikes, and it looked for all the world like he was going to strike out the final batter. Froemming called the next three pitches balls, and the batter took the walk. Regulars who were at the game hold that Froemming's calls were malicious, deliberately ruining the potential glory of the moment.

14. In other words, they were regarded as a lucky team rather than a talented one.

15. Giant in this case means something in the neighborhood of thirty-feet tall.

16. In 1932, Babe Ruth is credited with having pointed to the outfield stands at Wrigley Field during game 3 of the World Series, indicating that he was going to hit the next ball out. He did hit a home run that at bat, and photos exist showing him standing with his arm extended. Most regulars I've talked to about the shot agree that he was reminding everyone how many strikes there were on him, not claiming he was going to hit a home run. Historians still dispute the point, but the regulars have an obvious interest in the shot NOT being called.

17. This policy eventually changed; the pencil now automatically comes with the scorecard.

18. As noted elsewhere, when more than one regular in a section has the same first name, regulars tend to bestow nicknames to distinguish them from one another.

19. This was yelled more than once in 2004, around the time that the scandal regarding American treatment of prisoners at the Abu Ghraib facility in Iraq broke.

Chapter 4. Effervescence

1. A "sub-.500" team is one that has won fewer than half of the games they have played.

2. That is, he got a hit that enabled him to reach second base.

3. Augie Ojeda was a utility infielder for the Cubs in 2001. He was also my favorite player while he was with the Cubs.

4. That is, McGriff was removed from the game and Ojeda went out to second base to run in his place.

5. Most teams have five or six "bullpen" pitchers who only come in late in the game to face a few batters. If a pitcher is ineffective or is about to face a batter he has not been able to get out consistently, the manager will take him out of the game and put in a new pitcher. Once a pitcher has been removed from the game, he can't be put back in.

6. That is, a hit that both allowed Gutierrez to get to first base and Ojeda to score.

7. When the games are less meaningful, many fans leave after they have sung "Take Me Out to the Ballgame," and many more leave when beer sales are cut off in the bottom of the seventh inning at night games.

8. The logic here is that each team should have an equal number of outs, normally twenty-seven each. If the away team has already had their twenty-seven outs, and the home team manages to score the winning run after only twenty-six outs, there is no point in continuing to play. Even giving the home team all twenty-seven of their outs will not change the fact that they won.

9. Tucker ran too far off the base to get back to it safely and was also too far from the next base, and so he was chased by defensive players who eventually tagged him with the baseball, making him out.

10. I confess that this is a disingenuous claim. Wrigley Field has a long history of being marketed to casual fans or people who are looking for an escape from city grime and stress and to whom baseball is an incidental activity at the ballpark. See Peter Golenbock's 1996 book, *Wrigleyville,* and my 2007 article in *The International History of Sport.*

11. For those unfamiliar with Chicago, the city has two Major League Baseball teams, the White Sox on the Southside, the Cubs on the Northside. The Southside is generally identified with African Americans, Irish immigrants, and working class fans, while the Northside is perceived as affluent and WASPy.

12. The Red Sox were held by fans to be cursed by the baseball gods because they traded Babe Ruth to the Yankees in 1919. After the trade, the Red Sox were unable to win a World Series until 2004. More discussion on curses will be had in chapter 8.

13. Those interested in the significance and history of "Sweet Caroline" to Red Sox fans should consult Vosk 2005.

14. As the song played, Al from Rightfield reported in his blog, www.bleedcubbieblue .com, Howard from Rightfield said "if we really wanted to make the Red Sox fans feel at home, we should have dug up all the streets around Wrigley Field" (referencing the state "Big Dig" of the Massachusetts Turnpike Authority in Boston). In centerfield, several of us held our scorecards in front of our bodies and swayed with the music, singing along loudly until we began fumbling words in the second verse.

Linda from Centerfield, exiled to the boxes, reported the same intense energy in the grandstand.

15. I share many National League fans' opinion on this—the designated hitter rule is a perversion of the game. This particular debate is purely one of opinion, though, and outside the scope of this book.

16. He also had five complete games (that is, he pitched all the innings of a game) on the season. These stats are excellent.

17. Sammy Sosa was nationally known for his home run race with Mark McGwire in 1998 and is among the few players to hit six hundred or more home runs in a career. Kerry Wood's fame has proven more fleeting due to a series of injuries, but he electrified the nation in 1998 by tying the Major League record for strikeouts in a single game (twenty) when he was only nineteen years old.

18. I have termed this "effervescent bacchanal" in another work (Swyers 2003b). The crowd in this scenario lacks the knowledge of how/when to act or react and seeks some leadership.

19. That is, the time between the top and bottom halves of the seventh inning.

20. Bartman's name was released by the media the day after the game in a move many have since criticized.

21. A baseball game is usually over when the losing team has had twenty-seven outs (three per inning). There are two exceptions: tie games, which go longer, and rain-shortened games, which are considered complete if they have gone at least five innings and the losing team has had at least as many outs as the winning team.

22. Young pitchers and pitchers returning from injuries are frequently on a pitch count, meaning the manager will only allow them to throw a certain number of pitches in the game before taking them out. Before the game in question, no one was sure what Wood's pitch count was, but the consensus among the regulars was that it had to be around ninety, which was his pitch count in his previous rehab start in Iowa.

Chapter 5. Boundaries and Gatekeeping

1. During the mid-1990s, baseball was trying to run a balanced schedule, meaning every team would see every other team in the league the same number of times. This meant the Cubs visited New York more often than they have in recent years, when they only make one trip to play the Mets and play more games against rivals in the National League Central division.

2. In situations such as this one, where there is any possibility that someone might run into problems for some favor or kindness done for a regular, I have taken pains to mask their identities.

3. With rare exception, the bleachers are the warmest seats at Wrigley Field, owing to a combination of the physical layout of the ballpark and the prevailing weather patterns.

4. More about the Wrigleyville Tap is in chapter 7.

5. A doubleheader is two games played back-to-back on the same day, and it is usually the case that each team wins one game.

6. The story was undoubtedly prompted by a shooting death right outside the ballpark after a game on May 6, 2004. The shooting, reported as the aftermath of a traffic altercation exacerbated by the postgame congestion, produced a steady stream of media coverage of the "craziness" of game day Wrigleyville.

7. There is one exception to this rule. Home run balls hit by the opposing team are *expected* to be thrown back on the field, a symbolic rejection.

8. Veeck sat in upper centerfield, and I should properly say the regulars sit in *his* bleachers, given how much he was involved in the construction and development of the bleachers (see chapter 2). Some of the regulars got to know him, although it seems most took pains to respect his privacy and his right to watch a game in peace. More than one regular has expressed their regret that they never went to shake his hand while he was sitting there.

9. In 1998, the Cubs Sammy Sosa and Mark McGwire of the St. Louis Cardinals were the talk of baseball as they approached and surpassed Roger Maris's thirty-seven-year old record for home runs in a single season (sixty-one). The home run race of '98 is widely credited with bringing fans back after the 1994–95 baseball strike.

10. For perspective, I now regularly attend forty to fifty games a season.

11. As it happens, this was the infamous Brant Brown game, named for a painful defensive play that cost the Cubs a sure victory. Details about the game can be read at http://sportsillustrated.cnn.com/baseball/mlb/news/1998/09/23/cubs_brewers/.

12. In 2000, I struck a deal with another relatively new regular to purchase a season ticket that we continue to share.

13. In other words, they won only six games that month and lost twenty-four. Five of the games were lost by one run, and none of them were won by one run.

14. A Chicago Transit Authority elevated train line runs by the ballpark, with a station half a block east of the park on Addison.

Chapter 6. Organization and Hierarchies

1. In baseball, the "front office" is the designation for upper-level management. They are distinguished from "on-field personnel."

2. More on the Tap is in chapter 7.

3. With the bleacher renovation in 2006, the bleacher sections were renumbered. Before it became section 303, the leftfield corner was section 153. For clarity, I will refer to the section as 303 throughout unless it is specifically mentioned in a quote.

4. Most home runs, whether in games or in batting practice, go out to leftfield. Fans arriving early enough for batting practice are likely to try to get seats as close to the field as possible and in a location where they are most likely to get a ball.

5. That is, to catch them. The ball hawks take pride in their ability to gauge where balls are heading and to catch them on the fly. They'll call one another's names when

a ball is headed toward one or another of them, and when a well-hit ball is going to leave the ballpark completely, they shout that information down to the ball hawks waiting below, across Waveland Avenue.

6. In the 1990s, the Cubs outlawed smoking in the seating areas of the bleachers. People were allowed to smoke against the back fence, however, and the smokers in leftfield took over the last two rows or so of what was then a five-and-a-half-row section. After the renovation, smoking was restricted to a patio area behind the seating area, and in 2008, a statewide ordinance in Illinois combined with an early city of Chicago ordinance prohibited smoking anywhere in the ballpark.

7. At the time, Donna was affiliated with leftfield. She and several other regulars shifted their field affiliation after the bleacher renovation of 2006.

8. There are some leftfield regulars who do not sit in section 303, but 303 has something of a critical mass in defining leftfield, particularly for regulars sitting in right and center. See note 13 in this chapter.

9. "She kept the premises as clean as they could be in a seventy-five-year-old stadium, and always told the girls to 'pick a stall and stand it front of it, and the rest of you, move to the back wall' to keep the lines moving," Stephanie remembered.

10. In 2005, I was living three-and-a-half blocks north of the start of the line and had occasion to pass the ballpark on foot or on the El several times a day. The line moved quickly—about half a block every fifteen minutes by midweek—but it was always there during business hours.

11. In 2005, the Red Sox made their first appearance at Wrigley Field since the World Series of 1918.

12. Prior to 2006, this section was numbered 147.

13. To put this in terms of everyday experience, I walk into the bleachers each day and sit where I want. Most of the section placards are missing, and it is entirely possible that only the regulars and crowd control actually know the section numbers. The seat numbers, repainted on the bleacher benches for playoff games, wear off over intervening seasons. Identifying one's seat location simply doesn't *matter*. For playoff games, however, my ticket has a section number and a seat number, and ushers come and check that my ticket stub matches the number stenciled on my bench. In 2003, the row numbers were actually hand scrawled on bench ends with a black magic marker.

14. The "baskets" are the very first row of the bleachers. The wall is high enough that people in the front row are usually only visible from the shoulder up, and they seem to be sitting very low, practically *in* the chain link "baskets" that line the outfield wall at Wrigley Field. Note that rightfield used to also sit that close, but the benefits of the backrest on the back row and the desire to avoid Sammy Sosa groupies in the late 1990s pushed many of them back. It is also worth noting that until 2005, section 303 only extended six rows from baskets to back row. Section 311, in contrast, was fourteen rows deep, while section 313 was twelve deep. The renovation created more uniformity in the numbers of rows per section, exacerbating the front–back

row conflicts in leftfield and prompting an exodus of some back row leftfielders to center and right.

15. Bill from Centerfield heads a group of regulars who migrate depending on the temperature at game time. On hot days, they position themselves at the top of the ramp that opens onto the rightfield side of the bleachers to take advantage of the breeze that usually travels through the walkways. On colder days, they sit across the aisle from the section headed by Judy from Centerfield.

16. There were two Lindas in centerfield at this point, and regulars distinguished them by where they were from at the time they were both attending. The Linda from Centerfield mentioned elsewhere in this book is also referred to as Jersey Linda.

17. The regular who complained had already established a reputation as a trouble-maker and was systematically ignored for the rest of the game.

18. The knot of regulars in the rightfield corner (section 315) suffered a fate similar to the light side and was able to recover. The section fell apart when one anchor got married and another had a baby. Donna from Rightfield was left on her own. What made the situation bearable was Ray, a member of crowd control who "ran a tight ship over there." If no other regular was sitting with her, Donna at least knew Ray would be there, and he would maintain order in the section so a person could enjoy the game. During a White Sox series in 2004, Ray was not at his usual station. The crowd, always at its worst on White Sox weekends, grew raucous and uncontrollable. Donna was miserable. The next day, a couple of the leftfield crowd invited her to sit with them. By 2005, Donna had become a leftfield regular, but when the 2006 renovation altered the bleacher landscape, several rightfield regulars consolidated their groups and Donna moved back to her original corner.

19. Although I have not detailed rightfield's organization here, it is similar to that of centerfield. Rightfield, however, is even less centralized than center, with more small pockets of regulars. There are a couple of groups that are steadily present for every game, but there are also a few that appear and disappear—in other words, there are games where none of the familiar faces are in their usual seats. There are also a couple of leftfield pockets like this that have taken over parts of section 305. Carmella from Leftfield, mentioned earlier, used to sit at the top of section 306, and there are still occasionally some regulars there as well.

20. The name is a deliberate pun on the phrase "inside pitch," which refers to a pitch that is thrown between the edge of home plate and the batter. The "tighter" the inside pitch, the closer it is to hitting the batter.

Chapter 7. Ballpark Rituals

1. Readers interested in this question might want to look at Brian Soucek's work on the subject.

2. For a number of years, the regulars did gather inside a set of tensor barriers put up by crowd control. Changes in gate procedure have eliminated that option, but

when that was the case, there was a definite "insider" marking going on. Regulars would open the tensor barriers for other regulars and then reclose them, thus demonstrating very physically who was *allowed* inside.

3. It is not uncommon for female regulars to hug in greeting or to exchange greeting kisses. Male regulars will reciprocate or initiate similar greetings with females, although their greetings to one another are more muted in keeping with American conventions of masculinity.

4. Tom was a concession worker at Wrigley prior to joining the regulars. He got to know the regulars through his job, and when he stopped working at Wrigley, he claimed his spot next to Marv, which is where he was sitting when I first met him.

5. I did not record my exact words, but it was undoubtedly something along the lines of, "Oh my god, he's alive!" or something equally facetious.

6. In point of fact, there are many secrets in the bleachers, some kept within a small subgroup of friends, others within a given field, others tacitly known by everyone but never discussed. But in an important way, Judy is right. Because regulars can be trusted to discriminate between information that needs to be confidential and information that is just embarrassing in an entertaining way, they often know more about one another than many people outside the bleachers might know.

7. For a brief period of time, the rules were so stringent that all bags had to be checked at a trailer away from the ballpark. During that time, I still lived far enough away from the ballpark to rollerblade in regularly, and for a stretch, security requested I check my blades at the trailer. Eventually, that stricture loosened, and I was allowed to check my blades at the gate as I had before September 11. Security held them for me in a small office by the gate, and they began to meet me before the gate open with a claim check already filled out for me when I wheeled up every game.

8. After a particularly nasty stretch of poor behavior on the part of bleacher fans in general (excluding the regulars) in 1998, the Cubs began a "Respect Wrigley" campaign. This includes PA announcements played in a loop throughout pregame exhorting fans to respect "the honor and tradition of Wrigley Field by exhibiting responsible fan behavior." There are also signs posted throughout the bleacher area promoting the same message.

9. In much the same way Corona is always served with a lime to be squeezed into the beer, Leinenkugel Red seems to require a dash of pepper be shaken into it before it is consumed.

10. The regulars did in fact boycott Fuel, the bar that occupied the space that had been the Tap, for well over a year. Even when the boycott ended—and it largely ended when Jimmy was seen inside the bar, allowing regulars to be there without appearing disloyal—it did not become a central gathering spot. Eventually, Fuel's high concept did poorly enough that it was renovated into the Full Shilling, a more pub-like place. It has since received more of the regulars' business, but it has not become what the Tap was.

11. See http://www.bleedcubbieblue.com/section/Bleacher-Photos (accessed October 2009).

Chapter 8. Baseball Gods

1. The historical record suggests the goat actually was allowed into the ballpark, but was ejected during the game because people complained of its stench (Gatto 2004: 4–5).

2. See http://www.bleedcubbieblue.com/story/2005/7/13/184146/529#commenttop (accessed October 2009).

3. The late 1990s and early 2000s were a study in "déjà vu all over again" for Cubs fans. The team would have a good year and then a miserable year or two. In 1997, the Cubs lost 94 of 162 games. In 1999, they lost 95; in 2000, they lost 97; in 2002, they lost 95.

4. This particular occasion, the regulars were reviewing the poor decision in 1998 to trade prospect Jon Garland for middle reliever Matt Karchner. In 2005 Jon Garland was an All-Star and one of the top starting pitchers in the American League. Karchner finished his career in 2000 after pitching fewer than ninety innings for the Cubs over 2.5 seasons.

5. An almost identical play in the 1986 World Series cost the Boston Red Sox their chance at a championship. In that play, ex-Cub Bill Buckner let a ball go through his legs to let the Mets score and eventually win. Buckner, although much maligned in Boston, remains a Cubs fan favorite.

6. See http://www.youtube.com/watch?v=hABtv6W27Zo (accessed October 2009).

7. Explaining his number change, Blanco told the press: "Twenty-four is the number I wear in winter ball. I was looking to change my luck a little bit. It worked today" (MLB Newswire 2005). Before the number change, Blanco was batting .158 on the season with two home runs and six RBIs. In the first six games he played in after the number changed, he went 9 for 19 (.474), hit two more home runs, and got six more RBIs.

8. This line by Yogi Berra, uttered in response to questions about the National League pennant race in 1973, is often cited as an example of the former catcher's apparently nonsensical remarks. As this example shows, Berra's comments usually make perfect sense within the context of baseball.

9. ERA stands for "earned run average," a number calculated by the number of earned runs a given pitcher gives up over 9 innings. Ideally, starting pitchers in the National League have ERAs lower than 4. A sub-3 ERA is considered excellent, and a sub-2 ERA is "sparkling."

10. Cy Young pitched from 1890 to 1911, the years split primarily between teams in Cleveland and Boston, with a couple-year stint in St. Louis. Over that span, he won 511 games—the best record in baseball. For comparison, the second highest number

of career wins—a record held by Walter Johnson (active 1907–27 for the Washington Senators)—is 417 games.

11. As much as I would have liked to attend all the Cubs playoff games, I only made it to four of the six home playoff games. The other two I watched at the same bar where I watched the road games.

12. Note that batters can reach base by means other than getting a hit, so on rare occasion, a pitcher will have a no-hitter and still manage to give up a run (usually by issuing bases on balls). A *perfect game* is where the pitcher does not allow any runner to reach base. In Major League Baseball, there have only been seventeen games that have met that criteria since 1880. For perspective, the current MLB season (not including postseason games) features over 2,500 games.

13. Hindsight is 20/20, of course, and after several more games it became clear that Lieber, at this point in his career, was subject to sudden late-inning meltdowns. He would be completely dominant for six or seven innings, and then he would, without warning, be incapable of getting any more outs. The trick was to figure out if a home run or solid hit he had given up was just a one-off thing or the clue that he was done for the night. In late innings, the regulars came to believe it was better safe than sorry and would exhort the manager to go to the bullpen more quickly than they did with other pitchers. The September 20, 1999, game was dramatic enough that the regulars were able to use it to sense a pattern, and grumblings about broadcasters subsided, at least for a time.

Chapter 9. Births, Weddings, and Funerals

1. The Aragon Ballroom on Chicago's Northside.

2. Sitting "in the baskets" is local slang for sitting in the front row of the bleachers. The top of the bleacher wall is edged by chain link baskets designed to prevent people from jumping down, and sitting in the first row, a person can reach down into the baskets. For more information on the baskets themselves, see chapter 6, note 14.

3. In the conclusion to his second edition of *American Kinship*, Schneider points out that his generalized model is flawed in that it uses almost exclusively the white middle-class standard of family and kinship. This flaw, however, seems to affect his assumptions about residence patterns and "distance" in kin relationships rather than undermining the idea of these two interconnected domains of kinship reckoning.

4. The title of Al from Rightfield's blog.

5. Official records state that the home run Dawson hit that day was actually his 399th. Stephanie was in disbelief when I passed the information along. She emailed me: "I can't believe they claim it was number 399, as the significance of hitting number 400 right to the 400' outfield sign was amazing in itself."

6. There is usually no more than a half-hour between games of a double header. While this is increasingly rare, double headers traditionally were both played on the same ticket, so a fan with a ticket could stay in the stands for both games.

7. As discussed in chapter 2, Wrigley Field did not get lights until 1988. The battle against lights was hard-fought by the neighborhood.

8. There are exceptions, of course, and regulars will adapt their expectations to what they know of the child in question.

9. Judy's husband John is a roller coaster fanatic.

10. The game finally ended at 1:06 am, amid speculation about a possible curfew and the legality of starting an inning after midnight or 1:00 am. This involved a lot of debate about local vs. national rules, baseball in Boston, and a game in Atlanta that ended with fireworks somewhere around three or four in the morning, and speculation about what kind of noise could come over the Wrigley PA at any given hour.

11. At risk of doing injustice to an entire field, most people have encountered sociobiology in ideas like mothers caring for their children in order to guarantee their genes continue into the next generation or men cheating for the same reason.

Postgame

1. Gourevitch's book, *We Wish to Inform You That Tomorrow We Will Be Killed with Our Families: Stories from Rwanda,* is published by Farrar, Straus, and Giroux.

Bibliography

Anderson, Benedict. 1991. *Imagined Communities: Reflections on the Origin and Spread of Nationalism*. 2nd ed. New York: Verso.

Appadurai, Arjun. 2006. *Fear of Small Numbers: An Essay on the Geography of Anger*. Durham, N.C.: Duke University Press.

Arab-American Bar Association of Illinois, Inc. (AABar). 2005 [1992]. Report of the *Ad Hoc* Committee on the Civil Disturbance of June 14–15, 1992. Chicago. http://www.arabbar.org/art-civildisturbance.asp (accessed July 2005).

Barthes, Roland. 1967. *The Elements of Semiology*. Trans. A. Lavers and C. Smith. London: Jonathan Cape.

Benedict, Ruth. 1969 [1946]. *The Chrysanthemum and the Sword: Patterns of Japanese Culture*. New York: Meridian Books.

Berliner, David C., and Bruce J. Biddle. 1995. *The Manufactured Crisis: Myths, Fraud, and the Attack on America's Public Schools*. Reading, Mass.: Addison-Wesley.

Bourdieu, Pierre. 1984. *Distinction: A Social Critique of the Judgement of Taste*. Trans. Richard Nice. Cambridge, Mass.: Harvard University Press.

Brotman, Barbara. 1991. Lifelong Fan Dies at Home—Front Row of Bleachers. *Chicago Tribune*, October 11.

Buford, Bill. 1993. *Among the Thugs*. New York: Vintage Books.

Carr, Todd. 1999. Bleacher Bums: The Mystique of the Wrigley Field Bleachers. http://web.archive.org/web/20011107131108http://formen.ign.com/news/10222.html. (accessed November 2001).

Cohen, Anthony P. 1985. *The Symbolic Construction of Community*. New York: Routledge.

Comaroff, Jean, and John Comaroff, eds. 1993. *Modernity and Its Malcontents: Ritual and Power in Postcolonial Africa*. Chicago: University of Chicago Press.

Coontz, Stephanie. 1992. *The Way We Never Were: American Families and the Nostalgia Trap*. New York: Basic Books.

Darwin, Charles. 1981 [1871]. *The Descent of Man, and Selection in Relation to Sex*. Princeton, N.J.: Princeton University Press.

Devoe, Ken. 2000. View from Connecticut: The New Rules. *Bleacher Banter* 10(2): 12.

Durkheim, Emile. 1995. *The Elementary Forms of Religious Life*. Trans. Karen Fields. New York: The Free Press.

Editorial. 2003. Curses. *The Week*, http://web.archive.org/web/20050527173334/http://www.theweekmagazine.com/article.asp?id=478 (accessed April 2004).

Evans-Pritchard, E. E. 1967. *Witchcraft, Oracles and Magic among the Azande*. New York: Clarendon Press.

Firth, Raymond. 1961. *Elements of Social Organization*. 3rd ed. Boston: Beacon Press.

Freud, Sigmund. 1959 [1922]. *Group Psychology and the Analysis of the Ego*. Trans. and ed. James Strachey. New York: W. W. Norton.

Garner, Tricia. 2005. Fun in the Sun at Wrigley. *Sporting News*, August 12, http://www.sportingnews.com/mlb/article/2005-08-03/fun-sun-wrigley (accessed November 2009).

Gatto, Steve. 2004. *Da Curse of the Billy Goat: The Chicago Cubs, Pennant Races, and Curses*. Lansing, Mich.: Protar House.

Geertz, Clifford. 1973. Thick Description. *The Interpretation of Cultures: Selected Essays*, 3–32. New York: BasicBooks.

Gladwell, Malcolm. 2002. *The Tipping Point: How Little Things Can Make a Big Difference*. New York: Back Bay Books.

Goffman, Erving. 1981. *Forms of Talk*. Philadelphia: University of Pennsylvania.

Golenbock, Peter. 1996. *Wrigleyville: A Magical History Tour of the Chicago Cubs*. New York: St. Martin's.

Hareven, Tamara K. 1982. *Family Time and Industrial Time: The Relationship between the Family and Work in a New England Industrial Community*. Cambridge: Cambridge University Press.

Harvey, David. 1990. *The Condition of Postmodernity: An Enquiry into Origins of Cultural Change*. Cambridge, Mass.: Blackwell.

Heffner, Reid R., Kenneth S. Kurani, and Thomas S. Terrentine. 2008. Symbolism in California's early market for hybrid electric vehicles. *Transportation Research Part D* 12(6): 396–413.

Holmes, David, ed. 1997. *Virtual Politics: Identity and Community in Cyberspace*. Thousand Oaks, Calif.: Sage Publications.

Huizinga, Johan. 1950. *Homo Ludens: A Study of the Play Element in Culture*. Boston: Beacon Press.

Joseph, Miranda. 2002. *Against the Romance of Community*. Minneapolis: University of Minnesota Press.

Leach, E. R. 1965. *Political Systems of Highland Burma: A Study of Kachin Social Structure*. Boston: Beacon Press.

Le Bon, Gustave. 2001 [1896]. *The Crowd: A Study of the Popular Mind.* Kitchener, Ont.: Batoche Books.

Lévi-Strauss, Claude. 1963. *Totemism.* Trans. Rodney Needham. Boston: Beacon Press.

———. 1966. *The Savage Mind.* Chicago: University of Chicago Press.

Luhrmann, T. M. 1989. *Persuasions of the Witch's Craft: Ritual Magic in Contemporary England.* Cambridge, Mass.: Harvard University Press.

Major League Baseball News Wire. 2005. Prior, Blanco Help Cubs Open Second Half on a Winning Note. ESPN.com, July 14, http://sports.espn.go.com/espn/wire?section=mlb&id=2108026 (accessed May 2006).

Malinowski, Bronislaw. 1954. *Magic, Science and Religion.* Garden City, N.Y.: Doubleday Anchor Books.

———. 1961 [1922]. *Argonauts of the Western Pacific: An Account of Native Enterprise and Adventure in the Archipelagoes of Melanisian New Guinea.* New York: E. P. Dutton.

Mandelbaum, Michael. 2004. *The Meaning of Sports: Why Americans Watch Baseball, Football, and Basketball, and What They See When They Do.* New York: Public Affairs.

Marx, Karl. 1978 [1846]. The German Ideology. In *The Marx-Engels Reader.* Ed. Robert C. Tucker. New York: W. W Norton.

McPhail, Clark. 1991. *The Myth of the Madding Crowd.* Piscataway, N.J.: Aldine Transaction.

Mead, Margaret. 2000 [1942]. *And Keep Your Powder Dry: An Anthropologist Looks at America.* New York: Berghahn Books.

Mihoces, Gary. 2000. Players Get Rough with Fans; Bleacher Brawl at Wrigley Field Sets Dangerous Precedent. *USA Today,* May 18, 3c.

Putnam, Robert D. 1995. Bowling Alone: America's Declining Social Capital. *Journal of Democracy* 6(1): 65–78.

———. 2000. *Bowling Alone: The Collapse and Revival of American Community.* New York: Simon and Schuster.

———. 2007. *E Pluribus Unum:* Diversity and Community in the Twenty-first Century. *Scandinavian Political Studies* 30(2): 137–74.

Putnam, Robert D., and Lewis M. Feldstein. 2003. *Better Together: Restoring the American Community.* New York: Simon and Schuster.

Quotes by Bill Veeck. 2003. ESPN Classic Web site, November 19. http://espn.go.com/classic/s/veeckquotes000816.html (accessed October 2009).

Radcliffe-Brown, A. R. 1952. *Structure and Function in Primitive Society.* New York: The Free Press.

Red Eye. 2004. Front cover. June 1.

Robertson, James Oliver. 1980. *American Myth, American Reality.* New York: Hill and Wang.

Robson, Kenneth S. 1998. *A Great and Glorious Game.* Chapel Hill, N.C.: Algonquin Books.

Roundtripper, Annie. 1998. Inside Bitch. *Bleacher Banter,* October, 5.

Rousseau, Jean-Jacques. 1997. *The Discourses and Other Early Political Writings.* Trans. Victor Gourevitch. Cambridge: Cambridge University Press.

Rude, John C. 1996. The Birth of a Nation in Cyberspace. *The Humanist* 56(2): 17–22.

Sahlins, Marshall. 1985. *Islands of History.* Chicago: University of Chicago Press.

Saussure, Ferdinand de. 1983. *General Course in Linguistics.* LaSalle, Ill.: Open Court.

Schaaf, Phil. 2003. *Sports, Inc.: 100 Years of Sports Business.* Amherst, N.Y.: Prometheus Books.

Schneider, David M. 1980. *American Kinship: A Cultural Account.* 2nd ed. Chicago: University of Chicago Press.

Secrist, Horace. 1933. *The Triumph of Mediocrity in Business.* Evanston, Ill.: Northwestern University, Bureau of Business Research.

Sennett, Richard. 1970. *The Uses of Disorder: Personal Identity and City Life.* New York: Alfred A. Knopf.

Simmel, Georg. 1971. *On Individuality and Social Forms.* Ed. Donald N. Levine. Chicago: University of Chicago Press.

Smith, Adam. 1976. *The Wealth of Nations.* Ed. Edwin Cannan. Chicago: University of Chicago Press.

Stigler, Stephen M. 1999. *Statistics on the Table: The History of Statistical Concepts and Methods.* Cambridge, Mass.: Harvard University Press.

St. John, Warren. 2005. *Rammer Jammer Yellowhammer: A Journey into the Heart of Fan Mania.* New York: Three Rivers Press.

Stoecker, Randy. 2002. Cyberspace vs. Face to Face: Community Organizing in the New Millennium. Paper presented on COMM-ORG: The On-Line Conference on Community Organizing and Development. http://comm-org.utoledo.edu/papers .htm (accessed October 2003).

Sullivan, Paul. 1997. Cubs End Slump—Barely. *Chicago Tribune,* April 21.

Swyers, Holly. 2003a. Succeed Anyway: Life and Lessons of American High School. Unpublished manuscript.

———. 2003b. In the Madding Crowd: Preliminary Thoughts on Baseball Fan Violence. Unpublished manuscript.

———. 2005. Who Owns Wrigley Field? *International Journal of the History of Sport* 22(6): 1086–105.

———. 2007. The Opposite of Losses: Where Lies the Soul of American Sports? *International Journal of the History of Sport* 24(2): 197–214.

Thompson, E. P. 1993. *Customs in Common.* New York: The New Press.

Tonnies, Ferdinand. 1957. *Gemeinschaft and Gesellschaft.* Trans. Charles Loomis. East Lansing: Michigan State University Press.

Turner, Victor. 1974. *Dramas, Fields, and Metaphors: Symbolic Action in Human Society.* Ithaca, N.Y.: Cornell University Press.

Veeck, Bill, and Edward Linn. 2001. *Veeck as in Wreck*. Chicago: University of Chicago Press.

Vosk, Stephanie. 2005. Another Mystery of the Diamond, Explained at Last. *Boston Globe,* May 25, City Weekly, 1.

Wann, Daniel L., and Frederick G. Grieve. 2008. The Coping Strategies of Highly Identified Sports Fans. *Sports Mania: Essays on Fandom and the Media in the 21st Century*. Ed. L. W. Hugenberg, P. M. Haridakis, and A. C. Earnheardt, 78–85. Jefferson, N.C.: McFarland.

Wann, Daniel L., Merrill J. Melnick, Gordon Russell, and Dale Pease. 2001. *Sports Fans: The Psychology and Social Impact of Spectators*. New York: Routledge.

Watters, Ethan. 2003. *Urban Tribes: A Generation Redefines Friendship, Family, and Commitment*. New York: Bloomsbury.

Weber, Max. 1949. *The Methodology of the Social Sciences*. Trans. and ed. Edward Shils and Henry A. Finch. New York: The Free Press.

———. 1978. *Economy and Society: An Outline of Interpretive Sociology*. 2 vols. Ed. Guenther Roth and Claus Wittich. Berkeley: University of California Press.

Whyte, William Foote. 1993. *Street Corner Society: The Social Structure of an Italian Slum*. 4th ed. Chicago: University of Chicago Press.

Williams, Raymond. 1983. *Keywords: A Vocabulary of Culture and Society*. London: Fontana Paperbacks.

Word Spy, The. 2003. Bowling Alone. http://www.wordspy.com/words/bowlingalone.asp (accessed July 2004).

Yellon, Al. 2005a. Grrrrrrrr . . . July 1, 2005. *Bleed Cubbie Blue,* http://www.bleedcubbieblue.com (accessed April 2006).

———. 2005b. Out of the Mouths of Babes August 15, 2005. *Bleed Cubbie Blue,* http://www.bleedcubbieblue.com (accessed April 2006).

Zelizer, Viviana. 2005. *The Purchase of Intimacy*. Princeton, N.J.: Princeton University Press.

Index

Holly Swyers is an assistant
professor of anthropology at
Lake Forest College.

The University of Illinois Press
is a founding member of the
Association of American University Presses.

Designed by Dennis Roberts
Composed in 10.5/13 Adobe Minion Pro
with Avenir Lt. Std display
by Celia Shapland
at the University of Illinois Press
Manufactured by Sheridan Books, Inc.

University of Illinois Press
1325 South Oak Street
Champaign, IL 61820-6903
www.press.uillinois.edu